NORTH EAST ENGLAND

North East England

An economic and social history

Norman McCord

Department of History
University of Newcastle upon Tyne

Batsford Academic

First published 1979
© Norman McCord, 1979

Photoset in Great Britain by
Bristol Typesetting Co Ltd
Barton Manor, St Philips, Bristol

Printed and bound
in Great Britain by
Redwood Burn Ltd,
Trowbridge & Esher
for the publishers
B. T. Batsford Ltd
4 Fitzhardinge Street
London W1H 0AH

ISBN 0 7134 1261 5

Contents

This book is dedicated to those who
taught me at school and university,
and especially to the memory of
Professor W. L. Burn and Dr G. S. R.
Kitson Clark

List of Illustrations

Preface

In the Introduction some mention is made of problems encountered during the composition of this book. Here it is a pleasant duty to record a major advantage enjoyed by anyone working on the history of North East England: that is the presence within the region of a great variety of people who share on the one hand a deep interest in the region's history and on the other hand a notable generosity in making the results of their own work freely available to others.

Apart from that recognized in the dedication, my principal debt here is to my colleague David Rowe. The references given in the text do not adequately recognize the extent to which his work, both published and unpublished, has been pillaged for my purposes here, and I owe much to him. Dr Brian Barber helped a great deal in the collection of material, while working as research assistant in the economics department of Newcastle University. The biggest single repository of printed source material for the region's history lies in the local collection of the Newcastle Central Library; like many others concerned with the history of the region I am much indebted to June Thompson and Douglas Bond for the unfailing helpfulness and cheerfulness displayed in their care of this crucial collection.

Most of the work on which this book is based was done while on the staff of the department of economics in Newcastle University, and I am grateful to two successive holders of the David Dale Chair of Economics for their many kindnesses. S. R. Dennison is a scholar who early in his career made important pioneering contributions to the region's economic history; as head of department he provided active encouragement and help, an attitude fully maintained by his successor C. K. Rowley.

I am grateful to the Bank of England for permission to quote from the Newcastle Branch correspondence. There are many others to whom I am indebted for help related to this book, and I do not suppose that I shall be able to remember all of those whom I ought to mention in this connection. Be that as it may, I wish to thank Ray Barker, David Brewster, Gloria Cadman, Maureen Calcott, Alec Campbell, Frank Carr, Ray Challinor, Joe Clarke, Peter

Dunkley, Keith Gregson, Steve Jones, Stafford Linsley, Stuart Macdonald, Ross Mackay, Frank Manders, Steve Martin, Ross Miles, Maurice Milne, John Noddings, Bill Purdue, Bob Rennison, Frank Rogers, Jennifer Seeley, Doris Snowdon, Bill Sullivan, Colin Taylor, Pamela Thomson, Chris Warn and Peter Wood. Some of those who have provided me with useful information will not agree with some of the conclusions expressed here, and none of them bears any responsibility for the use to which I have put their aid.

Norman McCord

Department of History,
University of Newcastle upon Tyne

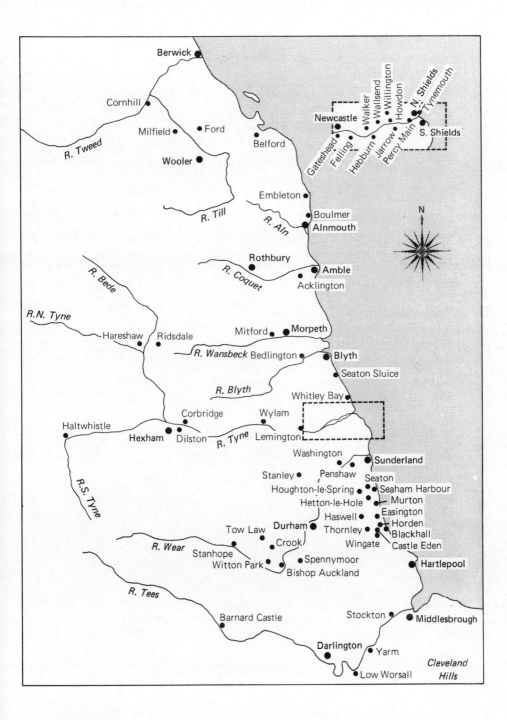

1. *The North East*

Introduction

The aim of this book is to give some general account of the economic and social development of North East England during the 200 years after about 1760. The region is for this purpose taken to include the two old counties of Durham and Northumberland, together with the city and county of Newcastle upon Tyne, while the border town of Berwick and part of North Yorkshire are annexed as essentially parts of the region during the period considered.

If the 200 years after 1760 are our main concern here, it must be remembered that this modern era represents in its time span only a very small part of human history within this region. The achievements of the post-1760 period were erected upon a foundation laid by the experience of many previous generations. When the counties of Northumberland and Durham emerged as settled units during the medieval period, some seven-eighths of the span of human activity within the region had already taken place since the arrival of the first primitive societies thousands of years earlier.

The area to be considered is very varied in terms of natural resources. From the point of view of surface advantages, both Durham and Northumberland possess a fertile coastal plain, an attenuated projection of the greater lowland areas in the more southerly parts of England. Both counties also possess important river valleys, providing other stretches of fertile land as well as useful routes. On the other hand, both counties also possess, especially in their western areas, large areas of relatively barren hills and moors. The region was endowed with a variety of mineral resources, including coal, iron, lead and silver. This buried inheritance itself varied in terms of quality and accessibility. The marked variations within the region's natural endowments, both on the surface and buried underground, have played key roles in determining the shifting patterns of human activity and settlement. They have not, however, been the sole determinants, for of crucial importance too has been the variation in human ability to exploit the opportunities offered by the region's natural resources. The patterns of human activity have also reflected the development of the social and political institutions which have been employed within the region at various times.

At no point in this region's long history, except possibly during the primitive stages of human occupation, is there any evidence for the effective destruction of an existing population and its replacement by another. At various different points in time there is of course clear evidence of substantial immigration into the region, but on the whole a substantial continuity of occupation seems to have accompanied the various cultural changes within the history of the region over the millennia.

Throughout the medieval and early modern periods the North East was a border region, distant from the main centres of English wealth and power. Although there were some lengthy gaps in the long tale of border warfare, fighting and destructive incursions were a common feature of the region's history. The strategic value of this border area remained high, but although Newcastle early became a trading town of considerable significance it could not be pretended that the North East can be seen as a major centre of sustained economic growth and development until the modern period with which this book is primarily concerned. Border warfare with its varied social and economic effects continued until after the Union of the Crowns in 1603. It would be too much to suggest that this happy event at once transformed the people of the border areas into paragons of industry and orderliness, but at least the effective cessation of large-scale Anglo-Scottish warfare provided a situation more conducive to economic development. The significance of these changed circumstances is eloquently represented in stone at Chipchase Castle in the North Tyne valley, where as early as the 1620s a medieval castle was graced by the addition of a sumptuous and essentially undefended Jacobean mansion.

In a number of categories of economic activity the seventeenth and early eighteenth centuries saw a significant quickening of the pace of development. Already during the medieval period the Tyne had acquired an important role in the shipment of coal. By 1600 coal shipments from the region's ports had probably reached an annual total of about 250,000 tons, a considerable commercial activity by the standards of the day. By 1700, however, this had grown to about 650,000 tons, with the growing appetite of London a major inducement. The increasing output of the region's collieries, clustered conveniently close to shipping points, was not all destined for shipment elsewhere, though we have no reliable estimates of local consumption at this early date. The collieries of North East England already enjoyed a high reputation for technical progress. In 1724 the indefatigable Sir John Clerk visited the area in pursuit of his search for information which could be turned to useful advantage; he came to this district because he 'understood that the perfection of coalery was to be learned both in relation to the Machines necessary above Ground and the easiest ways of working below Ground'. Among the developments which impressed visitors was the extension of the system of colliery waggon ways, which allowed the profitable operation of pits at some distance from the points of transfer to water carriage. Early forms of steam pumping engines to control water in the collieries were soon adopted in the region's more advanced coal mines during the eighteenth century.

In other ways too by the early part of the eighteenth century the North East appears to have been in the van of technical progress. From the latter part of the seventeenth century the region was one of the leading centres in the production of the country's small output of steel. It is probable that by the middle of the eighteenth century the North East manufactured about 800 tons of steel a year, and the Tyne was well placed for the import of Swedish wrought iron on which this process relied. This scale of production represented then well over half of the national output of steel. Other centres such as Sheffield were happy to borrow more advanced techniques in steel-making already adopted in the North East.

By 1720 the region's salt-pans, mainly concentrated on the lower Tyne, were making good use of the availability of cheap local coal to produce some 15,000 tons of salt annually. Shipbuilding, glass-making and lead-mining, with some extraction of silver from the lead ores, were other sectors of the region's economy which saw expansion during the late seventeenth and early eighteenth centuries, although of course farming remained much the most important economic activity. In commerce too there was increased sophistication during these years. While the leading Newcastle merchants were usually happy to buy and sell a considerable variety of goods rather than to specialize in a single product, a complex chain of contacts and agents abroad was gradually built up, with the western and northern districts of continental Europe the main focus of this activity.

It must be remembered, though, that these developments, however impressive they may have been in comparison with earlier periods, were very modest in relation to that which was to come later. It seems likely that at the beginning of the eighteenth century the total population of the North East was still well under a quarter of a million people. Moreover, in some respects the impetus towards rapid economic growth achieved in the North East by about 1700 seems to have faltered somewhat in ensuing years, in comparison with the increased pace of expansion in those other areas of Britain which were among the major centres of early industrialization. The lead in steel-making attained by the early eighteenth century was not maintained, and a relatively static figure for steel-making in the North East was to be rapidly overhauled by a booming growth in Sheffield and elsewhere. The peak in the prosperity of the region's salt industry was reached by about the middle of the eighteenth century, and thereafter unbeatable competition from Cheshire salt production drove the North East product from its principal markets. If in 1700 the North East seems to have been as advanced in technical developments as any region in Britain, the great days of the North East industrialization were to be considerably delayed, and this region was not one of the most obvious prodigies of early industrial Britain.

Nevertheless, the North East did not stand still, and during the century or so after 1760, as we shall see, there was a quickening of the process of economic development which had been marked in the late seventeenth and earlier eighteenth centuries. After about 1850, however, the pace of expansion in the North East was to show a spectacular acceleration, making the region one of the principal growth areas of late Victorian Britain. The twentieth century was to see more mixed fortunes, with serious economic problems and set-backs, but with overall a remarkable improvement in the standard of living of the region's inhabitants.

The task of trying to provide some general account of the evolution of the region during the 200 years or so after about 1760 is beset with a number of problems. In some cases these problems are simply those common to any attempt to comprehend the complicated story of the development of modern Britain. In the case of North East England we are dealing with first hundreds of thousands and then with millions of individuals. To make sense of the story these individuals must be considered somehow in categories, but our conceptual equipment for this task is seriously defective, for we do not possess any general theory of social development into which the complex and varied evidence can be fitted satisfactorily. The limitations of our conceptual framework can be readily illustrated by reference to the problems involved in relying on social class as a crucial determinant of human behaviour.

It would certainly make the historian's task much easier if we could use class terminology with reasonable levels of precision—if we could say with confidence that the middle class thought so-and-so or that the working class did such-and-such. In practice such an approach is fraught with many serious difficulties, so much so as to make the terminology of class of limited use in describing the evolution of modern British society. Class can certainly be used in many cases as a convenient social shorthand, as for instance when we talk of nineteenth-century urban terraces or colliery rows as working-class housing, where we can be reasonably certain that these houses were occupied by wage-earners and their families. The difficulties emerge, however, when we try to attribute to those who lived in such houses any very substantial uniformity or cohesion over a much wider range of activities and attitudes. On the whole the evidence suggests that any very comprehensive and continuous co-operation on the basis of a major social class has been abnormal and unusual rather than a typical situation.

The aristocracy always formed a relatively small grouping, and it might be expected that there if anywhere in British society would be found a pervasive spirit of class unity and concerted action. Even there, however, the level of class co-operation was distinctly limited, and the grouping often split by political, economic and social rivalries which were much more than superficial influences. For much of the nineteenth century county politics remained heavily affected by aristocratic influence; if Northumberland was largely Tory in this respect, Durham was largely Whig. Any solidarity among these ruling minorities did not prevent the occurrence of bitterly fought county elections, in which rival factions spent very large sums of money, sometimes more than the participants could readily afford. In the mid-1830s, if the Duke of Northumberland was a stout Tory, the Earl of Durham has a strong claim to be considered the decade's most important radical politician. No other radical politician of those years came as close to exercising effective influence in national politics, and Lord Durham's radicalism was impeccable in some respects at least—in 1834, for instance, we find him campaigning vigorously for the secret ballot, a vote for every householder and a general election at least every three years.

It is easy to define a middle class comprising those groups which occupied positions between the aristocratic establishment and the wage-earning sectors of society; it is, however, very much more difficult to find any substantial level of agreement, cohesion and co-operation within a middle class defined in some such way. To take only a scratch collection of likely contenders for inclusion within a middle class we might include shopkeepers, teachers, farmers, mine-owners, ships' captains, doctors, lawyers, bankers, hotel-keepers, factory-owners. It is impossible to find many, if any, instances in practice in which such diverse groups have exhibited any reasonable level of unity and cohesion in attitude or behaviour. It was common in the nineteenth century for certain behavioural characteristics to be firmly attached to the middle class—qualities such as respectability, thrift and hard work. It is plain, however, that such nominally *bourgeois* characteristics have never been the exclusive possession, or even a reliably distinguishing characteristic, of any social class. Thrift, hard work and respectability have been attributes much valued by many workers, while they have not been unknown among the country's aristocracy.

Similar difficulties are to be found in trying to use the concept of a working class as a reliable social category. Again contenders for inclusion in such a category would be many and diverse, and it is not easy to discover much in the way of mutual sympathy and co-operation between varied working groups in many different historical contexts within our period. In the middle of the nineteenth century, for instance, workers within our region would include domestic servants, farm labourers, coal-miners, merchant seamen and those employed in a great variety of industrial occupations; the evidence hardly supports the belief that there was any very substantial degree of co-operation between such diverse elements. Moreover, a grouping such as coal-miners which appears tolerably simple could in practice be much more complex. As in many other groups there were marked variations in status among those employed in coal mines, variations which meant a great deal to those concerned. There might not be a great deal in common in the attitudes and interests of a miner who was a devout Primitive Methodist and a miner for whom sport, drinking and gambling were important activities. Even at a much later stage in the evolution of industrial society the evidence scarcely supports the belief that workers in general shared much the same ideas and interests on a class basis. In 1935 Jarrow's electorate was dominated by workers and their families, and the town had already been very seriously hit by economic depression; in the general election of that year nearly 47% of the votes cast at Jarrow went to the Conservative candidate. In 1960 the growing strength of the trade unions was buttressed by the devoted work of those who acted as branch officials, committee members and delegates, but the level of attendance at branch meetings and participation in major union elections does not suggest that these priorities can be attributed to workers in general. A very good test of an individual's actual priorities is how he chooses to employ the time and the money of which he has free disposal; most workers do not seem to have felt impelled to devote such resources to either the political or the indus-trial wings of the labour movement, and there is little evidence to support any very widespread agreement on a class basis in such matters. It is possible to construct another kind of definition for a working class, by limiting it to those workers who felt that the interests of the workers in general as against the interests of other elements in society was a matter of paramount importance which should occupy a significant part of their energies and resources. The usefulness of such a category, however, would be severely limited by the large numbers of workers who would have to be left outside it.

Unfortunately, if social class does not provide us with a reasonably precise indicator of human behaviour, we do not yet possess any satisfactory alternative set of categories for social analysis which can be reliably applied to the understanding of a large and varied society. In these circumstances, however, it is better to avoid the misleading precision of class terminology and to accept that diversity and complexity of behaviour at all social levels have been the norm and any high level of class cohesion and uniformity distinctly unusual. Otherwise the historian can be easily misled; in some recent works, for instance, the miners' strike of 1844 has been described as an operation by the working class, despite the facts that the North East miners struck in defiance of the wishes of miners elsewhere, that other groups of workers in the region did not take sympathetic industrial action and that what sympathy and help the strikers did receive came from a variety of sources, not all of which were composed of fellow workers.

Another problem affecting the North East in common with the history of other areas in Britain relates to the curiously lop-sided approach evident in much recent writing about modern British history. This is the way in which a much higher degree of attention is commonly directed to those aspects where things went awry than is devoted to those aspects in which things went well. This is the more surprising since it requires the application of only modest powers of observation and common sense to appreciate that the story of the evolution of modern British society must contain very significant elements of success and achievement. Not only did this country see population growth on an unprecedented scale, but these vastly swollen numbers came to occupy a position which exhibited a standard of living and levels of health, leisure and opportunity which obviously transcended the experiences of any earlier period.

While there is no difficulty in finding ample evidence for oppression, conflict and cruelty, it is important to give adequate attention also to the very substantial elements of sympathy, progress and achievement.

There are a number of reasons why an undue concentration on the darker aspects of modern British history has taken place. One of these is the nature of some of the sources which have been much employed. We have learned a great deal from the reports of a great variety of enquiries undertaken especially in the nineteenth and twentieth centuries, but such a source can contain seeds of distortion. The reports of royal commissions, select committees and government inspectors are commonly directed in a concentrated fashion to things which have gone wrong. We do not normally expect to see royal commissions appointed to investigate the continuance of normality, tranquillity or progress though these attributes may be widespread. This kind of source material tends to give an unduly bleak picture of a past which included at the same time elements of achievement and success which were not obvious targets for deliberate investigation. Similarly, while the columns of the press have provided another major source we need not expect newspapers and other media of popular communication to be notably thorough and objective in the picture they present of contemporary society. The unusual and the untypical events tend to be the meat and drink of the press, while little attention is likely to be paid to the continuance of relatively satisfactory normality, though the latter condition may be very common.

Another related factor is the way in which modern British history has been directly affected by political and ideological controversy. Not all historical work in this field has been actuated by a simple desire to understand the past, and there is a constant temptation for historians who hold strong political opinions, whether those opinions be of the right or the left, to regard modern British history as a magazine of ammunition which can be drawn upon for our contemporary political and ideological controversies. It would probably be fair to say that the holding of strong political opinions is more common among modern historians than it is in society in general. It can be difficult for a right-wing historian to appreciate why a small group of workers might embark in the early nineteenth century upon a revolutionary plot which seemed foredoomed to failure; it can be difficult for a left-wing historian to appreciate that nineteenth-century methodism among workers was primarily a religious movement rather than an insidious form of social control.

In trying to understand any portion of modern British history it is important to bear these difficulties in mind, for they can lead to serious misunderstanding sometimes of a prolonged nature. For example, it would be difficult to find a general account of British history of the early nineteenth century which omitted to mention the Peterloo Massacre of 1819 and the Tolpuddle Martyrs of 1834 as events which can be taken to illustrate the nature of the society in which they occurred. Yet there is very good reason to doubt the validity of what is by now almost a traditional use of these two events. On 16 August 1819 eleven people were killed and hundreds injured when troops intervened in a mass public meeting at Manchester, an incident immortalized in British history as the Peterloo Massacre. If, however, the bloody dispersal of public meetings illustrated the usual reaction of contemporary authorities to popular pressures, it is odd that this single event has achieved such exceptional fame, instead of being submerged in a flood of very similar events. If in the 1830s workers were commonly transported to Australia for trade union activities, it is difficult to see why the conviction of the six Tolpuddle martyrs in 1834 caused such an exceptional stir both at the time and subsequently. The notoriety attached to these famous events arose not because they represented the usual and normal behaviour of that society but because they were distinctly unusual and abnormal, yet capable of prolonged political exploitation. This is only one significant instance of the ways in which widely received versions of modern British history have been powerfully affected by political and ideological attitudes, whether those attitudes have been held in the past or the present.

In other ways, too, the student of modern British history should adopt a spirit of healthy scepticism in approaching much recent writing in this field. It may well be that no other historical context has suffered more from the unthinking use of our modern ideas and beliefs about society as a yardstick by which to judge the affairs of past societies which were in many ways very different. The absence of trade unions from neolithic society, and the failure of Anglo-Saxon England to develop a national health service, are no doubt cause for regret, but as an approach to historical understanding such concepts are obviously worse than useless. A surprising amount of recent writing on modern British history has differed from these patent absurdities only in degree. Such errors commonly occur where a principal concern of the writer is to explore the past in search of materials with which to fight later twentieth century political battles. It is, however, of little use to pretend that what happened in the past ought not to have happened, and that something quite different should have happened instead. The problems of trying to comprehend the complexities of what did actually happen are difficult enough, without resort to that kind of futile romancing.

In the years around 1840, Macaulay was engaged on the composition of his famous *History of England*. In addition to being one of the most brilliant of all British historians he was an intelligent, humane and well-informed individual who was for many years close to the centre of British affairs. He also had ample opportunity for knowing how the experience of British society during his own lifetime could be transformed into a distorted version of history for political purposes. In the celebrated third chapter of his *History*, he included a number of illuminating reflections on such matters which are still well worth consideration by any student of modern British history. (In this passage Macaulay uses 'police' in an older meaning, equivalent to 'civil administration'.)

The more carefully we examine the history of the past, the more reason shall we find to dissent from those who imagine that our age has been fruitful of new social evils. The truth is that the evils are, with scarcely an exception, old. That which is new is the intelligence which discerns and the humanity which remedies them . . . We too shall, in our turn be outstripped, and in our turn be envied. It may well be, in the twentieth century, that the peasant of Dorsetshire may think himself miserably paid with twenty shillings a week; that the carpenter in Greenwich may receive ten shillings a day; that labouring men may be as little used to dine without meat as they now are to eat rye bread; that sanitary, police and medical discoveries may have added several more years to the average length of human life; that numerous comforts and luxuries which are now unknown, or confined to a few, may be within the reach of every diligent and thrifty person. And yet it may then be the mode to assert that the increase of wealth and the progress of science have benefitted the few at the expense of the many . . .

It will be sufficiently obvious from what has already been said that modern British history remains an arena of considerable disagreement and controversy among historians. There are no doubt many instances of interpretation and selection in the present book on which other historians working in this area would strongly disagree, and this is something which readers should bear in mind.

In addition to such problems which beset consideration of modern British history generally, the history of North East England from about 1760 presents difficulties of its own. Ironically, the available evidence is both over-abundant and deficient. It is over-abundant in the sense that the bulk of surviving evidence, whether in print or in manuscript, structure or artifact, is much too large for it ever to be comprehended by an individual, and much of this source material has never received adequate study. It would be foolish to pretend that the present account is based upon a survey of all the evidence, or all that has been written upon the region by other historians or by scholars working in such related disciplines as economics, politics, sociology or geography. The available source material is on the other hand deficient because of the very limited extent to which we can call upon earlier general accounts of the region's modern history or specialist studies of major elements within it. Some of the crucial elements in the region's history have received relatively little modern scrutiny. Most glaring deficiency of all is the absence of any comprehensive account of the development of the Great Northern Coalfield which played such a vital part in the evolution of the modern North East. This is not the only serious gap. There are as yet no major studies of the engineering or shipbuilding industries of the region. In the chemical industry and in agriculture there has been some distinctly useful recent work but the coverage is still far from complete. We are less fortunately placed than some other British regions in the extent to which a modern account can draw on adequate specialist studies of major industries and other important components of the region's history. This means that any general survey attempted at this stage must necessarily be limited and tentative in its coverage, with ample leeway remaining for future amendment of the picture as further work on the region's history accumulates.

It has not been easy to decide how best to divide up the subject matter of this book, and a variety of periods and patterns of organization could have been adopted. The choice has been to divide the book simply into three main parts, roughly corresponding to the most clearly defined stages in the region's economic development. The first part covers the period from about 1760 to around 1850, an era in which the predominantly rural society was expanding into a more industrialized and urbanized form but at no very spectacular rate. The second part deals with the period from the middle of the nineteenth century to just after the First World War, the years of the region's most prodigious economic growth. The shorter third part deals with a shorter period of about forty years from around 1920, a time of much more mixed fortunes and one which is in some ways even less well served in terms of previous historical work than its predecessor. In dealing with these three main parts no precise chronological limits are strictly observed, since the periods chosen are merely rough points of convenience rather than exact times of transition. Each of the three main parts has been divided into two chapters. In the first of these attention is concentrated on more specifically economic developments, while the second looks also at some other aspects of the society in which those economic developments took place. No attempt has been made to stick rigidly to this division either, since it is often impossible to make a meaningful separation between economic and social developments.

The book is not intended as a presentation of meticulous research for the benefit of the specialized historian, but rather to offer a more general account of the region's history during this period. If the deliberate absence of many tables and graphs may come as a disappointment to some readers, perhaps this omission will be borne with equanimity by those with less specialized interests in the subject. For the same reason references have been restricted both in number and in function. The references are essentially confined to the citation of some of the more useful sources on which the account in the main chapters has been based, and they contain no significant part of the book's main subject matter. Readers who are not concerned to follow through the sources employed here may cheerfully ignore them.

Part One
1760–1850

1 Agriculture, Industry and Commerce

During the period 1760–1850 North East England saw increasingly rapid change in its economic, political and social organization, though these were to be far outstripped in scale in the succeeding period. We do not know with any precision the population which Northumberland and Durham supported in the middle of the eighteenth century, but it seems certain that it had already been growing during the decades before the first national census of 1801, which credited Northumberland with a population of 168,000, and Durham with a population of 149,000. By the middle of the nineteenth century there had been an unprecedented growth, with the census of 1851 attributing a population of 304,000 to Northumberland and 391,000 to Durham.

The development of the region's economy provided the basis for the support of the increased population, and from about 1760 onwards the pace of economic change was clearly quickening. By 1850 what had previously been a society of small scattered largely agricultural communities was already advanced in the transformation into an industrialized and urbanized society. When we look back at these changes of the late eighteenth and early nineteenth centuries, it is tempting to see in them some kind of sweeping inexorable process of growth, for with the hindsight of history we can select what attracts us as general lines of development which dictated the course of events. However, for those who lived in this period of rapid, and often puzzling, change this was not nearly so easy, and the processes of change were in reality much more complex and haphazard than a superficial consideration might suggest. There was not in the later eighteenth century any coherent determination to produce the kind of trans-formed society which had substantially appeared by 1850; instead the North East of 1850 emerged in an unplanned and unforeseen fashion from a myriad of individual actions and decisions. In trying to understand the economic and social changes of this period of transition it is important to try to avoid the imposition on them of a misleading concept of purposefulness and deliberation. It is highly unlikely that anyone in 1760 was consciously working for the transformation of North East England into a part of a capitalist industrial society, even though the result of the complex interactions of individual ambitions and efforts was to move towards that end.

The economic development of North East England in the later eighteenth and early nineteenth centuries was remarkable for its diversity. From about 1760 onwards heightened activity affected a wide range of different forms of production, and the degree of success or failure attained was equally diverse. In some cases, the foundations were laid of industrial growth which was to continue for generations; in others, enterprises embarked upon with great energy and high hopes produced either failure or very limited success.

Agriculture

In 1760 agriculture remained far and away the most important economic activity within the region. Even the coal-mining industry, the most obvious non-agricultural activity, was confined within narrow limits, constrained in its capacity by technical limitations in extraction and transport. By 1850 the relative importance of these two elements had markedly altered; the 1851 census showed 41,089 employed in coal-mining, as against 35,522 in farming. It is clear, however, that this shift in proportion was then a recent one, derived mainly from a very rapid expansion of mining in County Durham during the preceding decades. Northumberland in 1851 still showed farming as the biggest single occupation group, and for most of the preceding century agriculture had remained the region's principal economic resource.

A large body of contemporary opinion testified to the importance of changes in the region's agriculture during this period. (This discussion of agriculture is largely based on two sources which are given in reference 1; both of these works contain useful guides to other relevant reading.) Many aspects of farming were affected by these developments. There were improvements in the quality of cultivated crops and in crop rotation, in the breeding of sheep, cattle and other livestock, and in the application of agricultural machinery. The improved farms of the region attracted a stream of visitors, both British and foreign, many of whom expressed themselves in terms of high praise for the innovations they observed. Improving farmers within the region kept themselves well informed of progress in farming techniques elsewhere and showed themselves capable of considerable skill in adapting new ideas to the particular needs of their own districts. Surviving records demonstrate a constant pattern of visits and tours, and a voluminous correspondence on technical and commercial matters between farmers and landowners in various regions affected by agricultural change.

By the end of the eighteenth century North East England was regarded as an area from which distinctly useful farming methods could be exported to other regions. A visitor to northern Scotland in 1801 noted[2a]:

A farm, belonging to a Mr Middleton, originally from Northumberland, struck our attention, as being cultivated in a superior style to what is customary in this part of the world. Saw a field of excellent wheat, and many other instances of good husbandry; but the country, in general . . . is barren and uncultivated, though very susceptible, in many places, of receiving beneficial improvement, provided any exertions were made by the possessors.

(For a similar instance, see reference 2b, in which the same farmer is described.) Middleton had moved there only 4 years previously, bringing into that district its first horse gin for threshing and other purposes, and establishing the first thriving trade in wheat there. The third Earl Spencer, himself a notable agricultural reformer, thought it worth while to recruit skilled farm labour from the North East, asking a northern friend to find for him[3] 'not only a first-rate ploughman, *but the sort of fellow you have in Northumberland*, who can be trusted to overlook the other labourers'. This was not the only contemporary tribute to the quality of farm workers within the region. Farming wages in the North East were higher than in other regions, perhaps because of the proximity of various other forms of employment.

By 1800 contemporaries had no doubt that one of the most important centres of agricultural development lay in Northumberland and Durham. Yet it would be very misleading to translate this reputation into an assumption that advanced farming was characteristic of the region as a whole. There is ample evidence to show that the favourable comment was essentially won by groups of farmers in a few select areas and that the region could also show wide areas of farming of a very different nature. (A number of examples of failure are given in reference 4.) The publicity centred largely around the attainments of a few well-known innovators, such as the Culley brothers in North Northumberland, the Collings family in the Tees valley and John Grey of Dilston on the Greenwich Hospital estates. If there were some very notable success stories, there were also many much less publicized cases of ineptitude and failure, and ample evidence of caution and conservatism among farmers in many parts of the region. On the whole Durham was less affected by improved techniques than Northumberland, and in general the less fertile western areas of both counties lagged behind in the adoption of new methods. Even in more easterly areas improvement was distinctly patchy, and as late as 1851 a report for *The Times* included this account of an area of eastern Northumberland[5]:

> It must surprise many who have hitherto been led to consider the agriculture of Northumberland as a model for the rest of the kingdom, to learn that a great portion of the county, extending from near Newcastle on both sides of the railway as far north as Warkworth, is as little drained and as badly farmed as any district we have yet seen in England, and that the occupiers of the small farms can only eke out a scanty subsistence by careful parsimony, and by employing no labour except that of themselves and their families.

The district described in these terms lay between two well-known centres of improved farming, the Tyne valley and the coastal plain of North Northumberland.

These marked variations within the region derived from a variety of causes. In part they simply reflected the marked variations in terrain within the region; the light but fertile soils of districts such as the Milfield plain in North Northumberland were much more susceptible to improvement by existing techniques than the western moors or the boulder clay of South East Northumberland. This is not, however, a sufficient explanation, for areas of comparable natural advantages did not always show comparable improvement in farming techniques. Contemporary commentators tended to stress the significance of certain aspects of the region's pattern of landownership and tenure. Northumberland, where some of the most striking advances were made in this period, was to an unusual degree a county of large estates and large farms, though careless observers tended to exaggerate the extent to which this was the case. Arthur Young stressed this point during his tours of the 1760s[6]: 'The farms become large almost immediately on entering it, after the small ones of Yorkshire and Durham, and rise in many parts of it to be as great as any in the kingdom, if not the greatest.' It was suggested that large estates and large farms should be characterized by the availability of larger resources and so present more favourable circumstances for sustained investment in improvements by both landlord and tenant. The mode of letting farms was also widely regarded as a factor which could advance or retard the rate of improvement. In those parts of North Northumberland which were among the most celebrated areas of improvement, leases for 21 years were common, and leases for terms of years rather than annual tenure were the norm. Surely, it was suggested, the relative security which leasehold tenure conferred would predispose tenants to embark upon improvements from which they could be sure to reap the profits.

It is, however, probable that contemporary publicists exaggerated the significance of these factors, and certainly some of those concerned to sing the praises of leaseholding were more concerned to improve the tenant's security of tenure than to measure with any precision the advantages of leases in economic terms. Moreover, it was by no means certain that the ownership of a large landed estate was necessarily a guarantee that the landlord's other interests and activities would leave him with a substantial surplus of income with which to finance estate improvement. The region's largest landed estate, that of the Duke of Northumberland, was certainly not regarded as a centre of improvement until after the Fourth Duke of Northumberland succeeded in 1847. Nor were large farms necessarily the nurseries of major change, and some of the most famous innovators began their farming careers on a small scale and only built up more extensive holdings on the basis of earlier achievements. The importance of leases was also exaggerated. On the estate of the Duke of Northumberland leases were not granted, but the estate's normal and accepted practice was to allow sitting tenants virtually automatic continuity of tenure; this did not lead to marked innovation in farming efficiency.

Other traditional explanations of improved farming cannot have much relevance in North East England. Most of the cultivated land had been enclosed long before the great spate of statutory enclosure in the late eighteenth and early nineteenth centuries, so that the enclosure movement cannot be credited with any responsibility for improvement within the region. There were further enclosures of land during this period, but they were mostly concerned with the division of common pasture, often of very moderate quality. Common land at Hexham and Allendale was divided in 1792, and Weardale common in 1799, for example, but these Acts cannot be seen as significant spurs to improved farming methods. Progressive farmers such as John Grey certainly developed land which had previously lain undrained and substantially unexploited, but this had little to do with the availability of statutory enclosure.

In seeking to understand how some areas within the region emerged as noted centres of progressive farming other factors must be taken into account. Innovations in farming were rarely embarked upon out of disinterested scientific zeal or a desire to serve the community as a whole by increased production of food. Much more commonly useful changes were adopted because the landowners and farmers concerned believed that they would contribute to their own profit and advancement. The widespread adoption of the horse-driven threshing machine within the region was not due to any particular delight in mechanical innovation but rather to the savings in expenditure which the improved threshing machines of the years after 1786 could bring, in an area of scattered population and high agricultural wages.[7] Developments in livestock-breeding were not directed to produce animals of attractive appearance but animals which carried the kinds of meat and wool which might be more profitably disposed of in the existing market situation. The kind of society which existed at that time was one which in a variety of ways provided a favourable climate for the application of a vigorous farmer's energy and skill. Many farmers, in the North East as elsewhere, lacked the resources or the ability or the enthusiasm needed to enable them to exploit these opportunities. In a largely experimental period of development, success in the application of new farming techniques was very far from being assured. Yet for those who persisted and succeeded there were very substantial rewards to be won.

British society was still very much dominated by the landed interest, and a man responsible for a marked success in farming improvements could experience a gratifying rise, not only in his income but also in his personal status and prestige. Many prominent landowners were themselves much concerned with agricultural improvements, and during the late eighteenth and early nineteenth centuries there was a great deal of emulation and rivalry in such matters within this dominating minority. Sometimes the search for distinction as a farming expert could reach absurd heights; Thomas Bewick, the Newcastle engraver, recorded how such extreme ambition could involve a question of artistic integrity[8]:

My journey, as far as concerned these fat Cattle makers, ended in nothing—I would not put lumps of fat here & there to please them where I could not see it—at least in so exaggerated a way as on the painting before me—so I got my "labour in vain"—many of the Animals were, during *this rage* for fat Cattle, surely fed up to as great a weight & bulk, as it was possible for feeding to make them, but this was not enough, they were to be figured monstrously fat before the owners of them could be pleased—some painters were found who were quite subservient to their wishes, but nothing else would please.

In such a world success in farming could bring not only increased profits but also gratifying notice, favour and patronage from the country's leaders. The careers of two of Northumberland's most successful farmers during this period illustrate the various ways in which farming success could lead to personal advancement and the variety of the complex factors which could lie behind the process of agricultural improvement.

George Culley was born in 1735, younger son of a farmer in the Darlington area[9]. The family farm would not be his to inherit, but his father did his best to provide his younger sons with an adequate training, sending George and his brother, Matthew, to work under Robert Bakewell in Leicestershire. This certainly brought the brothers into contact with the contemporary world of farming improvement. In 1767 George and Matthew entered upon the tenancy of a farm at Fenton, in North Northumberland, taking with them their experience both on Teesside and in Leicestershire and such acquisitions as a herd of thirty of the improved shorthorn cattle developed in the Darlington district by the Collings and other successful local breeders. By 1800 the brothers had prospered markedly, by dint of hard work, technical skill and commercial acumen. Their early contacts with improving farmers elsewhere were sedulously maintained, and potentially useful ideas devised in other regions were studied and considered and, when they appeared likely to prove profitable, were applied with such local modifications as might be needed. George Culley was visiting Leicestershire in 1765 and 1771, he toured Scotland in 1771, the Midlands and East Anglia in 1784. Matthew was in Soctland in 1770 and 1775, in Leicestershire in 1794 and 1798.

The brothers improved the efficiency and the profitability of their farms in a wide variety of ways. They took great care in the manuring and liming of their land, and varied the known Norfolk four-fold rotation into a 5-year rotation of oats, turnips, wheat or barley, then 2 years of pasture, which a process of trial and error showed to be more appropriate to local conditions and needs. In stock-farming the Culleys, and George especially, established a national reputation as a leading livestock-breeder. Just as an importation from Teesdale had formed the nucleus of their shorthorn herds, so the importation of Bakewell's improved sheep from Leicestershire, and their inter-breeding with older Northumbrian strains, produced a sheep which combined hardiness with significant increases in meat production. These successes brought the brothers status and influence, increased income and readier access to credit when they needed it. Their hard work in earlier years produced especially good results during the periods of high prices during the French Wars. In 1801 their profits from farming amounted to at least £4,100, an income equal to that of many gentry families. Such profits, and their ability to borrow on the strength of an established reputation for successful farming, enabled them to buy land. The first estate was bought for £24,000 in 1795, a second 6 years later cost £13,000, and the transition from tenant farmer to landowning gentry culminated in 1807 with the purchase for £45,000 of a substantial estate centred on the country house of Fowberry Tower. Even such a hard-bitten commercially minded man as George Culley was impressed by the social as well as the financial gains; in 1810, 3 years before his death, he included this passage in a letter to his heir[10]: 'Whenever I am at Fowberry, I am struck with astonishment, when I reflect on our beginning in Northumberland 43 years ago. To think of my son, now inhabiting *a Palace!* altho' his father in less than 50 years since worked harder than any servant we now have, & even drove a coal cart.' A society which offered this kind of prize for success was well fitted to encourage rapid economic growth.

Our other example of the notably successful agriculturist John Grey was born in 1785 at Milfield. (See reference 11 for the account of Grey.) The Greys of Milfield were a minor landowning and farming family, with a remote family link with the more important Greys of Howick Hall. John Grey's father died when he was a young boy, and after a good education at Richmond he took up management of the family interests while still a teenager. As a schoolboy he had already come into contact with new ideas in farming, and his home at Milfield was situated in one of the major areas of improvement within the region. Within a short distance a number of celebrated innovators, including the Culley brothers, were already active. John Grey rapidly established himself as a member of this circle and learned much from the Culleys. His own rise to fame, however, was determined by more complex considerations, and his reputation was not built entirely on his agricultural achievements. He was born to a position among Northumberland's minor gentry, and he allied to skilful farming a considerable involvement in the social and political life of the county. In a predominantly Tory county Grey steadily adhered to the minority Whig interest headed by the senior line of the Grey family, and his combination of good farming and political enthusiasm brought him into flattering and profitable contact with men of much heavier metal. By the time that the Whigs came to power in 1830 Grey enjoyed strong links with members of the new cabinet such as Lord Grey himself, Lord Durham and Lord Althorp. Althorp, the new Chancellor of the Exchequer, shared John Grey's Whig allegiance and enthusiasm for farming improvement. Grey's daughter later described one meeting between these two men during the Reform Bill crisis of 1832[12]:

My father, happening to be in town, called on him in Downing Street. Lord Althorp carefully shut the door, looked round to see if they were alone, and then, before uttering a word on the political crisis in which they were so deeply interested, he asked eagerly, "Have you been to Wiseton on your way up? *Have you seen the cows?"* The two cattle-loving men indulged in a hearty fit of laughter at their own expense and then proceeded to speak of politics.

During the critical general election of 1831, Grey's influence in county society and among farmers was exerted to the full and helped to swing even Northumberland's two MPs behind the Reform Bill. His abilities in agriculture were undoubtedly genuine, but it is likely that he owed his opportunity to shine on a much more extensive stage as much to his political as to his agricultural achievements. Greenwich Hospital owned large estates in North East England, mostly from the estates of attainted Jacobites of the early eighteenth century, and the administration of this extensive property was effectively in the government's gift. The estates were in poor condition by 1830 and stood badly in need of expert management, but it is highly unlikely that his plum of patronage would have come Grey's way as a result of farming skills alone. Althorp placed him in this position in 1833, and it was from this new base rather than from his inherited property that as John Grey of Dilston he made his major rise to fame. During the next 30 years he transformed the Greenwich holdings into a prosperous and well-managed estate, with an increase of some 50% in rental. His work here enhanced his own income and his own status and elevated the social position of his family. His younger son, Charles, succeeded him in the management of the Greenwich estates, while his eldest son, George, inherited the old family home at Milfield and became a county magistrate and deputy lieutenant; John Grey's daughter became, as Josephine Butler, a national figure of considerable note in the history of Victorian social reform.

The careers of John Grey and George Culley varied both in detail and in timing, but it is possible to discern personal qualities which they held in common and which contributed materially to their success. Both men were shrewd as well as hard working. They had good noses for scenting which suggested innovations would serve their own ends, and which would not. They were also very good salesmen, taking deliberate care in fostering personal reputations for skilful farming which enhanced the prices they could charge for their products or their services. Both of them were ambitious and embraced agricultural improvement not simply for its own sake but for the rewards which they knew it could bring. For example, in breeding his improved sheep, Culley was not concerned to produce the finest or most highly bred animal but to produce a breed which combined a decent fleece, the hardiness to withstand Northumberland conditions, and above all the ability to produce larger quantities of mutton. He was not primarily concerned to produce meat which would satisfy the sophisticated palate of the rich—one contemporary contrasted the meat of the older local sheep which was 'like dark juicy Venison' with that of[13] 'the *improved* Breed, with their fatting qualities . . . the latter puts one in mind of blubber'. What Culley had in mind was the growing market presented by the expanding urban, mining and industrial areas, where there was a growing demand for lower-priced meat in considerable quantities, in itself evidence for the spread of higher standards of living among at least some working groups. Culley's eye for a profitable opportunity was apparent here, as in many of his activities. When he did breed prize animals it was primarily because of the high prices he could obtain by their sale or their hiring-out for breeding purposes. The kind of landowner or farmer who indulged in expensive innovation without keeping very firmly in mind the likely commercial results could easily part with a great deal of money to little effect except to earn ridicule from more practical men.

Both Culley and Grey were very sharp, and not overly scrupulous, in their commercial dealings. During his long work with the Greenwich estates, Grey made a number of local enemies, and the single-mindedness with which he set about his task earned him a reputation for ruthlessness. While perfectly willing to help tenants who saw things just as he did, he showed little mercy in weeding out those who he judged 'incompetent and incorrigible'. It is unlikely that his achievement in reducing arrears of rent from about £7,000 to £8,000 down to £30 was made in an entirely painless way, although complaints were normally little heard among the chorus of congratulations at his undoubted success in skilled estate management. In agriculture, as in other areas of economic growth, success did not normally go to the meek.

Grey and Culley were exceptional, both in the extent of their farming and social success and in the widespread publicity engendered by their work; yet such achievements played a considerable role in facilitating the adoption of more efficient and productive farming techniques. Their patent and obvious success, together with that of a variety of lesser-known names, was the best inducement to other landowners and farmers to emulate their efforts, and the patchy areas of advanced agriculture with which such men were associated were sources of inspiration from which better techniques gradually permeated the region, though this was to be a slow piecemeal process. If some areas remained backward, there was a substantial increase in the production of the region's agriculture. Already in the third quarter of the eighteenth century there was a period in which coastal ports such as Alnmouth flourished, as an agricultural surplus was exported from Northumberland. The development of the town of Berwick also testified to increased resources[14].

Berwick was an old established town and seaport, and by the 1820s possessed a range of small-scale industry, including textiles, rope-making and iron-working. These were not, however, the core of the town's economy. Early nineteenth-century Berwick depended much more on its role as part of the machinery which was already expanding to provide food for the growing non-agricultural population, and especially London, the country's greatest industrial centre as well as the centre of government. Berwick grew as a fishing port and as a port for the export of agricultural produce from North Northumberland and the Tweed valley. In 1816, for instance, Berwick sent nearly 5,000 chests of eggs to London, of value around £30,000. Large quantities of salmon were also shipped to London, either packed in boxes with ice or transported alive in smacks specially fitted with water tanks for that purpose. The Berwick Shipping Company formed in 1820 with a capital of £20,000 in £100 shares replaced earlier and smaller companies in this trade. In 1822 the company imported 440 tons of ice, mainly from Bergen, at a cost of £1,082, and also found another £600 worth of ice from other sources. The town's fleet of sailing smacks, carrying fish and other foodstuffs down the East Coast to London gradually gathered to itself much of the other trade of the East Coast. However, Berwick proved unable to sustain this high level of prosperity. French competition came to replace the Berwick smacks in the supply of eggs to London, while an injudicious piece of imperialism lost the town much of its share of routine East Coast trade. An attempt to extend Berwick's network of services to the Forth provoked a spirited response from the Leith merchants, who built bigger and better vessels to beat off the challenge and went on to annex much of the East Coast trade which Berwick had won in the recent past. By 1828 the Berwick fleet had dwindled to a total of only seven trading smacks in regular service.

If this growth point contracted by the late 1820s, its earlier importance in the food-shipping trade is further evidence of increased production on many of the Northumberland farms which used Berwick as an outlet. Another consequence of the existence of improved farming was an increase in farm rents in the areas affected. The Culley brothers leased a farm in 1775 at a rent of £260 and another in 1778 at £350; after considerable improvements had been effected, renewals of these leases in 1796 and 1793 respectively saw the new rents at £393.15s.0d and £483, marking substantial increases in the landowner's rent income[15]. This kind of increased income played a part in bolstering up the position of the dominant landed interest during a period of considerable economic change generally, while in many cases landowners also derived substantial new income from non-agricultural sources, such as royalties or way-leave rents from coal-mining, urban rents, or the profitable sale of land to railway companies. When the Newcastle and Carlisle Railway was being planned, Charles Bacon of Styford Hall was bought off by the company paying him the extravagant price of £3,000 for 7 acres of land, while he and other landowners also insisted on the inclusion in the railway's Act of a stipulation that the railway must not obtrude any of its installations into the views of the mansion houses along the planned route [16]. The continued prosperity of most landed proprietors during this period had political and social consequences in the maintenance of their predominant influence in national and regional affairs, while the real if patchy improvement in the region's food-producing resources was an important factor in feeding the growing population involved in non-agricultural interests.

Industry and commerce

In turning to consider some of the non-agricultural interests within the region's economy, it is important not to exaggerate or anticipate the clarity of such a distinction. By the end of the nineteenth century it was much easier to distinguish between industry and farming than it had been a century earlier. In the late eighteenth and early nineteenth centuries the contacts and the similarities were in many ways close. Landowners owned the minerals under their estates and concerned themselves either directly or indirectly with their exploitation. A successful mine-owner would naturally aspire to join the landowning dominant groups, without necessarily withdrawing from mining interests. Moreover in the late eighteenth century the technology applied to industry, including mining, was often not very different from that used in farming. If the application of steam power to mining was an important innovation, it remained true that much of the work in the pits was still carried out with simple hand tools, not very different from those employed on the land. Horse gins virtually identical with those used on many farms were also employed by many collieries. The early steam engines used for pumping water from collieries often required skills no more sophisticated than those possessed by many blacksmiths. A manuscript in the library of the Newcastle Literary and Philosophical Society describes the techniques and apparatus used in more advanced early nineteenth-century lead mines: one illustration, 'Draughts of the several Instruments necessary for the Dressing of Lead Ore so as to fit it for Smelting', depicts a group of objects which could easily be mistaken for a set of gardening implements[17]. In these early years of industrial growth, much of the equipment used in industrial activity would have presented no great mystery to a rural craftsman.

It was common for early industrial activity to be grafted on to a pre-dominantly farming community. Thus a militia return for 1762 presented the following breakdown of occupations from Acomb, a village a few miles North of Hexham—16 farm workers, three tailors, four blacksmiths, 23 miners and pitmen, one shoemaker, one shovel-maker, three sinkers of colliery shafts, one wright, three potters, one schoolmaster, one painter, two joiners, two weavers, one mason and one gardener[18]. It was relatively easy for a rural craftsman to transfer his talents to an early industrial setting, and the existence of a substantial reservoir of men skilled in working both wood and metal for farm-ing purposes was a distinctly useful asset in facilitating early industrialization; there was a considerable amount of overlap and movement of workers between rural crafts and urban or industrial employment. The widespread use of horses in industrial and urban contexts—in coal-mining, for example—necessi-tated the employment of many men with skills identical with those used in farming communities. During the nineteenth century the North Shields firm of Pow and Fawcus became one of Britain's biggest manufacturers of anchors, chains and other maritime ironwork; its founders owed much to early training in rural blacksmiths' shops. Similarly F. C. Marshall, who was by 1870 a partner in the great engineering firm of R. and W. Hawthorn, also came from a family of country blacksmiths. Mixed employment in agriculture and industry was also common. A combination of mining with small-scale farming was normal in the lead-mining districts.

The intimate connection between farming and non-agricultural activities existed in the management of many estates in the North East. For example, during the early eighteenth century the Ridley family became established as important landowners in South East Northumberland, after many generations as successful Newcastle merchants. The acquisition of this substantial landed estate brought a marked accession of social prestige and political influence, but successive generations of Ridleys were not simply members of the landed gentry, but the proprietors of an estate of varied interests, all of which were sedulously cultivated. They certainly took care that their farms should be profitable, but they were quick to exploit all of the other opportunities for profit embodied in this substantial investment. Banking, coal-mining and the growth of the small port of Blyth were all Ridley interests which combined to make the family richer and more influential. The spirit with which this landed family, well established in county society before 1800, exploited their territory may be illustrated by two examples. The *Newcastle Journal* of 17 January 1744 carried the following advertisement:

> At Blyth a good seaport in Northumberland, good convenience for carrying on any trade, with liberty to build warehouses, granaries, and other things necessary; also a new windmill built with stone and well accustomed, a fire-stone quarry for glasshouse furnaces, a draw-kiln for limestones, two large sheds for making pantiles and stock bricks, with a good seam of clay for that purpose.

The dignity of a baronetcy made little difference to the family's multifarious commercial activities. In the mid-1780s Sir Matthew White Ridley, Bt, MP, built a substantial new brewery at Blyth and operated it directly for nearly 10 years, making an average annual profit from it of some £400. When in 1800 he leased a butcher's shop in Blyth, he inserted in the lease a prudent stipulation that, if at any time during the lease period the premises became a public house then the tenant must buy all the ale and porter involved from the Blyth brewery owned by Ridley. (The book cited in reference 19 discusses the family's varied interests.) No clear distinction between the landed interest and the developing concern with mining and other industry existed at this time.

Coal-mining

Of all the industrial activities in the region the growth of coal-mining was far and away the most significant, not only because of its direct role in the region's economy but also because it attracted other forms of productive enterprise which could be provided with cheap supplies of coal. The principal spur to the expansion of coal-mining was the existence of a ready market, especially in the sea (i.e. ship-borne) route to London which facilitated the sale of coal. By 1826 the capital was importing about 2 million tons of coal by sea, of which only about 125,000 tons emanated from other coalfields. To meet this, and other, demands in the last decades of the eighteenth and the early part of the nineteenth centuries some of the technical barriers which had previously hindered expansion in coal production were partially overcome. The increased use of waggon ways reduced the previously prohibitive cost of leading coal from collieries at a distance from shipping points, while the increased use of steam power for pumping out water made it possible to reach deeper seams. New deeper pits were sunk at Walker (1765), Willington (1775), Felling (1779), Wallsend Main (1781), Hebburn (1794), Percy Main (1802), Jarrow (1803) and

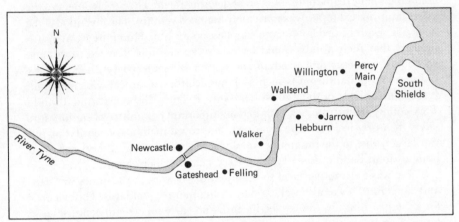

2. Some Tyneside collieries of c. 1800.

South Shields (1810). All of these Tyneside pits were over 100 fathoms in depth. Most of the increased production at this time was destined for consumption either in the region, or elsewhere in Britain, but there was already a small export trade with a long history. In 1776, for example, the Tyne exported some 77,000 tons of coal, mostly to northern Europe, with Germany, France and Scandinavia each taking about a quarter of the total[20].

The venture into greater depths in pursuit of greater coal output was pushing contemporary technology to its limits, and the toll of death and injury expanded with the number and depth of pits. Apart from a stream of small-scale accidents involving death or injury to an individual or a small group the larger, deeper collieries, with their larger work force, were the scenes of a long list of tragic large-scale disasters. In one two-year period at the beginning of the nineteenth century Ashton and Sykes[21] claim that as many as 600 North East miners were killed in pit explosions. There were at least 538 deaths in the period 1816–34, and between 1767 and 1815 there were at least seven explosions which each caused more than 30 deaths. It is probable that the first three decades of the nineteenth century saw the peak of danger in coal-mining, and the annual death rate reached a peak of around eight per thousand men involved[22]. During these years many pits had been sunk deep enough to reach seams rich in inflammable or asphyxiating gases before there was sufficient technical knowledge of how such dangers could be mitigated. Even when some safety precautions were taken, complete security was not to be attained. Human error could have disastrous consequences, as in the Harraton Row explosion in 1817[23]. An overman had warned a group of hewers that naked lights must not be used in the area in which they were working. As soon as he had moved away, one of the hewers lit a candle, complaining that the safety lamps gave inadequate light; 38 men died in the explosion which followed.

There was not in this little-governed society any official agency capable of enforcing safety regulations, or even of devising them. The development of the safety lamp, for example, was a privately financed venture. The invention of the device is securely tied to George Stephenson and Sir Humphrey Davy; it is unlikely that their ability would have been successfully directed to this end without the energy imparted to the search by some coal-owners and by disinterested philanthropists such as James Mather, a radical wine merchant from South Shields, or the Rev. Robert Gray, Rector of Bishopwearmouth and a Tory county magistrate, who chaired an important committee of enquiry into safety measures in 1813. The creation of improved methods of ventilating pits was largely due to the pragmatic work of active viewers, or colliery-managers, notably John Buddle, Lord Londonderry's chief colliery agent.

There was too another facet to the situation. If work in the mines was hard and dangerous, it was also well paid by contemporary standards. The evidence for actual earnings in the late eighteenth and early nineteenth centuries is so scrappy and defective that no reliable picture can be reconstructed in detail, but there is no reason to suppose that Adam Smith was in error when he stated in *The Wealth of Nations* that[24] 'a collier working by the piece is supposed, at Newcastle, to earn commonly about double . . . the wages of common labour . . . from the hardship, disagreeableness and dirtiness of his work'. A well-known local song from eighteenth century has a similar message:

When aw came to Walker wark
Aw had ne coat nor ne pit sark
But noo aw've gotten twe or three—
Walker Pit's dyun well for me.

While the large pits such as Walker were responsible for the lion's share of expanded production in the years around 1800 there remained also very many small collieries, serving primarily a restricted local area, usually employing a small work force and not mining to any great depth. Thomas Bewick's[25] autobiography describes the unsophisticated atmosphere associated with such small-scale enterprises, which remained largely unpublicized in the background while the limelight centred on bigger colliery undertakings elsewhere.

The second quarter of the nineteenth century saw further rapid growth in coal output. Shipments from the Tyne alone jumped from an annual total of 2.2 million tons in 1831 to 4 million tons in the early 1850s[26]. One contributory cause of this growth was the removal of export duties on coal; these were reduced in 1831, were abolished for British-owned colliers in 1845 and were finally ended in 1850. Increased demand, however, played a more important role, and from the 1830s demand abroad became increasingly significant. The Tyne was the main beneficiary of the increased export trade; foreign shipments there which stood at only 161,000 tons in 1831 passed the million tons figure in 1845, and by that time exports had moved from 7.3% of total shipments to 30.6%.

As in farming, the expansion and improved techniques in coal exploitation provided both additional resources to the older landowning interests and opportunities for new men to attain to positions of importance and affluence. Mining expertise in this period was not normally the fruit of academic study but much more of practical experience, with colliery-viewers, or colliery-managers, playing a key role, which often presented an opening for individual advancement for men of ability and ambition. An account of 1813 describes the career of an early member of this group[27]. William Brown was born at the mining village of Throckley in the mid-eighteenth century and

> . . . notwithstanding at that period the duty of coal-viewing was so little known that there were few if any to teach him precepts . . . from his close application and being endued with a solid judgement, he so far succeeded in the science of coal-mining, as enabled him to give lessons to others, and made himself highly respected as the father of the trade.

Again, as in farming, such prestige went hand in hand with more obvious financial success. Brown's services as colliery-viewer were rewarded first by substantial salaries and eventually with a share in the ownership of some of the collieries with which he was connected, some of them notably profitable undertakings.

The cost of sinking new collieries continued to grow as greater depths were reached and more expensive equipment was required. As with most branches of the economy in this period coal-mining was an uncertain business, and the history of the coalfield is scattered with instances of failure and bankruptcy. For those who succeeded, however, there were valuable prizes. In 1819, for instance, a Gateshead colliery made £7,000 clear profit on an initial capital outlay of £15,320, though this was a distinctly unusual achievement. Figures of profit of 27% and 18% are also recorded from the early nineteenth century, but profits of this amount could not be foreseen and the problems involved in sinking and working collieries during this period were so great that failure was a common event[28].

One development which increased coal output considerably and altered the configuration of the coalfield was the exploitation of the East Durham plateau. In much of that area a spread of magnesian limestone overlaid the principal seams, and there was prolonged uncertainty as to whether it was possible to find workable coal under this covering. The first breakthrough here came with the sinking of the Hetton colliery in the early 1820s. This involved penetrating nearly 60 yards of the limestone, and the sinking of the pit cost some £50,000. By contemporary standards this was a huge sum to be invested in sinking a shaft, and the cost was sufficient to break the original investors, although it served to demonstrate the viability of this section of the coalfield. Hetton was speedily followed by new pits at South Hetton, Haswell, Murton, Seaton, Thornley, Wingate, South Wingate and Castle Eden. The technical difficulties involved in this district continued to be reflected in high capital costs and frequent set-backs. The geology of the district was still only imperfectly understood, and there was a strong element of chance in some of these expensive undertakings. The first shaft at Haswell, begun in 1831, was one early disaster, and it was abandoned when, after £60,000 had been spent on it, the inflow of water proved uncontrollable. The first shaft at Murton was also abandoned, and coal was not won until after 5 years and many set-backs. At Shotton Grange sinking began in 1841, but it was not until 8 years later and after an expenditure of £120,000 that the colliery began to return a profit[29].

Developments such as these involved changes in the structure of the industry. At the beginning of the nineteenth century individuals or small partnerships could usually raise the necessary capital to open a colliery, but, when faced with such sums as the £¼ million spent before the Murton colliery began to return a profit, the number of men who could afford to embark on major new colliery schemes became more limited. The increased costs, and the continued un-certainty of success, induced most landowners to lease coal royalties rather than to exploit their coal measures directly, but this still involved a considerable amount of aristocratic interest in the profitability of coal-mining. The Marquess of Londonderry and the Earl of Durham were two leading local landowners who persisted in large-scale colliery operations for long after the middle of the nineteenth century, but by that time this activity on their part was unusual.

Another feature of the increased depth and size of colliery undertakings was an increase in the work force employed in the larger collieries, and in the complexity of their organization. A list of the workers at the South Hetton colliery in the early 1850s includes an office and managerial staff of 12, with 200 surface workers in 22 separate categories, and 316 underground workers, again with a degree of specialization; the 140 hewers were uniform enough, but the 140 putters included 'many assistants of different styles and ages,' and there were 36 men exercising supervisory functions or carrying out ancillary special-ized tasks underground[30]. This kind of complex work force was very different from the relatively unsophisticated arrangements which sufficed for the small shallower pits of an earlier period.

The history of coal-mining in the past had seen repeated attempts on the part of coal-owners to protect their interests by combining together to maintain prices, by fixing quotas of output allowed and by regulating the amount of coal which came on to the market at any one time. The last great 'Regulation of the Vend' ended in 1845, as many of its predecessors had done, in mutual recriminations among the coal-owners about the scale of quotas and their observance, though in this case the situation was complicated by the arrival on the scene of the first of the large East Durham collieries, and the problem of fitting this large-scale newcomer into the pattern[31]. Attempts by coal-miners to protect wages by similarly limiting output were no more successful in overcoming the tug of individual interests. In 1843, for instance, we find that *The Miners' Journal* complains of the behaviour of hewers in some East Durham collieries. With some difficulty the miners at South Hetton had been induced to agree to a scheme for limiting output and earnings, with a view to serving the interests of miners as a whole by limiting production and by hopefully enhancing the coal prices out of which wages were paid. When the new Murton colliery opened a group of South Hetton hewers emigrated there and at once abandoned any idea of restrictive practices of this kind. This was perhaps not very surprising when, after being limited to 3s. a day at South Hetton, they could easily realize 5s. at Murton[32]. For both miners and owners, individual interests proved more powerful than group interests within the coalfield.

The development of coal-mining was a major factor in increasing the density of population in the areas affected. The rapid growth of collieries in East Durham drew this comment in the evidence presented to the Royal Commission on the Employment of Children[33] in 1841:

> Within the last ten or twelve years an entirely new population has been produced. Where formerly there was not a single hut of a shepherd, the lofty steam engine chimneys of a colliery now send their columns of smoke into the sky, and in the vicinity a town is called, as if by enchantment, into immediate existence.

South Durham also provided a major component to the increased coal output of the second quarter of the nineteenth century, but that development can be more conveniently considered in connection with the effects of railway development later in this chapter. Together the developments in East and South Durham saw the southerly county outstrip its northern neighbour in population growth, as the newer Durham pits attracted miners and new mining communities were rapidly established. For example, Hetton-le-Hole, described as 'a hamlet' in a directory of 1821, saw its population expand from 264 in 1811 to 5,900 in 1831; thus the place that had been in 1829 merely 'a hamlet in the parish of Houghton-le-Spring' was by 1831 already emerging as a local centre to serve the needs of smaller mining communities that were springing up in this area of rapid mining expansion[34a]. (Further information on the effects of mining development exists in reference 34b.)

During the first half of the nineteenth century the output of the Great Northern Coalfield rose from some 4.5 million tons to around 10.5 million. The number of jobs on the coalfield rose from about 12,000 to about 40,000. The impact of this substantial development was, however, felt over a much wider area. The increased flow of coal necessitated expansion too in the commercial facilities involved in the sale and shipping of coal, the expansion in port and dock facilities, and a substantial expansion in the fleet of wooden sailing colliers which was a major segment of Britain's merchant marine, and one of the main centres for the employment of merchant seamen. Moreover, the importance of the coalfield's increased output was reflected too in the growth of a wide variety of coal-using industries which grew up on or near the coalfield which supplied this crucial input.

Chemical industry

One of these industries was the chemical industry, transformed in the course of the first half of the nineteenth century, though with important precedents in the long-standing participation of the area in salt manufacture[35]. The principal spur to the growth of the North East's chemical industry was the existence of a serious and notorious bottleneck in the supply of soda or alkali, which had become a vital ingredient for a number of industries; the needs of the growing textile industries were the most pressing, but this impediment in supply also hindered other industries such as glass-making and paper manufacture. Until the end of the eighteenth century the available sources of alkali were limited and subject to marked variation in quality which was a severe handicap to those who used it. The usefulness of finding a method which would be easier, cheaper and more consistent in quality of product was appreciated for many years before a solution was propounded. There had been many experiments both in Britain and elsewhere, but the decisive breakthrough was made by the French chemist, Leblanc, at the end of the eighteenth century. An interested Tynesider was already keeping a watchful eye on Leblanc's work. William Losh had been born in Cumberland, from a family of small landowners who enjoyed connections by marriage with the Lowthers and other major Cumbrian families. Losh had as a youth studied chemistry in Cambridge and metallurgy in Sweden, and in the early 1790s he had worked in Paris with the French chemist, Lavoisier. This visit made him aware of Leblanc's work, and he began a series of experiments in his new home area on Tyneside with a view to taking Leblanc's line of work to a successful conclusion. His principal associate in this work was Archibald Cochrane, Ninth Earl of Dundonald, a Scottish aristocrat who combined a keen interest in science with an almost total lack of commercial sense, an ingredient which, happily, Losh and some of his other friends possessed in ample quantity. Losh was in Paris again in the first years of the new century, to keep an eye on Leblanc's further progress, and pioneered the manufacture of alkali on Tyneside. From his inheritance of a large share in the ownership of the Walker colliery Losh obtained ready access to a supply of cheap fuel and a copious supply of brine—a nuisance in the pit but a useful ingredient in alkali manufacture by the Leblanc process. His first installations were built at Walker in 1796 and sparked off a period of massive growth in the Tyneside chemical industry. By the middle of the nineteenth century the value of the produce of the Tyneside chemical works was estimated by a local banker to be at least £700,000, probably a conservative estimate. By the early 1850s chemical-manufacturers in the Tyne area employed 3,067 of the national total of 6,326 in the industry and consumed nearly $\frac{1}{4}$ million tons of coal a year. These firms produced about a third of the national supply of alkali and two-thirds of the national output of crystal soda[36]. By that time two centres dominated the British chemical industry—Tyneside and Merseyside—which between them supplied most of the national output.

The Leblanc process was a marked improvement on any process which had gone before, but it was in fact inherently wasteful and also dangerous. Much of the technical development which took place in the Tyneside industry in the first three-quarters of the nineteenth century was directed to an increasingly complex system of ancillary processes designed to make more efficient use of plant by the manufacture of a wide range of by-products. Throughout the first half of the century the booming chemical industry of Tyneside continued, not only to provide well-paid jobs, some of which were both dangerous and uncomfortable but also to pump into the atmosphere large quantities of hydrochloric acid gas, a waste product of the Leblanc process, which also disastrously affected the environment. In the 1830s and 1840s chemical works were repeatedly assailed by farmers and householders who sought to obtain legal sanctions against this pollution. In some cases it seems reasonably plain that the attempt was a concealed attempt to blackmail the manufacturers into making substantial payments to the complainants, but other actions were sincere and amply justified. One chemical works was forced to close down, but when others were threatened there tended to be a rally of a wide range of local interests in their defence. In 1839 and 1841 the important firm of Cookson at South Shields was threatened with legal action against pollution; the firm employed more than 700 men, who demonstrated unmistakably their hostility to any attempts to destroy their employment. In 1839 the chemical-manu-facturers concerned were supported openly by the South Shields Chartists[37]: 'However we may differ from the owners of those Works in our Political Creed, yet we must express our approbation and acknowledge the benefits we receive in common with our Townsmen from those enterprising and spirited under-takings.' By mid-century the Tyneside chemical industry was still an expanding sector. The Merseyside centre was closer to the major British textile areas, while Tyneside firms came to depend on overseas orders for the sale of a high proportion of their produce. Exports of alkali, bleaching powder and soda reached about 100,000 tons a year in the third quarter of the century[38]. This dependence on overseas markets was to prove a future weakness, but it played a major part in the growth of the industry. In addition, however, the Tyneside chemical-manufacturers sold much of their output to a group of related local industries which required the same basic chemicals. These included glass and pottery manufacture, paper-making and soap-making.

The glass industry had a long record within the region, with an important contribution to its technology being made by refugee families of the seventeenth and early eighteenth centuries. It was, however, only in the nineteenth century that very-large-scale glass-making enterprises developed on both the Tyne and the Wear. In 1772 there were 16 glass-makers on Tyneside alone, but the works were not yet very large; by 1812 this number had risen to 30, and the output included a variety of glass forms, including bottles, sheet glass and window glass. By 1827 around two-fifths of the national glass output came from Tyneside alone, with Sunderland another important producer[39]. Considerable amounts of capital were involved in this industry. For example in 1838 Hartley's works at Sunderland were extended at a cost of some £50,000, and 20 years later the firm was producing one-third of the national output of sheet glass[40]. In the 1830s Cookson's glass works at South Shields was the biggest single glass-making enterprise in the country, and when it was sold in 1845 the price was £140,000. The purchasers provided an interesting example of a local commercial partnership. Nicholas Wood and William Hutt, MP for Gateshead, were both partners in the extensive coal-mining enterprise of John Bowes and Partners, George Hudson and Robert Stephenson brought engineering and railway contacts, R. P. Philipson had banking interests and a wide range of commercial contacts, while R. W. Swinburne, the existing manager of Cookson's glass works, provided technical knowledge and day-to-day management of the new firm, which traded as R. W. Swinburne and Company[41]. In this new form the company retained for many years the distinction of being the country's biggest glass-making plant, and both Swinburne and Hartley made major contributions to the 1851 Crystal Palace. The intimate connection between coal-mining and the chemical- and glass-making industries was illustrated by a high degree of multiple ownership, with interested individuals participating in the financing and control of firms in two or three of the related interests, with a view to the integration of control over vital supplies of fuel or other ingredients.

The growth of other industries

Pottery-making was another related industry which expanded in the region during this period. In 1730 John Warburton set up a pottery works at Pandon Dean, Newcastle, which used local supplies of clay and local coal to make coarser brown wares. About 1750 the works was moved to Carr's Hill, near Gateshead, and for some time finer wares were also made there. The coal trade provided another advantage here, for special clays for finer products could be cheaply imported as ballast in returning colliers. From 1817, however, with increasing competition, the Carr's Hill works reverted to coarse wares only until its final demise in 1892.

By 1800 there were at least ten sizeable potteries on Tyneside alone, and by 1850 one Tyneside firm, C. T. Maling, was the biggest manufacturer of pottery in the country, again with a concentration on the mass production of coarse wares such as containers of various kinds. Wearside was another important centre of this industry, and by 1818 as many as 300,000 pottery pieces were annually shipped from Sunderland. Sunderland made a local speciality later in the century in the production of huge quantities of decorative and colourful items—jugs, plaques, etc.—in 'Sunderland pottery', items now regarded as collectors' pieces, but then an increasingly common household embellishment. Both on Wearside and Tyneside the pottery industry was a considerable employer by mid-century, with well over 1,000 workers involved on Tyneside alone.

Soap-making and paper-making were other local industries connected to both the chemical trade and local coal supplies during this period which showed significant expansion, and in general this group of trades—the production of alkali, bleaching powder and soda, and the manufacture of glass, pottery, soap and paper—provided a useful source of wealth and employment. By 1851, for instance, glass and pottery provided 7% of all the jobs in South Shields and 5.5% in Gateshead as well as substantial numbers in other centres[42]. During the first half of the century their growth was more impressive than that of some other local industries in which a greater future still lay ahead in 1850.

Lead-mining was another regional interest which showed strong growth during the late eighteenth and early nineteenth centuries. This form of mining was carried on in areas remote from the main coal-mining districts, and it was organized with very different conventions, largely owing to the very different nature of the deposits to be worked. A system of indirect employment was normal in lead-mining, in the form described in a report[43a] of 1842 which gives the fullest account of the lead industry:

> The miners, with few exceptions, speculate on the produce of the mines in which they work. Four miners . . . form a partnership together, and they make a bargain that they will work in a certain part of a certain mine for the next three months, for so many shillings for every bing of ore which they dig out: the expense of washing and cleaning the ore, and making it fit for the furnace, being charged to them. All the other men in the mine, in parties of 4, 5, or 6 or more make bargains in the same way. These bargains are entered into a book, and the miners sign them.

(A shorter but useful account is given in reference 43b.) Lead-mining was never as dangerous an occupation as coal-mining, and there was an almost complete absence of the dangerous gases which caused so many disasters in coal mines. Lead-mining was also an occupation commonly carried on in conjunction with the working of small hill farms. Some of the subsequent processes involved in the preparation and industrial use of lead were, however, distinctly less healthy. Like contemporary coal-mining, success in lead-mining was often uncertain; the siting of the ore deposits was not easily predictable, and disappointments were common. A lucky strike could, however, be extremely profitable; in 1835 a Newcastle banker referred to the owners of the Hudgill Burn mine who[44] 'by the unprecedented success of that mine have been raised from the condition of labouring miners to very great opulence'. Among the dominant interests in northern lead-mining were the London Lead Company, employing about 1,500 employees in 1840, and the Beaumont family who then had some 2,000 workers in their employ. By the middle of the nineteenth century lead-mining

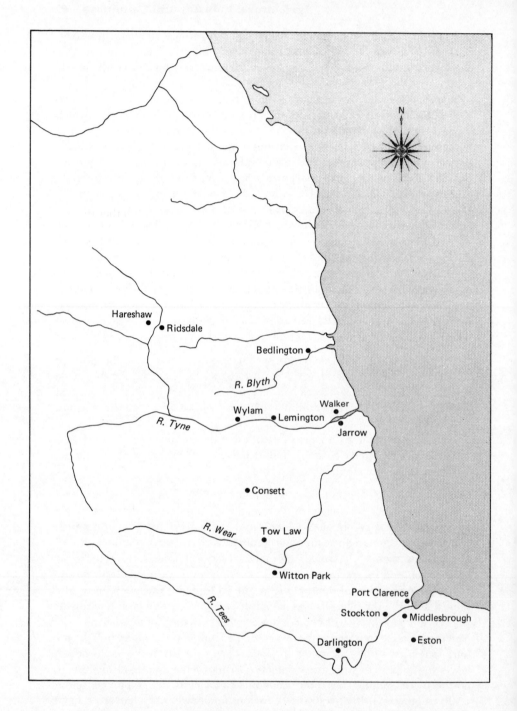

3. *Some iron-working sites within the region.*

in West Durham and South West Northumberland was approaching the peak of its prosperity.

The iron industry also expanded in the late eighteenth and early nineteenth centuries. Even before the building of the railway system produced a major increase in demand there had been a number of incentives to increased activity. Prolonged periods of war expanded demand for weapons and other articles of iron connected with warlike purposes. Even while shipbuilding was concerned with wooden ships there was a considerable maritime demand for such items as anchors and chains, a demand which grew significantly as the shipping of coal and other products increased. There was also an increasing tendency for iron to replace wood in the making of implements used in agriculture and a variety of other fields. Transport developments played a major part in increased iron consumption. From 1753 the use of iron wheels in coal waggons began to spread, while from the 1790s onwards iron rails increasingly replaced wood in colliery waggon ways[45]. With these varied incentives it is not surprising to find new iron works springing up in various places where a conjunction of coal and iron ore deposits seemed to provide particular opportunities. In Northumberland such plants were established at Lemington-on-Tyne (1799), Wylam (1836), Ridsdale (1836), and Hareshaw (1836). Iron-using firms were naturally interested in encouraging such developments; for example Pow and Fawcus of North Shields, a rapidly growing firm engaged in the making of marine ironwork, took a leading part in the Ridsdale Iron Works, in the hope of securing control over the supply of this vital raw material. However, the future of iron-making within the region was not to lie with these scattered Northumberland sites, and even before 1850 significant developments had taken place further south within the region, though these can be more suitably considered later in connection with the rise of the industry in the second half of the century.

Although the increased supplies of iron achieved in the first half of the century appear very limited in comparison with later achievements, there was already a significant drop in prices. Between 1812 and 1844, for example, waggon wheels dropped from 17*s*. to 5*s*. or 6*s*. per cwt, rails from 15*s*. to 5*s*. 6*d*. per cwt, engine grate bars from 13*s*. to about 4*s*. and bored steam cylinders from 34*s*. to 16*s*. per cwt, while the price of pig iron on Newcastle Quay sank from 8*s*. per cwt in 1812 to 2*s*. per cwt in 1844[46].

Even before this period the region presented some very notable examples of iron-using industry. During his late eighteenth-century tours Arthur Young visited Crowley's famous iron works, west of Gateshead. The firm's annual wage bill of £20,000 impressed him, as well it might, and he noted that some of the key supervisory workers there earned as much as £200 per annum. Young's[47] fertile imagination was also stirred by the metal-working machinery installed there:

As to the machines for accelerating several operations in the manufacture, the copper rollers for squeezing bars into hoops, and the scissors cutting bars of iron—the turning cranes for moving anchors in and out of the fire—the beating hammer, lifted by the cogs of a wheel; these are machines of manifest utility, simple in their construction, and all moved by water.

During the first half of the nineteenth century the scale of the iron-manufacturing industry continued to expand. At Bedlington, for example, the iron works, founded in 1736 mainly as a nail-making enterprise, branched out into the manufacture of a wide variety of iron products, and by 1850 it was employing some 2,000 workers.

Shipbuilding and ports

Shipbuilding was another industry with a long record in the region which showed considerable expansion during this period. Most shipbuilding enterprises before 1850 were, however, on a small scale, occupying riverside sites, building small wooden ships with little in the way of complex equipment and employing relatively small work forces. The one striking exception to this rule was not encouraging. At Howdon-on-Tyne Hurry's shipyard was constructed in 1758–9 and in the next few decades grew to a size and complexity unknown in other local yards[48]. By the end of the century the site included a dry dock capable of handling two ships at once, building slips which enabled four ships to be built at the same time, a quay nearly 800 feet long, a ropery, sail-making lofts and a variety of ancillary installations—this at a time when most local shipbuilding was carried on in open sites, with one vessel at a time being the usual situation. In the event the Howdon project proved overambitious; the employment of a large work force, well paid by the standards of the time, and the need to lay out considerable sums of money before any profit on ships built could be realized, proved too much for the family's financial resources. After further expansion during the early years of the French Wars and an increased reliance on orders from the government (not the speediest settler of accounts), a shipping recession in 1806 and a drying-up of government orders broke the firm, with Francis Hurry being declared bankrupt in 1806. Subsequently the various parts of the previously integrated enterprise passed into separate hands, and eventually much of the Hurry site was disused until the second half of the century.

Shipbuilding firms that operated on a smaller scale were more typical. Two Tyneside firms with a long history before them were associated with the Smith family and the Edwards family. In 1756 William Rowe owned a small shipyard at St. Peter's, on the Tyne just east of Newcastle. Later in the century Thomas Smith, of Heaton Hall, Newcastle, provided for his second son William by apprenticing him to the Rowe yard to learn the trade of shipbuilding; in 1810 the Smith family bought the yard and began shipbuilding under the name of T. and W. Smith. Between 1810 and 1836, when Thomas Smith died, the firm achieved a considerable reputation, establishing a connection with the East India trade which produced a series of orders for substantial ships. A number of celebrated East Indiamen, including the *Blenheim*, the *Hotspur* and the *Marl-borough*, were built there. Nevertheless the scale of operations, and the ships built, were small by later standards. When the *Marlborough* was completed in 1846 she was, at 1,500 tons, the largest vessel yet built on the Tyne and was regarded as a considerable achievement. In 1849 the Smith enterprise was moved to a more convenient site down river at North Shields, with the family combining for many years shipbuilding, ship-owning and ship-repairing.

At South Shields the High Docks shipyard began in 1768 and, like Rowe's yard at St Peter's, was taken over early in the next century by expanding local business interests. In this case the purchaser was George Straker, who combined farming near Blyth with important commercial interests at Newcastle. Straker's interests were subsequently inherited by his son-in-law and subsequent gener-ations of the Edwards family; like the Smiths the Edwards family combined shipbuilding, ship-owning and ship-repairing, but again their interests re-mained on a relatively small scale until the second half of the century.

By 1848 there were 36 shipbuilding yards on the Tyne alone, but none of them was very large. The Wear also was an early centre of shipbuilding. In 1800 there were probably about 1,000 shipwrights employed on the Tyne and perhaps half that number on the Wear. During the first half of the nineteenth century the Wear showed the greatest capacity for expansion in shipbuilding, and by the 1830s Lloyd's Register recognized that Sunderland was 'the most important shipbuilding centre in the country, nearly equalling as regards number and tonnage of ships built, all the other ports together'. This was something of an exaggeration as far as normal years went, but it was during this period of considerable growth that some of Wearside's most famous firms, such as Doxford and Austin and Pickersgill, began their long careers as notable shipbuilders. Between 1830 and 1850 the output of Wearside shipyards fluctu-ated markedly, annual figures of tonnage built ranging between 20,000 and 64,000 tons but settling at around 50,000 tons per annum in the 1850s.

While Wear shipyards far outstripped the Tyne yards in tonnage built during the 1830s and 1840s, the firms on the northern river were showing greater initiative in experiment and innovation in ways which were to prove immensely profitable in the years after 1850 and would cause the Tyne to regain its earlier predominance. In 1839 Marshall's yard of South Shields built the *Star*, a small passenger steamer but the North East's first iron ship. In 1841, the same yard launched another vessel, the *S.S. Bedlington*, which represented a much more startling leap forward in design convention, for she was an iron-built twin-screw train ferry, intended to carry loaded coal trucks in her hold. In this case the many new ideas incorporated in the design outstripped the practical resources of contemporary technology, and she was a commercial failure, but her building marked one important step in the evolution of merchant ship design in the region[49].

The expansion of shipbuilding was one facet of a more general improvement in transport facilities characteristic of the late eighteenth and early nineteenth centuries. In this extended service coastal shipping provided one important element. There had of course been a pattern of shipping down the East Coast for many years, but this period saw an increase in its scale, its regularity and the sophistication with which the trade was organized. We have already noted how Berwick ships played a part in this coastal trade. Advertisements make it plain that by the 1840s the tentacles of the main coastal shipping companies reached far inland in their search for profitable traffic. For example, in 1842 the six ships of the Stockton and London Shipping Company ran weekly voyages in each direction between the coast of the North East and London. Nearly 100 established pick-up points in various parts of Northumberland, Durham and North Yorkshire had by that time been organized to feed into the work of this one company. Despite the improvement of land transport facilities during the period, coastal shipping remained, as it was to do for long afterwards, a major artery of commerce, carrying huge quantities of coal but many other com- modities too and providing also a relatively cheap passenger link[50].

The increased volume of shipping concentrated attention on the state of the region's harbours. The Wear was the first major port to embark upon a systematic improvement of its harbour facilities and the Wear Commissioners were established at the very early date of 1717; in 1752 the area of their powers was extended, and from that date they always employed a full-time salaried harbour engineer[51]. Money for port improvement was raised by a statutory levy on all coal shipped from the river. The work of this harbour authority played a part in facilitating the growth of the Port of Sunderland which by 1817 ranked as one of the country's major harbours. In that year, for example, about 7,000 vessels used the port and about 1 million tons of coal were shipped there; the river improvements had ensured a minimum depth in the main channel, and over the entrance bar, of 17 feet at high water of ordinary spring tides. The South Pier was rebuilt in extended form in 1832, and the North Pier was completed in 1842. On the Tees there was nothing at all equivalent to this, although, like some Northumberland coastal ports, the later eighteenth century saw some increased activity involved with the shipping of agricultural produce from areas of increased production. There was also a limited trade in lead and in some textile materials and finished goods. Much of the Tees trade, however, was comprised in the coastal shipping of various foodstuffs, especially to London. Various small-scale efforts to improve and cheapen shipping facilities were undertaken, such as the work initiated by the Peirs family at Low Worsall, but not much progress was made; in fact harbours such as Stockton and Yarm were less satisfactory at the end of the eighteenth century than they had been earlier[52].

The Tyne also failed to imitate the Wear as a centre of harbour improvement, and this is more surprising than the inaction on the Tees, because the economic base on Tyneside had expanded markedly long before Teesside began its period of rapid growth. The question of port improvement on Tyneside, however, provides an almost classical instance of the interaction of economic, political and social factors, and the difficulty of separating history into such separate strands. By ancient chartered privileges, the town and county of Newcastle upon Tyne controlled the whole harbour of Tyne from the mouth of the river to a point well to the west of Newcastle itself. It would be difficult to maintain that Newcastle had proved in the late eighteenth and early nineteenth centuries an adequate conservator of the harbour. The most that the Newcastle authorities could claim by about 1850 was that the harbour had become no worse during the last half-century. In fact the Tyne was a treacherous and inconvenient port, with no defences at the entrance against gales which frequently strewed the Black Midden rocks with wrecks, and with a channel beset by shoals and obstructions. During the first half of the nineteenth century Newcastle took over £1 million in dues from shipping which used the port, but only about a third of that amount was spent in maintaining or improving the harbour.

Both political and economic factors developed to challenge the existing situation. Towns such as Gateshead, North and South Shields were growing in importance and population, their industry expanding and their interest in the state of the harbour becoming more acute. The Reform Act of 1832 gave these towns M.P.s of their own for the first time; whatever their party affiliation an indispensable qualification for candidates was a clear expression of hostility to Newcastle's monopoly control of the port. In 1849 Tynemouth (of which North Shields formed the larger part) and in 1850 South Shields received borough councils—Gateshead had enjoyed this status since 1835—and again Newcastle's rivals received political institutions which could join in the attack on the river monopoly. Throughout the 1830s and 1840s the other riverside towns, backed by a variety of other interests hindered by the unsatisfactory nature of the harbour, pressed the attack on the chartered privileges of the unsatisfactory custodian. Minor victories, such as the creation of separate customs facilities at the Shields end of the harbour, were followed by the major success at mid-century. Newcastle fought long and hard in defence of its privileges, and the reformed council after 1835 was every bit as fierce on this issue as its predecessor; however, the opposition and the irrefutable evidence, both of the need for improvement and of the little that had in fact been done, proved too strong, and by an Act of 1850 control of the Port of Tyne passed to the Tyne Improvement Commission. The Commission consisted of nominees from the principal towns, the interests involved in shipping, and the Admiralty. With its establishment the Tyne saw the commencement of a major sequence of port improvements, but before 1850 the performance of the region's major port on this score had been distinctly meagre.

Transport
Road transport also saw some improvements during this period. Turnpike trusts took over and improved some of the main roads during the later eighteenth century. The Great North Road had been turnpiked from 1741, but in many parts it left much to be desired until the nineteenth century. Arthur

Young on his late eighteenth-century travels found a stretch near Darlington 'execrably broke into holes, like an old pavement; sufficient to dislocate one's bones'; leaving Newcastle for Morpeth he found the first few miles adequate, 'all the rest vile'.

However, in general there was a significant improvement in the extent and condition of the region's roads. The increased export of agricultural produce from Northumberland coastal ports in the third quarter of the eighteenth century was facilitated by the construction in 1753–4 of a turnpike road which linked Hexham via Rothbury and Alnwick to the port of Alnmouth. During the early nineteenth century roads were built to connect the lead-mining districts with Tyneside and other shipping points, and the strings of lead-carrying pack ponies ceased to be a familiar sight in the lead-mining valleys. As with coastal shipping services the organization of this branch of transport became increasingly organized and comprehensive, both for goods and for passengers. In 1795 there were seven daily coach services from Newcastle, including scheduled services to Carlisle, Edinburgh and London as well as to nearer places like Morpeth and Durham. The number had more than quadrupled by 1831, when the fastest coaches aimed to reach London from Newcastle in 37 hours, though at a fare of £6 or £7 such rapid travel was beyond the normal reach of most people. Directories of the period show also the many scheduled services operated by the much slower stage waggons, with their broad wooden wheels designed to minimize road damage. By the mid-1820s, for example, the waggons of Pickersgill and Company left Newcastle for Birmingham on 6 days each week, omitting Sunday, while a rival carrier's vehicles set off for the same destination on Tuesdays, Wednesdays and Fridays. A small Northumberland village such as Barrasford in the North Tyne valley received one regular carrier's visit weekly, as did a relatively small distant town such as Brough in Stainmore.

The most striking revolution in transport during the first half of the nineteenth century was the coming of the railway. The use of waggon ways from collieries to shipping points was an old practice, and a variety of motive power had been applied to these systems. Responsibility for 'inventing the railway' need not detain us, since it is sufficiently plain that a number of innovators made contributions which together made the railway a practical possibility; there can be no doubt, however, that the North East played a crucial role in the pioneering of the new system. The pioneer Stockton and Darlington Railway was in its inspiration merely an extended waggon way, with locomotive haulage an afterthought and passenger-carrying very much an unexpected later development. The Stanhope and Tyne Railway, completed in 1834, was a good example of the way in which the early railways drew on the experience and the technology of the colliery waggon ways; on this line when first completed $10\frac{1}{2}$ miles were worked by horses, 11 miles by fixed steam haulage engines, 3 miles by self-acting inclined planes and only $9\frac{1}{4}$ miles by locomotive engines[53]. The Stockton and Darlington Railway of 1825 is celebrated in railway history as the first public railway to use locomotives; perhaps it should be remembered more as the first clear demonstration of the commercial transformation which could be produced by the construction of a railway. The impact of the Stockton and Darlington line on the collieries of South Durham was startling, the motive behind the plan an obvious one.

In the early nineteenth century land transport facilities were such that a ton of coal which fetched 4s. at a colliery near Bishop Auckland cost 8s. when carted to Darlington and 12s. at Stockton. When, in 1825, Joseph Pease was calculating the probable impact of his proposed railway he estimated that this more economical carriage would reduce the price of coal at Darlington by nearly half and at Stockton by more than half[54]. The success of the project in this respect vindicated these hopes, but in fact the value of the line came from a more extended advantage: the coming of the railway provided for the first time a viable access to the lucrative sea-sale markets for the produce of the mines of inland South Durham[55]. At the beginning of the century it cost less to move a ton of coal from Newcastle to London by sea than to move it overland from Bishop Auckland to Stockton, a distance of 19 miles. Rail carriage soon produced a reduction in coal transport costs in that area from the road figure of some 4d. to 5d. per ton per mile to the average cost on Durham coal railways by 1840 of about 1.3d. per ton per mile; this startling reduction made a crucial difference to the competitive situation of many inland collieries. The opening of the Stockton and Darlington line in 1825, and its anticipated effect on local coal prices, marked the beginning of the process, but the impact of the innovation was only limited until in 1830 the line was extended from Stockton's unsatisfactory shipping facilities to a deeper riverside terminal which was to be the first nucleus of the boom town of Middlesbrough. This railway carried 46,216 tons of coal in the operating year 1828-9, 152,262 tons in 1830-1 and 336,000 tons in 1832-3. Middlesbrough had shown a total population of 25 in the first census of 1801; the figure was 150 in 1831 and 5,463 in 1841.

Elsewhere in South Durham the impact of the coming of the railway was equally dramatic. There were coastal sites which might prove better coal ports than the difficult estuary of the Tees. In 1832 the Hartlepool Dock and Railway Company obtained powers to build a railway from that ancient harbour into adjacent colliery districts, and also to rebuild and extend the old and largely moribund port of Hartlepool. By 1841 this railway was carrying more coal than any other line in North England, and 27% of the coal shipped from the ports of the North East passed along its tracks[56]. In 1839 the line derived only 6% of its revenue from passenger traffic, and only 4% from the carriage of goods other than coal. Again the effect on the communities involved was immediate; apart from expansion in the colliery districts affected, the population of the old borough of Hartlepool shot up from 1,330 in 1831 to 5,256 in 1841. The building of a further line from Stockton to Hartlepool a few years later diverted substantial further supplies of coal from the Tees port to the new dock at Hartlepool. Continued rivalry and friction between the proprietors of the two lines prompted the owners of the later line to take steps to build their own shipping facilities, and in 1844 they obtained parliamentary powers to build their own docks outside the territory controlled by the Hartlepool Dock and Railway Company. Their first coal-shipping installation, in what was then called Hartlepool West Harbour, opened in 1847, and within the next decade a completely new town grew up with the new harbour as its nucleus and soon outstripped the older Hartlepool in size and importance.

Further north along the Durham coast a similar story had already begun. We have already seen that the Third Marquess of Londonderry was one of the active coal magnates of the period. At Seaham there had been plans for the construction of a port before Lord Londonderry acquired the estate, but such plans were not viable before the railway came on the scene and provided the cheap carriage of coal which could make such a port competitive. Londonderry owned a number of collieries in the Penshaw district, the coal being shipped through the port of Sunderland and subject therefore to significant port dues. The advantages of creating a unified system of mines, railway and port all in the same hands were obvious enough. Between 1828 and 1831 Londonderry built a new harbour, Seaham Harbour, previously a mere fishing hamlet with an open beach. Here, however, there was not to be the same spectacular growth which marked the rise of Middlesbrough and West Hartlepool. Although some £300,000 was spent on its creation, the new harbour could not in its original form cope with the rapidly expanding output of Londonderry's pits. In 1854 the Londonderry Railway was therefore extended to a terminal at Sunderland's Hendon Dock; although Seaham Harbour saw further development in both the nineteenth and twentieth centuries it never experienced the scale of growth of its southern neighbours. Railway-building also brought major developments in opening out the hinterland for both Tyne and Wear coal-shipping installations, which showed marked extensions. In general the coming of the railway produced a multi-lateral effect on the regional economy; improved access and cheaper carriage enabled some key inland areas of the coalfield to enter the home and overseas markets on a large scale, while the continued building of railways at home and abroad brought with it a significant increase in demand for labour and materials, notably the demand for iron rails and the development of works for the construction of railway engines and rolling stock.

Railway-building within the region brought considerable demands for capital investment. Two phases can be distinguished[57]. The first, typical of the 1830s, was concerned with the building of relatively short local lines designed to carry coal from mines to a point of shipment. The second phase, more typical of the 1840s, saw further building of the same kind, but also the construction of major lines linking the region and joining it to other areas. In the first phase the necessary capital came mainly from sources within the region, but in the second outside capital played a more important role. This is scarcely surprising in view of the wider interest in trunk line construction, and the greater costs involved, as well as the greater degree of sophistication reached in railway investment by the 1840s. Of the 537 £100 shares in the Stockton and Darlington Railway

issued in 1823, 267 were held by residents of North East England, only 137 by
London sources; the relatively large number, 75, of shares held in Norwich was
a reflection of the family connections of the Teesside backers of the project. One
of the early trunk line companies, the Great North of England Railway, showed
a very different pattern as early as 1835; of a total capital raised of some
£850,000, £¼ million was raised in London and well over £200,000 in Manchester and Liverpool, while less than a third came from the area in which the
railway was built.

By 1850 the region was served by a network of railways, even if the system was
far from complete. A process of amalgamation and rationalization soon began,
with an early culmination in the creation in 1854 of the North Eastern Railway
which was to be one of the best managed and most profitable of all British
railways for the remainder of the century.

Engineering
Railway development gave a major spur to the development of the region's
engineering industry. The Newcastle works of Robert Stephenson and
Company were one of the first locomotive-building plants to be established.
This enterprise originally had four partners—Edward Pease, Michael Long-
ridge, George Stephenson and Robert Stephenson—all of them major railway
pioneers. Much of the original capital came from Pease, whose family had
played a crucial role in the financing of the Stockton and Darlington line, and
he had no cause to regret his further investment. In 1839 he received at least
£1,000 as a return on his original £1,600 shares; in 1848 he received £7,000,
while in 1853 he received £2,000, having refused part of the sums due to him as
they represented profits derived from the building of engines for warships[58].
Little love was lost between Pease and Robert Stephenson, but this did not
impair the company's fortunes. Like other engineering enterprises, the firm
depended heavily not only on the contribution of the governing partners but
also on the work of key employees both in the works themselves and in the
equally important task of maintaining an adequate flow of orders from
customers both at home and abroad. On the shop floor George Crow was first
chief foreman and subsequently works-manager. In the drawing office design
work owed much to Ralph Whyte and William Wheallans, the latter becoming a partner in 1855. Many lucrative contracts came to the Forth Street
Works as a result of the skill and persistence of John Starbuck, the company's
roving sales representative abroad. Robert Stephenson was also fortunate in
having the services of William Hutchinson, who gradually took over from him
much of the immediate management functions as other commitments obliged
Stephenson to spend long periods abroad, and Hutchinson too entered the
partnership in 1845, after working with the Stephensons for more than 20 years.
The firm's success raised these men to financial and social positions of some
note, as well as providing what was in contemporary terms well-paid
employment for many Tyneside workers.

Not surprisingly, however, it was Robert Stephenson himself who displayed the rewards of success most plainly. He became one of the country's most distinguished engineers, with an international record of distinction. When Robert was born in 1803 his father, George, was a colliery workman, unknown outside a limited circle. By 1850 Robert Stephenson had an income of some £30,000 per annum, equal to the patrimony of many an aristocratic family; part of this wealth was inherited from his father's successful career, part of it of his own making. Robert was Hon. D.C.L. (Oxon), MP for Whitby (and a staunch Tory), Knight Grand Cross of the Order of St Olaf, Chevalier in the Legion d'Honneur, Knight of the Order of Leopold. When he died in 1859 he was buried in Westminster Abbey. On the day of the funeral shipping on Thames, Tyne, Wear and Tees lay silent with flags at half-mast, while on Tyneside all business activity ceased at noon. The workers of his Forth Street Works at their own request marched 1,500 strong, to a memorial service.

A similar, if less grandiose, success story in the engineering industry on Tyneside, from even smaller beginnings, was the partnership of Robert and William Hawthorn. These two brothers were sons of an older Robert, who was for more than 50 years employed as an engineer at the Walbottle colliery, a few miles west of Newcastle. In January 1817 the younger Robert set up a small engineering workshop at Forth Banks, Newcastle, with a view to the manufacture of steam engines and general engineering work. His original work force consisted of four men, but the enterprise prospered and succeeded in winning contracts and a reputation for reliability. For example, in 1820, the year in which William Hawthorn joined the works, the Hawthorn Company built a steam-driven crane for hoisting ballast out of ships at St Anthony's Quay, just east of Newcastle. In 1822 steam power was first applied to the firm's own machinery, when some of the work was done by steam-powered lathes. The growth in demand for steam engines and similar equipment brought considerable expansion. The work force rose from four in 1817, to ten by 1818, 34 by 1820, 185 by 1830, 550 by 1840 and just under 1,000 by mid-century, all of this growth being concentrated in premises in central Newcastle near the works of Robert Stephenson and Company. Part of the Hawthorn success was due to a reputation for sound design and good workmanship; for example, an engine built in 1824 for the plate glass factory of Cookson and Cuthbert was still working away satisfactorily 40 years later. Like many other contemporary enterprises financial problems arose from time to time; two fires, for example, involved substantial rebuilding operations. Colliery engines and other mining equipment formed an important market, and colliery companies were notoriously slow payers. In 1847 the Hawthorn brothers had a narrow squeak when they nearly burnt their fingers through involvement in the North of England Joint Stock Bank, but they were fortunate enough to extricate themselves from its affairs before the final collapse. One notable strength of the firm was its very good record in industrial relations; even when the firm had grown to considerable size the brothers proved kindly and paternalistic employers, and industrial strife was unknown during the long period in which they directed the company's affairs.

The Stephenson and Hawthorn firms provide good examples of the potential growth to be derived from success in the engineering industry. There were other firms of similar size and similar success; there were others which began with equally high hopes, but whether because of ineptitude or adverse circumstances, they failed, for, while demand for engineering products expanded, it was a competitive trade in which a great deal of skill and perseverance was a prerequisite for success. By 1850 engineering in various forms had established an important place among the region's industries, but its expansion still had far to go.

Textile industry in decline

Hitherto the elements in the regional economy to be considered have been areas of continuing development. That was not, however, the whole story, and there were other sectors in which failure was equally marked. If the Merseyside chemical industry owed much to the continued growth of textile manufacture in nearby areas, the textile industry of North East England told a different story. No one now would automatically think of this region as a notable textile centre, except perhaps for modern man-made fibres, but this would not have been nearly so clear to an observer at the end of the eighteenth century. By that time the region included in Darlington one significant textile-manufacturing town, while Barnard Castle and Durham also showed sizeable enterprises in this sector. Darlington certainly possessed other industries, such as the making of optical glass, but it was primarily a textile town. River Skene provided ample water power and by the late 1820s there were nine linen and seven woollen or worsted mills in the town. Surrounding villages provided further contributions to the local textile industry. Barnard Castle had four mills for spinning wool, Durham shared its interests between linen and wool, with three mills for the former and four mills for the latter.

However, the North East textile industry spread much more widely than this. In Northumberland, for instance, there were textile works at Alnwick, Mitford, Berwick, Corbridge, Haltwhistle, Hexham and Morpeth. A few of these early textile factories enjoyed a long life. At Acklington Park an old iron works converted into a blanket mill in 1791 continued at work until 1930. The Otterburn tweed mill, built in 1821, survived into the last quarter of the twentieth century. Most of the textile enterprises of the North East, however, proved short lived. A good example of how transient they could be comes from South East Durham. A directory of 1793 recorded the building of a large cotton mill on the outskirts of Castle Eden, but a directory of 1828 tells a different story[59]: 'Factory—a hamlet half a mile south of Castle Eden where there was formerly an extensive cotton manufactory, but it has long since gone to decay, though the cottages built for the workmen are still remaining'.

Even in Darlington the importance of textile manufacture did not persist, although in 1831 25% of the town's adult males were directly employed in the industry, in addition to a good deal of employment in neighbouring communities and the employment of a significant number of women. Darlington's industries in the later nineteenth century were to be railways, iron and steel, and not linen, wool and worsted. We do not know in detail the reasons for the decline of the region's textile industry, but the existence of so many and perhaps more attractive alternative outlets for the region's capital may have played a part, and there is no reason to suppose that the causes which crippled such other textile areas as East Anglia and the West Country did not also apply here. These could include such factors as poor organization in comparison with the growth areas of Lancashire and Yorkshire, the slower adoption of new technology and fewer opportunities for economies of scale.

In addition to the failure of such an industry to follow up earlier expansion, there were numerous instances within the region of individual initiative which failed to realize the high hopes with which they were inaugurated. In the later eighteenth century and earlier nineteenth century the pace of economic growth clearly quickened, and it was as if a wave of energy spread through many sectors of the region's economic activity. Many individuals saw in a period of change opportunities which should be seized and exploited, but not all of these attempts were well conceived or fortunate enough to spark off sustained growth. Scores of examples of this kind could readily be collected from directories, local newspapers, banking correspondence and bankruptcy proceedings, but perhaps one example may serve to illustrate this category. When in 1770 Arthur Young[60] visited Belford in North Northumberland he described how the principal local landowner, Abraham Dickson, had established there a woollen mill, a tannery, collieries and large lime kilns, '13 years ago it did not contain above 100 souls . . . they now amount to six times that number'. Even the enterprise of an alert landowner of considerable means could not, however, overcome the inherent disadvantages of Belford's limited natural resources and remote situation. The village's emergence from a predominantly rural aspect was to be brief, and half a century later directories were silent as to the village's industrial activities.

Growth of prosperity and banking

The overall result of the complex history of improvement and growth on the one hand, failure and disappointment on the other, was a considerable increase in the region's revenue and employment. This was reflected not only in the field of productive enterprises themselves but also in the various commercial and financial institutions employed in the service of the region's economy, though here again an overall pattern of significant growth must include also a variety of set-backs, some of them distinctly damaging.

Newcastle had been for centuries a major trading centre, and during the late seventeenth and the eighteenth centuries there was a marked expansion of the town's mercantile interests and contacts. Well before there was any very great industrial expansion there had been considerable expansion in trade from the Tyne in a wide variety of commodities—coal, lead, agricultural produce of various kinds, grindstones, glass, for instance—and the principal merchant houses gradually built up complex chains of contacts and agencies in other parts of Britain and throughout West Europe. The emergence during the first half of the nineteenth century of a more sophisticated pattern of company structure and investment was marked; by 1841 there were nine men acting as stockbrokers in Newcastle, and the number had risen to about 20 by 1845. At least some of these brokers had moved into that business from an original base in Newcastle's mercantile trading interests. In 1845 the creation of the Newcastle Stock Exchange signalled the consolidation of this aspect of the regional economy[61].

Similar activities, such as the provision of insurance services, saw a similar growth, but perhaps the history of the region's banking facilities illustrates best how the expanding economy produced additional resources of financial organization. Already before the mid-eighteenth century the need for orderly arrangements for the transmission of funds had become clear. Delays in the sailing of the collier fleet caused by adverse weather could send shivers of uncertainty through many sectors of the region's affairs, as the receipt of credits from coal sales in London and elsewhere had become an important feature of the region's livelihood. The increase in trade and in the region's output in various forms, together with the desire to find profitable outlets for investment of the increasing resources available, produced a developed system of banking facilities.

The first local firm recognizable as a bank, Bell, Cookson, Carr and Airey, was set up in Newcastle by 1755 at latest, and was probably the second oldest of Britain's country banks. The capital of the firm at its foundation consisted of £2,000, in four equal shares held by the original partners, all of them men of considerable means, active in a wide variety of agricultural, commercial and industrial activities within the region. The bank returned a profit of £3,705 in 1771, £3,000 in 1772 and £5,712 in 1776. Not surprisingly this early example soon found imitators, with a second bank founded at Newcastle in 1768, a third in 1777, a fourth in 1784 and a fifth in 1788. As early as 1788 Newcastle bankers had already created a standing committee to deal with matters of mutual concern. Other local centres also joined in. The Backhouse bank at Darlington, founded in 1774, was the most famous bank in the North East outside Newcastle. James Backhouse and his son, Jonathan, were originally Quaker linen- and worsted-manufacturers in Darlington, though their interests were by no means confined to these trades. The commercial side of their operations brought a gradual extension into the provision of financial services to their customers, and then to others also, and developed into a range of banking operations.

The partners in these early private banks emerged from groups already possessing considerable resources and active in interests within the region which were increasingly in need of banking services. Many of them provided access to resources much greater than the bank's nominal capital. The Backhouses, for example, were part of a close-knit and co-operating network of wealthy Quaker families,which included the Gurney family and which could be relied upon to rally round in any time of stress. The first Newcastle bank—the 'Old Bank' as it became known locally—attracted into partnership members of the wealthy Ridley family which, as we have already seen, combined extensive landowner-ship with a wide range of other interests. The fifth Newcastle bank, founded in 1788 largely with money acquired by the original partners in India, later passed into the hands of the Lambton family, and so was linked with one of the richest of Durham's landowning and coal-owning families.

Even where such important connections to wealthy backing existed, banking could be a precarious business within a relatively unsophisticated and unregu-lated economy. Unlimited liability existed for partners, and subsequently for shareholders in joint stock banks, until legislation of 1862. However cleverly a bank invested the resources entrusted to it, an unpredictable financial crisis might blow up and cause serious pressure to build up on the resources immediately available to local banks. It remained difficult to reconcile profit-able application of deposited funds with the maintenance of adequate liquidity to enable the bank to meet unexpected calls for money; any sign that a bank was finding it difficult to meet immediate demands for payment could be disastrous. Six times between 1772 and 1816 local banks found themselves under acute pressure, and on each occasion they were sustained by the local dominant minorities from which the partners were normally drawn and which fully appreciated the value of these institutions to local interests. On those occasions when rumours spread that local banks were under pressure, large meetings of leaders of the region's society and economy were held and firmly expressed their confidence in the banks and their continued willingness to accept the payments of sums due to them for any reason in the notes issued by the banks. In 1793, by which time local banks already had nearly £¼ million of their own notes in circulation, local landowners and business men provided guarantees of support to the local banks amounting to almost £½ million, when a wider financial crisis in Britain brought about a temporary run on banks in the North East. Even this kind of massive support could not always save the region's financial institutions. Newcastle's second bank, founded in 1768 by two prominent local figures, Aubone Surtees and Rowland Burdon, failed catastrophically in 1818; the entire estates of the partners were put up for sale in the consequent bankruptcy proceedings. However Rowland Burdon, the son of the bank's founder, was very well known and very popular in the area, and, although he lost all of his other assets, a consortium of sympathizers contrived arrangements which allowed him to retain the core of his family estates in County Durham, although for many years they were mortgaged to pay off the failed bank's liabilities. Not all bank partners were so fortunate in their friends.

A major period of banking instability marked the years 1826-57, with the establishment of joint stock banking companies after an Act of 1826. The advantages appeared very great. The profits of banking operations in an expanding economy could now become readily available to many people who could not conceivably find the resources needed for a partnership in a viable private bank. In North East England the movement began with the foundation of a joint stock bank at Darlington in 1831, followed by the Newcastle-based North of England Joint Stock Bank in 1832. The mid-1830s saw the foundation of a number of other joint stock banks, of which much the most important was the Northumberland and Durham District Bank, which expanded rapidly to take a prominent place in the region's economy. This bank's mushroom-like growth was greatly assisted by its acquisition in 1839 of the business of New-castle's 'Old Bank'. This junction arose out of the decision of the new head of the Ridley family to withdraw from the banking business in which his father and grandfather had taken a leading role, in order to concentrate his energies on the family's other varied interests. The remaining partners, instead of continuing on the old basis with the recruitment of suitable new partners, decided to amalgamate their established interests with the joint stock Northumberland and Durham District Bank. But, before going on to the subsequent history of the region's joint stock banks, it is necessary to note the arrival on the scene of what was to prove a crucial influence on the region's financial institutions, the Newcastle branch of the Bank of England.

Banking legislation of 1826 provided for the creation of branches of the Bank of England in the provinces. The Newcastle branch was the ninth to be set up and began business in April 1828. The decision to establish the branch was met, in the North East as elsewhere, by strong local opposition. Bank of England branches carried out all normal banking transactions, and existing local banks were understandably angry at the irruption into their bailiwick of this formidable competitor. Relations between the local banks and the newcomer were strained for a number of years. Resentment at this serious competition was sustained by the realization that the central bank intended to attack the independent note issue of existing local banks. The first Agent of the Bank of England in Newcastle proved tactless in his dealings with the existing banks, but fortunately his successors were cast in a different mould and sought instead to attain their ends by a policy of sweet reasonableness, sympathy and co-operation. The aim of replacing the note issue of local banks was still pursued strongly, but much more by a policy of offering sufficient inducements to local banks to persuade them to give up their independent issue voluntarily and to act instead as distribution points for Bank of England notes. These tactics, backed by experience of how useful a cordial co-operation with the Bank of England could be in practice, proved successful. For example, in 1840 one of the area's oldest and strongest private banks, the Lambton Bank, accepted the Bank of England's terms for the ending of its own note issue in return for generous allowances for acting as an issuing agency for Bank of England notes. By that time the branch Bank of England had arrived at a position of influence and acceptance within the regional economy. As with other local banks the branch operated in a variety of ways. With co-operation established with existing local banks, the branch became a major link in a chain of commercial intelligence which steadily developed in scope and reliability about the credit-worthiness of a wide variety of company and individual, which contributed to establishing wider areas of business confidence and higher standards of commercial integrity. The ways in which a series of skilful and flexible Agents built up the prestige and influence of the Newcastle branch proved of immense value to the region's economy during the mid-century years.

The many joint stock banks founded in the wave of euphoria of the 1830s proved in the end a serious weakness in the region's financial arrangements, although during their brief lives their role in channelling resources into economic developments was by no means insignificant in the region's expansion. Joint stock banks were not at all immune from the perils which had already become plain with private country banks. However impressive a bank's resources might be—and they usually appeared much more impressive in appeals for investment and deposits than they were in reality—there remained the serious difficulty of reconciling profitable investment of funds with the ready availability of money to meet calls for withdrawal from depositors. Joint stock banks attracted funds from a wide variety of sources, and their apparent strength and soundness in their early days proved a magnet for small as well as large investors. While large holdings of bank stock were common, lists of shareholders included also the nest-eggs of the elderly and of widows, while such investment still entailed unlimited liability.

The early joint stock banks also had their own peculiar weaknesses. In order to attract funds, promoters regularly succumbed to the temptation to exaggerate their resources and the glittering prospects of success. Moreover the directors of these new banks were generally men who had other interests of their own, and the temptation to direct bank funds into their own personal concerns was often irresistible. It was less easy for shareholders in a large joint stock bank to keep tabs on the bank's operations than it was for the partners in a private bank. The failure of some of the early local joint stock banks was due to ineptitude or what could fairly be considered to be downright bad luck. In other cases, however, the reality was more sinister. When the Sunderland Joint Stock Bank, founded in 1836, collapsed in 1851 a contemporary described its affairs:

> The managing clique of *Tartuffes*, over a series of years, employed the capital in their own shipping transactions—concealed these transactions from the other directors and clerks—had fictitious accounts opened—closed these accounts, when the speculation that originated them failed, by crediting them with cheques drawn against their previously overdrawn private accounts—released each other from liabilities to the bank—made arrangements out of bank funds with their creditors—manufactured, amongst themselves accommodation paper to carry on an unprofitable business—and continued this business until it broke down under the weight of helpless and hopeless ruin.

The directors responsible for this mess included men of great prominence in the commercial, social and political life of Wearside, such as Andrew White, three times Mayor of Sunderland and one of the borough's M.P.s from 1837 to 1841. The liabilities incurred by the 'managing clique' fell upon the other shareholders, and it was not until 6 years after the bank's collapse that these victims managed to clear off the remaining debts.

This Sunderland bank was, however, very small compared with the two great joint stock banks founded in the region during this period—the North of England Bank of 1832 and the District Bank of 1836. Both of these banks grew rapidly and came to play important roles in the region's economy, and yet both were in reality unsound from the beginning. It was here that the presence of the Bank of England branch proved a crucial asset to the region's financial machinery. The failure of banks as important as these two became was not just a disaster for directors and shareholders but brought sudden and serious problems to the many institutions and individuals who had come to rely on the services provided. The North of England Bank faced recurring crises but struggled on until it collapsed during the financial panic of 1847. The calamitous effect of this failure on the bank's customers, who included many of the large employers in the region, was alleviated by the responsible reaction of the Newcastle Agent of the Bank of England who, on his own authority, made available enough funds to meet wages and similar needs to the customers of the failed bank, and he thereby prevented a commercial failure from leading to considerable local distress.

The District Bank, of even greater regional importance, was hard pressed in 1847, but here again the Bank of England acted to shore up a major financial institution, the failure of which would damage many sectors of the regional economy. The Bank of England also embarked upon a prolonged campaign of persuasion and pressure to induce the District Bank to put its distinctly ricketty structure into order. The Bank of England Agent extracted from the directors of the District Bank information as to the latter's actual position, in return for the proffer of continued support. Among the facts elicited in this way was the information as to the ways, or some of them, in which District directors had exploited the bank for their own purposes. When the Bank of England learned that one director, R. P. Philipson, had unsecured loans from the bank of more than £100,000, his exclusion from the directorship was made a condition of further help. In this persistent attempt to shore up the region's principal joint stock bank—and a principal competitor—the Bank of England acted with the best of motives, but it was backing a loser. In the years after 1847 the District Bank, despite repeated and profuse promises of amendment, floundered on from crisis to crisis and from expedient to expedient. Although nominally possessed of large capital resources, its means never in practice matched its claims, while bank funds were continually used to buttress the speculations of some of the principal directors. The worst single instance of this was the lavish support given to the Derwent Iron Company of Consett, with which some of the bank's directors were deeply involved. However strong the future prospects of iron-making at Consett were to be, this first company there was distinctly weak, and yet the District Bank locked up in its affairs such huge sums of money as to deprive the bank of the necessary amounts of liquid working funds. The insecure bank was in no state to resist the pressure of a second financial panic in 1857. Time and time again in the past the Bank of England had come to the rescue, time and time again the District Bank directors had failed to mend their ways, and now in 1857 the Bank of England threw in its hand as far as sustaining the ailing bank was concerned. It seemed obvious that there was no point in continuing to shore up an inherently mismanaged and insolvent firm, and in 1857 the Bank of England refused frantic pleas for a huge extension of further credit. However, the lesson of the crisis of 1847 had been learnt, and the Bank of England made careful preparations to minimize the regional impact of the impending failure. The Newcastle Agent was not this time faced with a crucial personal responsibility. Once the decision had been taken to refuse further support, the Deputy Governor of the Bank of England came to Newcastle, fully authorized to use his discretion in providing funds to help the customers of the failed bank to surmount the collapse. In two days after the District Bank's failure was known the Newcastle branch of the Bank of England made available more than $£\frac{1}{4}$ million to customers of the failed bank, including for example leading local colliery companies, in order to enable them to pay their workers. Both in 1847 and 1857 the action of the Bank of England had been taken, not on commercial grounds primarily, but explicitly to cushion society in the area against the sudden stoppage of funds normally provided by the failed bank. Here for example is part of a letter from the Newcastle branch during the 1857 crisis:

> I beg to acknowledge . . . the former authorizing me to assist as much as possible the manufactories and collieries in this neighbourhood in meeting the pays of their workmen . . . I beg to say that this liberal concession has been of the utmost benefit, as by it all the workmen in this district will this day receive their pays as usual, and thereby a calamity of the most disastrous kind has been averted from this locality; for it is impossible to say what would have been the consequence had a mass of workmen infuriated by the loss of their hard earned wages been let loose on the community . . . our counter has been completely besieged by parties wanting assistance to meet their wages . . . not one person having a pay to make either large or small has been sent away without getting the required assistance.

The catastrophe to the District Bank in 1857 involved the disappearance of the last of the local joint stock banks founded during the 1830s and the end of a period of instability in local banking. With this failure local banking pre-dominance returned to the sounder private banks of the area, many of which continued important independent financial institutions until the end of the century, and to the local branch of the Bank of England. The bitter experience of the first half of the century, together with increasingly effective legislative controls, ensured that the region's vital banking facilities during the second half of the century were more soundly based and responsible, and this was to be a matter of some importance in the accelerating economic growth of the latter part of the nineteenth century. It is, however, unlikely that this marked improvement in prudence and integrity would have come about without the very plain lessons taught in the first half of the century during a period of experiment and discovery in banking practices.

(This account of regional banks is drawn from two principal sources, references 62a and 62b. The first source is the extensive correspondence of the Newcastle branch in the Bank of England's record office, and the second is a book, written by a man who served for many years in the Newcastle branch of the Bank of England, which contains a very full and well-informed account.)

By 1850 North East England had seen a degree of economic development startling in the light of the region's experience in any earlier period, though during the late eighteenth and early nineteenth centuries other regions of Britain had achieved markedly greater growth rates, particularly evident in the achievements—in every sense prodigious—of the main textile areas. The second half of the century was to see important changes in these relative positions.

References

1 S. Macdonald, *The Development of Agriculture and the Diffusion of Agricultural Innovation in Northumberland, 1750-1850, Ph.D. Thesis*, Newcastle University, 1974.
   J. Bailey and G. Culley, *General View of the Agriculture of Northumberland, Cumberland and Westmorland*, 1805, modern edn, 1972, ed. D. J. Rowe.

2a A. Farmer, 'Sketch of a Tour through the Northern Counties of Scotland', *Farmer's Magazine*, no. 2, 1801, p. 421.

 b H. C. Pawson, *Cockle Park Farm*, 1960, p. 19.

3 Josephine E. Butler, *Memoir of John Grey of Dilston*, 1869, p. 167.

4 J. C. Hodgson, 'Elsdon Lairds', *Proceedings of Berwick Naturalists Club*, vol. 22, 1914, pp. 3-13.

5 Bailey and Culley, op. cit., 1972 edn, p. xxii.

6 A. Young, *A Six Months' Tour Through the North of England*, vol. II, 2nd edn, 1771, p. 91.

7 S. Macdonald, 'The Progress of the Early Threshing Machine', *Agricultural History Review*, vol. 23, 1975, part I, pp. 63-77.

8 T. Bewick, *A Memoir Written by Himself*, 1862, modern edn, Oxford University Press, 1975, pp. 140–1.

9 D. J. Rowe, 'The Culleys , Northumberland Farmers, 1767–1813', *Agricultural History Review*, vol. 19, 1971, part II, pp. 156–74.
  S. Macdonald, 'The Role of George Culley of Fenton in the Development of Northumberland Agriculture', *Archaeologia Aeliana*, 5th ser., vol. III, pp. 131–41.

10 Rowe, op. cit., p. 174.

11 Butler, op. cit.

12 ibid., p. 153.

13 Bewick, op. cit., p. 7.

14 Parson and White, *Directory of Northumberland and Durham, etc.*, vol. II, 1828, pp. 374–5.

15 Rowe, op. cit., p. 170.

16 W. Fisher Cassie, 'Early Civil Engineering in Northumbria', *Department of Civil Engineering Bulletin*, Newcastle University, no. 43, June 1972, p. 14.

17 James Mulcaster, manuscript, c. 1805.

18 S. Wrathmell, *Deserted Villages in Northumberland*, vol. I, *Ph.D. Thesis*, University College, Cardiff, 1975, p. 243.

19 W. R. Sullivan, *Blyth in the Eighteenth Century*, 1971.

20 N. R. Elliott, 'A Geographical Analysis of the Tyne Coal Trade', *Tijdschrift voor Econ. en Soc. Geografie*, April 1968, p. 85 et seq.

21 T. S. Ashton and J. Sykes, *The Coal Industry of the Eighteenth Century*, 1929, p. 52.

22 H. and B. Duckham, *Great Pit Disasters*, 1973, p. 53.

23 ibid., pp. 42–3.

24 Quoted by Ashton and Sykes, op. cit., pp. 147–8.

25 Bewick, op. cit., p. 28.

26 Elliott, op. cit., p. 85.

27 R. Edington, *A Treatise on the Coal Trade*, 1813, pp. 123–4.

28 Ashton and Sykes, op. cit., appendix C, 'A Note on Profits'.

29 W. A. Moyes, *Mostly Mining*, 1969, chapter 7.

30 Anon. (J. R. Leifchild), 'Our Coal and Our Coal Pits', (1853), pp. 182–3.

31 A. J. Taylor, 'Combination in the Mid-nineteenth-century Coal Industry', *Transactions of the Royal Historical Society*, 5th ser., vol. III, 1953.
  R. W. Sturgess, *Aristocrat in Business*, Durham County Local History Society, 1975.
  D. Large, 'The Third Marquess of Londonderry and the End of the Regulation, 1844–5', *Durham University Journal*, vol. LI, 1958–9, pp. 1–9.
  A. J. Heesom, 'Entrepreneurial Paternalism: The Third Lord Londonderry and the Coal Trade', *Durham University Journal*, vol. LXVI, 1974, pp. 238–56.

32 *The Miner's Journal*, 21 October 1843.

33 Royal Commission on the Employment of Children, *First Report of Commissioners, Mines*, 1842, part I, appendix, p. 143.

34a B. F. Capper, *A Topographical Dictionary of the United Kingdom*, 1829, p. 414.

  b R. Barker, *The Houghton-le-Spring Poor Law Union, M.Litt. Thesis*, Newcastle University, 1974.

35 W. A. Campbell, *The Old Tyneside Chemical Trade*, 1964; *A Century of Chemistry on Tyneside*, 1969.

36 Bank of England, Newcastle Branch, correspondence, 20 April 1850, 3 May 1851, 10 February 1853.

37 D. J. Rowe, 'The Economy of the North-East in the Nineteenth Century', *Northern History*, vol. VI, 1971, p. 131.

38 Anon., *Notes on the Leading Industries of the River Tyne*, 1886, pp. 2, 7.

39 Parson and White, op. cit., vol. I, p. lxxxii.

40 Bank of England, op. cit., 24 December 1838.
  Anon., *A History of the Trade and Manufactures of the Tyne, Wear and Tees*, revised edn, 1863, p. 178.

41 Bank of England, op. cit., 25 July 1845.

42 D. J. Rowe, 'Occupations in Northumberland and Durham, 1851–1911', *Northern History*, vol. VIII, 1973, pp. 119–31.

43a C. J. Hunt, *The Lead Miners of the Northern Pennines*, 1970, p. 35.

  b L. Turnbull, *The History of Lead Mining in the North East of England*, 1975.

44 Bank of England, op. cit., 11 April 1835.

45 R. L. Galloway, *Annals of Coal Mining and the Coal Trade*, vol. I, 1898, pp. 283, 318, 366.

46 Anon., *Inventions, Improvements and Practice of Benjamin Thompson*, 1847, p. 89.

47 Young, op. cit., vol. III, pp. 10–11.

48 W. Richardson, *History of the Parish of Wallsend*, 1923, pp. 199–204.

49 S. B. Martin and N. McCord, 'The Steamship *Bedlington*, 1841–54'. *Maritime History*, vol. I, no. 1, 1971, pp. 46–72.

50 Principal local libraries and record offices, posters and handbills giving details of coasting services.

51 A. W. Skempton, *The Engineers of Sunderland Harbour, 1718–1817, First Rolt Memorial Lecture*, September 1975.

52 P. Barton, 'Low Worsall: the Shipping and Trade of an Eighteenth-Century "Port" on the River Tees', *The Mariner's Mirror*, vol. 55, no. 1, 1969, pp. 57–76.

53 L. T. C. Rolt, *George and Robert Stephenson*, 1960, p. 263.

54 N. Sunderland, *A History of Darlington*, 1968, pp. 61, 67.

55 Sir G. Head, *A Home Tour through the Manufacturing Districts of England in the Summer of 1835*, 1836, pp. 298–306.

56 R. Wood, *West Hartlepool*, 1967, p. 13.

57 A. G. Kenwood, *Capital Investment in North Eastern England, 1800–1913, Ph.D. Thesis*, London University, 1962, p. 63 et seq.

58   Sir A. E. Pease, *The Diaries of Edward Pease*, 1907, pp. 147, 168, 213, 264, 303, 323.
      Rolt, op. cit., pp. 257–9.
59   Parson and White, op. cit., vol. II, p. 265.
60   Young, op. cit., vol. III, pp. 50–8.
61   J. R. Killick and W. A. Thomas, 'The Stock Exchanges of the North of England, 1836–1850', *Northern History*, vol. V, 1970, p. 121.
62a   Bank of England, op. cit.
  b   M. Phillips, *A History of Banks, Bankers and Banking in Northumberland, Durham and North Yorkshire*, 1894.

2 Social Change and Social Problems

Crime and vice

The economic developments of c. 1760–1850 occurred within the framework of a regional society which was neither simple nor uniform but which instead presented complexities and contrasts in modes of behaviour at all social levels.

There were some aspects of the life of this period in which North East England could claim to exhibit high levels of orderliness and internal peace. For example, figures of committals for the deliberate firing of crops, property and other forms of arson during the years 1842–51 showed that Durham and Northumberland were among the areas little affected by agrarian disorder of that kind[1]. Durham notched up a total of 11 such cases during this 10-year period, but six of these were in the single year of 1844, marked by a major mining strike. Northumberland saw only three such cases during this 10-year period.

However, not all of the evidence is of this tendency, and there is ample proof of the existence within the region of much that was cruel, rough and vicious. It is important to emphasize that there was nothing particularly new in this. There is little foundation for the belief that the pre-industrial eighteenth century was a time of harmony and good living compared with that which came later. In the North East, as elsewhere in eighteenth-century Britain, crime and vice were common, while social evils were often regarded with a callous unconcern which the nineteenth century was to prove unwilling to emulate. When in 1771 John Howard, the prison reformer visited Newcastle, he noted the conditions which contemporary society provided for accused persons awaiting trial[2]:

> During the Assizes at Newcastle the county prisoners are, men and women, confined together seven or eight nights in a dirty, damp dungeon, six steps down in the old Castle, which, having no roof, in wet seasons the water is sometimes inches deep. The felons are chained to rings in the wall.

In 1761, 10 years before this description was penned, a riot at Hexham against ballotting for the militia recruits had the result that 18 rioters were shot dead by troops (some accounts put the death toll as high as 45)[3]. One of the leaders of the anti-militia agitation, Peter Pattison, 'a man of substance and well over 70 years of age' was subsequently hung, drawn and quartered at Morpeth. In 1798 Mary Nicholson, a maidservant, was condemned to death at Durham Assizes for poisoning her mistress, but the sentence was not carried out for almost a year after her conviction. During this period the condemned woman remained in Durham employed as a kind of prison servant, sometimes running errands in the town on behalf of prison staff. When her public execution finally took place, on 22 July 1799, the rope snapped at the first attempt. Nicholson recovered and was able to talk with members of her family for almost an hour until new arrangements had been made; a new rope was then rigged up, and she was hanged[4].

Recreations of this period were frequently marked by a degree of cruelty, with blood sports a common attraction. At a bull-baiting at Newcastle's Sandhill in January 1768, two bulls were involved, and a soldier in the audience ventured too near in his excitement and was fatally gored[5]. Visitors to the region in the later eighteenth century often expressed high praise for the more advanced features of the region's economy, but some of them also had other things to say about other features of the region. John Wesley visited Newcastle in 1742 and confided to his diary the following comments on some of the inhabitants of the regional centre[6]: 'I was surprised: so much drunkenness, cursing and swearing (even from the mouths of little children) do I never remember to have seen and heard before, in so small a compass of time.' In the following year Wesley took his investigations further[7]:

I had a great desire to visit a small colliery village near Newcastle. It is inhabited by colliers only, and such as had been always in the first rank for savage ignorance, and wickedness of every kind. Their grand assembly used to be on the Lord's Day: on which men, women and children met together to dance, fight, curse, and swear, and play at chuck ball, span farthing, or whatever came next to hand. I felt a great compassion for these poor creatures, from the time I heard of them first, and the more because all men seemed to dispair of them.

The picture is much the same if we turn our attention to the other end of the period covered by this section. It is plain that in the middle of the nineteenth century North East England still contained much that was rough and vicious, though as we shall see there were also signs of influences at work which exercised a taming effect. In 1837 the Chief Constable of Newcastle presented to Newcastle Town Council a prosaic tabulation of the town's less salubrious activities[8]:

17 houses for the reception of thieves.
 8 houses the resort of thieves.
31 the average numbers of thieves.
71 brothels where prostitutes are kept.

4 average kept in each house.
46 houses of ill-fame, where they resort.
31 houses where they lodge.

In 1850 the Tynemouth superintendent of police reported that[9]:

> In one house, the notorious "Sally Joyce" on the Steam-Mill Bank, I found one night eleven persons who had been living for a considerable period of time on no other visible means than that of pilfering. The most of them had been convicted thieves and were the associates of thieves. They were regaling themselves with a piece of beef, eggs, tea and some hot whisky toddy.

Prostitution remained a common social problem. In 1827 the Newcastle historian, Eneas Mackenzie, wrote that[10] 'Plumber Chare was noted, a few years ago, as the receptacle of Cyprian nymphs, whose blandishments were of the most coarse and vulgar description'. In 1854 a conscientious social investigator was able to visit more than 100 brothels in Newcastle alone[11]. Accounts of local courts reveal something of the substantial world of vice and crime which characterized the period. Year by year a procession of cases involving prostitutes were heard, as a normal occurrence rather than as a shocking novelty. In the single court year 1829-30, for example, one of Mackenzie's 'Cyprian nymphs', the redoubtable Hannah Rickaby, was before Newcastle magistrates on five occasions[12]. Routinely described as 'a common prostitute', some form of disorderly conduct was the usual charge she faced. On one occasion that year, however, she was charged with stealing 2s. 6d. from a man's pocket—the complainant, perhaps prudently, failed to appear in court, and she was discharged; on another occasion she was involved with two friends in a suspicious death but was again discharged when a coroner's jury returned a verdict of accidental death. Accounts of the late eighteenth and early nineteenth century often include references to the large number of young girls involved in prostitution.

Drink also provided a major social problem which was not a new one. Beer duty at Newcastle netted for the national revenue a handy £43,000 in 1825-6, and in the later 1830s the town brewed some 50,000 gallons of beer; some of this was exported, but much of it was not. Illicit distilling was a common criminal charge, and we need not suppose that all of it appears in the surviving records. In May 1822, for example, a large illicit still was found inside the abandoned workings of a colliery on the outskirts of Newcastle. The smoke from this installation had been emitted into the old workings in the hope that it would disperse unnoticed, while the necessary supplies of fuel had been frugally obtained by the use of unworked coal in the pit[13]. For much of the nineteenth century there was a substantial difference between rates of duty charged on spirits in Scotland and England, and a substantial smuggling trade developed on the border; in 1834, 56 excise officers were employed, with but modest success, in dealing with this traffic[14]. In 1838 the Newcastle courts heard 1,366 charges of being drunk and disorderly[15]. Newspapers of the time abound with accounts of disturbances and violence arising from excessive drinking.

The process of building up the necessary organizations for a more sophisticated regional economy were often adversely affected by these weaknesses in contemporary society. Absconding clerks, embezzlement, fraudulent bankruptcies and alcoholism were frequent hindrances in the development of firms during this period, and the economic development which occurred is the more remarkable when set against this background of an unsophisticated and often very rough society.

Yet the evidence also shows that there were factors at work tending towards amelioration. The figure of prosecutions on drunk and disorderly charges at Newcastle, for example, dropped from 1,366 in 1838 to less than 1,000 by 1852[16]. One of the most important of these refining influences was the religious revival of the early nineteenth century.

Religious revival

The spread of religious fervour during this period and its impact on society have been matters of considerable controversy among historians. Yet the general outline seems reasonably clear, in this region as elsewhere. The early visits of John Wesley in the eighteenth century seem to have been largely ineffective, at least as far as the workers were concerned, but the pattern changed in the first half of the nineteenth century. During that period substantial numbers of people at all levels of society were affected by the spread of religion; however, substantial numbers of people at all levels of society remained either little affected or totally unconverted. There can be no doubt, however, of the significance of the development and its social impact. In many working communities the effects of the evangelical missionaries were considerable. Here for instance is part of an account of a Primitive Methodist crusade in County Durham in the 1830s[17]:

> The most impressive scenes were witnessed. Fallings were common, as many as fourteen being seen on the floor at once. At a lovefeast at Bishop Auckland the people fell in all directions, and there was a strange mingling of shouts, groans and hallelujahs. During the revival at South Side, centres of gambling were broken up; confirmed gamblers burnt their dice, cards and books of enchantment; drunkards, hopeless incurable sots, were freed from the dread tyranny of fiery appetite; pugilists, practiced and professional, and cock-fighters of terrible experience, turned from their brutalities. The miracle was repeated at Evenwood, West Auckland, and elsewhere, and at each place the converts became church workers and several of them local preachers.

The missionaries who effected such changes among the workers were usually workers themselves, invested with a burning sense of mission. (Reference 18a gives a very good example of the type; for a different slant on such events, see reference 18b.) It is, however, plain that the effects produced were uneven rather than uniform. Even works of nonconformist hagiography contain references which show that, if some colliery villages early acquired and retained a strong religious influence, others required periodic revivals to keep them up to the mark, while yet others remained relatively immune to these ministrations. (Reference 19 includes much evidence on the unevenness of conversion, and the need for frequent revivals in many places.) In many communities there was marked disunity in life styles, with some families committed to religion and respectability, others remaining in a popular culture which remained untouched by religious zeal.

Yet overall the spread of evangelical religion must be accounted a major factor in establishing over wide reaches of local society higher standards of respectability, responsibility and personal behaviour in general. For example, the results of the work of methodist missionaries among the lead-miners in the 1830s was described by a contemporary observer in these terms[20]:

> They have been the principal engine in effecting moral change in this wild district, and instead of insult and a volley of stones, strangers are met with civility and good behaviour . . . They have reclaimed and reformed individuals who were enemies to their families and themselves, as well as a perfect pest and a disgrace to the neighbourhood.

Moreover since the spread of religious fervour was not confined to any particular social level, there were other significant implications. There were evangelical peers and evangelical bankers and mine-owners as well as evangelical miners, and, even if the sects and the theological faiths might cover a considerable variety of belief and practice, the religious revival meant that important elements within different social groupings shared an area of common belief and common attitudes in matters to which they attached crucial importance. In many ways there might be more in common between a devout pitman and a devout employer than either of them had with the unregenerate among their own brethren. Religious faith encouraged responsible and law-abiding behaviour in a society which possessed much that was rough, cruel and vicious. Even those who did not share the intense personal experience of religious conversion could be affected by the changing canons of conduct which the spread of religion inculcated. Church and chapel also provided for increasing numbers of people social and recreational facilities of innocuous kinds and diminished the appeal of the popular blood sports and the less attractive aspects of popular recreation.

Even by 1851, however, if evangelical religion had achieved a remarkable degree of penetration in a couple of generations, there still remained very wide areas of society which it had not reached. The contrasts which existed between the extensive world of vice and crime and this other extensive world of the religious revival show that we are not dealing with a simple and uniform society, but with a complex and diverse one.

Role of local and central government

There was no substantial umbrella of government under which these varied interests could be moulded and contained. It is difficult for those who are accustomed to life in a society in which the agencies of central and local government play crucial roles to appreciate just how little governed was the society of late eighteenth-century and early nineteenth-century Britain. The economic developments already discussed took place in a context in which official authority played a very small role. Not only were the resources at the disposal of local and central government meagre, but there was no widespread and sustained demand at any level of society for their expansion, despite the social problems which certainly existed. Even contemporary radical propaganda concerned itself more with denunciation of government waste and extravagance than with policies of expanding government resources to tackle social problems. Campaigns for the reduction of official expenditure were much more vociferous and common than any constructive plans for raising additional revenue from rates and taxes and applying them to social amelioration. The belief in the effectiveness and integrity of government agencies was a very slow growth and began from a distinctly low level in eighteenth-century Britain.

Even where substantial attempts at the reform of official agencies were undertaken, the results were often for many years unimpressive. The 1835 Municipal Reform Act's impact in Newcastle is a case in point. Here the unreformed council had spent nearly £100,000 on town improvement schemes between 1780 and 1832. Its 'reformed' successor, closely responsive to the opinions of a ratepaying electorate, proved distinctly more economical for many years and showed no great enthusiasm for spending money on schemes to improve the town's health and cleanliness. One of their first acts was to sell off at derisory prices the Mansion House and its contents, in what one historian has described[21] as 'an insensate and wasteful piece of vandalism'.

The key to understanding the way in which the region was governed during this period is to appreciate that power flowed mainly from unofficial rather than from official channels. As late as the 1851 census half of the region's population still lived in communities of less than 2,000 people, and in the relatively small inward-looking locally orientated towns and villages of this period authority resided not primarily in the holding of official position but rather in the exercise of the unofficial forms of control which emanated from wealth, status or personal influence. In practice official and unofficial controls centred in the same hands. In the counties, for example, in which the magistrates were the most important official powers, it was not the case that a man became a figure of influence because he was a county magistrate but rather that men who already possessed power from other sources, such as birth, wealth, land ownership, possessed a strong claim to be appointed to the county magistracy and thereby to add an extra official dimension to the authority derived from unofficial attributes.

The situation in the growing towns was essentially similar. Town councils were dominated by men drawn from local oligarchies already deeply embedded in the community's economic and social life. In early nineteenth-century Newcastle, for example, the town council and local offices of importance were dominated by members of a handful of leading families possessing close links with the town's commercial affairs. Claytons, Bells, Andersons, Cooksons and Brandlings passed municipal offices among themselves[22]:

> Thus, in 1817 Nathaniel Clayton was Town Clerk; he had held that office since 1785, and was to be succeeded in 1822 by his son, John; his brother Robert was mayor and Robert's son, William, was sheriff: in the following year, although Robert and William were out of office, Henry, another son of Robert's, was sheriff.

It was not so very different in the reformed town councils after 1835. Gateshead provides a good example. For many years after 1835 the council there was effectively led by William Henry Brockett, who, in addition to his own links with a variety of Tyneside commercial activities, possessed a significant range of family contacts. He was connected by marriage with the Crawshays, partners in Gateshead's leading iron works. His father-in-law, Thomas Wilson, was a partner in a major chemical works and a Gateshead alderman. John Trotter Brockett, his brother, was an important Newcastle lawyer with close ties to the Claytons and other leading families in Tyneside's municipal and economic affairs[23].

Alike in county and borough, local government represented these close links between official position and unofficial individual influence. There was no very strong desire on the part of these local oligarchies to make local government more expensive by embarrassing reforming zeal, though they were willing enough to forward the economic interests of their communities, with which they were closely concerned, by exploiting any influence conferred by official positions.

The general distrust of government and its agencies reflected for instance in the unflattering portraits of officials to be found in contemporary literature (Mr Bumble, the beadle of *Oliver Twist*, is not unique) was not simply derived from the meanness of ratepayers and taxpayers. Government agencies were not in this period marked by any very high level of general competence or skill. There was certainly no profession of government service, most of the limited number of posts which existed in local government were part-time, and there were many instances of a low level of performance. In offering the fruits of the 1831 census, for example, the plaintive comment was added that 'the Male Population of the (Lemmington) Township are all returned 20 years of age and upwards, but no explanation of this incredible Return, nor of the cause of the decrease of the Population (40 persons) can be obtained from the Overseer'. When, especially in the rural districts, census returns depended on the varying activity of unpaid and conscripted parish officers this kind of dereliction is intelligible.

There was only one administrative agency which covered the whole of

England and Wales and employed substantial numbers of paid officials, the machinery of the poor law. The early nineteenth-century corps of poor law officials were far from an *élite* body. It is probably true that the system was better able after the Poor Law Amendment Act of 1834 to weed out poor staff and to replace them with better, but the process of improvement was slow and difficult[24]. In 1836 William Pickering, a relieving officer in the Northumberland Castle Ward Union, was sacked for drunkenness and neglect of duty. In the South Shields Union Thomas Wilson was sacked in 1844 for embezzlement. Both of these men had been officials for many years, and there is no evidence to suggest that they had been exemplary public servants earlier. The Sunderland Poor Law Union inherited three relieving officers from the old poor law; of these three, one turned out to be an embezzler, another a drunkard. Of the three inherited rate-collectors there, one was subsequently sacked for embezzlement, another for incompetence.

Nor did such administrative difficulties apply only to lesser officers. The first Clerk to the Houghton-le-Spring Poor Law Union in County Durham served from the union's creation in 1836 until his death in 1853. In 1851 a meeting of the Board of Guardians had to be adjourned because its Clerk was hopelessly drunk—the minutes of the meeting are a mere series of doodles; he was severely reprimanded, but the same thing happened again in the following year. However, his successor was a competent and reliable official.

The task of building up adequate staffs was by no means easy, and only limited progress had been made in the evolution of an administrative profession by the middle of the nineteenth century. Local government agencies like town councils and poor law unions were subject to a ratepaying electorate, and ratepayers in these smaller communities of that time were able to keep a wary eye on what was done with their money. There was constant pressure to keep official salaries down, which tended to exclude able and reliable candidates, while the poor performance of some officials seemed to justify a refusal to pay adequate salaries. The second half of the century saw a quickening in the process of government expansion, but it was hard work in earlier years.

Social Enquiries

There was, however, one very significant area of growing expertise during the first half of the nineteenth century. This period saw a continual proliferation of enquiries and reports on an unprecedented scale, as the dominant minorities which controlled the machinery of central and local government made increasing efforts to comprehend the social problems which faced their society, with a view to mitigating them. Of course not every member of the governing groups shared these ambitions, but it is difficult to see how effective social reform could have come about without the systematic collection of information which increasingly marked the second quarter of the nineteenth century. Although in this region as elsewhere the official inquiries into municipal government and poor law administration which preceded the legislation of 1834–5 were in some ways defective, they did mark a significant extension of the state's machinery for the investigation and description of administrative and social conditions. Such agencies as royal commissions and select committees of enquiry into social problems provided for the first time an increasingly systematic body of evidence. This has of course tended to exaggerate the extent to which early nineteenth-century social problems were new, for the existence of a copious body of evidence from this period contrasts with the absence of such evidence from a pre-industrial society which lacked both the will and the ability to undertake such appraisals. The series of enquiries which published a great deal of evidence on mining conditions, poor relief, local government and the like culminated during the first half of the century with the major series of sanitary and public health reports which provided an unprecedented range of detailed evidence on social conditions. It was no longer possible for members of the governing minorities to take refuge in a real or feigned ignorance of what conditions really were like.

A few examples will suffice to give the flavour of these descriptions of the worst social conditions which accompanied the rapid growth of population brought to a little governed society by unregulated economic growth. For instance, the comment on Gateshead in 1849[25]:

> Several of our streets, courts and entries are not only undrained, but remain unpaved and uncleansed, and without any side channels to carry off the liquid matters, so that in wet weather they become almost impassable from rats and filth. The inhabitants (have) no other method of disposing of their refuse water, excrement, etc., but throw them on the streets and lanes, where they spread, become decomposed, and evolve a most disgusting odour, more particularly when the weather is warm and close. . . . In some portions of the town (no privies) are provided; in other portions, as in Hillgate, Oakwellgate, etc., there is frequently only one privy common to 20 or 30 families, and these are in such an abominable dirty condition as to excite surprise that they should ever be used. . . . There are no public baths and wash-houses in Gateshead; the poorer class of the inhabitants invariably wash their clothes in their confined and crowded rooms, and hang them out to dry in the thoroughfares.

Also a description of Sunderland in 1845[26]:

> Under a large free school in the Low-row, Bishop Wearmouth (and in which a very great number of children are daily educated) there are a series of vaults in which already upwards of 60 or 70 bodies are deposited, and where it intended to deposit more. . . . on those vaults being opened, the effluvium which escapes is most offensive and dangerous, so much so, that some of the medical gentlemen in attending funerals take the precaution of not entering the vaults, and even remaining at some distance from the entrance during the interments.

Similar descriptions of sanitary conditions, poor housing, overcrowding, suscep-
tibility to disease and high child mortality accumulated during the last years of
the first half of the century, and these excerpts could be paralleled in North and
South Shields and Newcastle as well as Gateshead and Sunderland, and indeed
within the region's growing towns in general.

Two rather unexpected elements emerge from this increasingly full body of
knowledge of social conditions in the North East at mid-century. One is that,
although the poorer sections of society suffered disproportionately from such
conditions, they were not the only victims. At North Shields many of the newer
streets built for more opulent citizens were as badly drained as some of the older
slums, and this was also true of parts of Gateshead. If many people of
considerable means were much better housed, a high proportion of local
businesses were in fact carried out in or near town centres which produced the
stench and the filth described so often in these reports. It is worth remembering
that the Prince Consort was to die of typhoid at the age of 41 years in 1861, in a
Windsor Castle surrounded by brimming cesspools.

The second feature worth noting is that the mid-century reports make it plain
that, if the worst black spots were to be found in the developing towns, the kind
of social problem associated with bad housing and sanitation was not specifically an industrial or an urban situation but was to be found in a wide variety of
community within the region. The following description comes not from
Newcastle, Gateshead or Sunderland but from the White Hart yard at
Alnwick, not a place powerfully affected by the industrial revolution[27]:

> Great filth of every description may always here be found, and it has long
> been noticed as much subjected to fever. An open sewer, containing all kinds
> of putridity, which is seldom or never cleansed, runs from the Green Batt so
> far down the yard, and, where it becomes covered, its place is supplied by a
> large midden, into which all the blood and offals from the slaughterhouses
> are thrown, and frequently for a considerable time to remain.

Nor were the poor conditions confined to towns; here is part of a description
of a Durham mining community in 1853[28]:

> Where a line of houses opens to the fields, there is generally a foul ditch or
> channel full of liquid and solid refuse sufficient to poison the atmosphere as it
> enters the dwelling rooms. If a catalogue of nuisances were made, it must
> include almost every house in the place. . . . Privies and cesspools are
> crowded close to many of the cottages, wells and pumps are in some places
> close to middens and cesspools. Many cottages have no privy or water
> supply. Refuse is thrown out in heaps, or over the surface. Children ease
> themselves in the road in front of the houses, and not infrequently adults also.

Scattered rural communities were by no means immune from the same evils.
Mid-century sanitary reports condemned conditions in a fishing hamlet such as

Boulmer or a rural village such as Embleton[29]. A housing reformer in North Northumberland included the following description of rural cottages of 1842[30]:

> In many, human beings and cows are littered together under the same roof. Of the whole number 174, which I am discussing, there are but 27 which have two rooms each, and which are supplied with that convenience which is indispensably necessary to cleanliness and decency.

We should be cautious then in supposing that the social problems facing North East England at mid-century were necessarily a phenomenon associated with the process of industrialization. Although the concentrations which occurred in the main towns of Tyneside and Wearside made them plainly the worst black spots, they were essentially concentrations of social problems which could be found in other parts of the region's society too and which probably already had a long history in many places.

By 1850 the nature of the social problems facing this and kindred regions was increasingly exposed in a wide range of published studies carried out either by the agents of central or local government or by keen social reformers drawn from the more influential sections of contemporary society. There is much less evidence to suggest that these efforts represented a response to any very widespread popular enthusiasm on these topics. When in 1850 a determined social reformer investigated some of the worst slums in the region and then published a detailed account of what he had found, there was no sign that the centres of appalling poverty and hardship which he described were in any sense centres also of political agitation or subversion[31].

Popular involvement in politics

The extent of popular involvement in political and ideological controversies has been a subject of considerable difference of opinion among historians, and interpretations of this aspect of the region's history differ widely. There seems little evidence, however, for the existence of a continuous, very widespread, popular support for radical political agitations, though this leaves ample room for the continuous existence of small dedicated minorities active in this way, and it is plain that from time to time their activities could attract a wider degree of popular support than was normally the case. During the Chartist period of the late 1830s and 1840s, for instance, support appears to have fluctuated in this region as elsewhere, with the peak of interest in the North East occurring during the first major wave of Chartist activity in 1839-40. This subject is somewhat controversial: Maehl (for example, reference 32a) has argued that it had an extensive effect, while Rowe (for example, reference 32b) argues for a less extensive effect. The latter view is preferred here.

Certainly there is a good deal of evidence for the existence of other aspects of popular activity. The growth in population, and the growth of the region's economic resources, were matched by a great increase in the number of local public houses. Newcastle alone had 425 pubs and 76 beer shops in the early

1850s[33]. These varied considerably in character from the markedly disreputable to the distinctly respectable. A few of them certainly acted as centres of radical political activity, but this was unusual rather than typical. There is also evidence of a continued, and probably growing, interest in other areas of sport and recreation. In the years around 1850, for instance, competitive rowing, by then the principal spectator sport of the day, seems to have attracted a high degree of popular interest.

If there is reason to doubt the extent to which politics aroused popular concern, this does not mean that workers were generally incapable of acting strenuously in defence of their own interests. This is illustrated, for instance, in the protracted survival of holidays during this period. On 21 December 1786 a leading colliery-manager noted[34]: 'This day laid in all ye pits till ye commencement of the new year being ye time usually allowed for ye holidays.' On 2 January 1787 he noted: 'This day ye pits commenced workg. after ye holiday recess but as customary very few coals were wrought—nor is it expected that any of ye pits will get their full stated quantities till after ye next pay day.' In this case coal-owners could of course view with relative equanimity such a prolonged stop in production during the winter months before the collier fleet began its main sailings in the spring. However, holidays were in practice much more widespread; in 1811, for example, 16 public holidays, including a 3-day Christmas break, were observed in the Newcastle district, and this was about the usual number[35].

The ability of ordinary people to defend their common interests was sometimes demonstrated in more striking fashion. The eighteenth and early nineteenth centuries were punctuated by incidents involving widespread popular demonstrations, often forcibly expressed, where immediate practical grievances involved widespread hardship. The causes could be diverse; a rapid rise in the cost of living was a frequent cause, but in 1816, for example, Sunderland saw large-scale disturbances against the circulation of large quantities of silver coins of dubious authenticity which were used in wage payments but were viewed with suspicion by many shopkeepers. The normal reaction of local authorities was to try to maintain order without resort to harsh repression and at the same time to try to do something to remedy the causes of the outbreak. At Sunderland in 1816, for example, there was an immediate official pronouncement that coins in circulation should be accepted, while local magistrates strongly urged the central government to hasten an impending major recoinage[36].

Industrial disputes

The story of industrial disputes within the region during this period was similar. From an early date some of the more coherent groups of workers showed very impressive capacity in the defence of their own interests, and in strike situations the workers' leaders often outclassed their employers in skill and ingenuity.

Some of the many strikes which took place were marked by considerable violence, scarcely surprising perhaps in the context of the rough society in which they occurred. During a miners' strike in 1789, sparked off by rapidly rising prices, colliery machinery was smashed at the Shiremoor, Wallsend and Longbenton collieries[37]. During a keelmen's strike in 1819 troops fired in retaliation against a stone-throwing crowd, and one man was shot dead[38]. In 1825, during a seamen's strike on Wearside, four men were shot dead in similar circumstances[39]. During the 1832 miners' strikes a blackleg miner and an elderly magistrate were brutally murdered. The bitter miners' strike of 1844 also saw sporadic outbreaks of violence. Many other strikes were marked by the use of force on a much smaller scale, such as assaults on blacklegs or on workers who disobeyed the orders of the men's leaders.

As with many aspects of the history of this period, however, there was another side to the story of industrial disputes. Throughout the late eighteenth and early nineteenth centuries trusted leaders from local ruling minorities often appeared in a mediating role, with a considerable record of success in bringing serious disputes to peaceful solutions. Rowland Burdon, son of the founder of a Newcastle bank, Tory magistrate and M.P., successfully mediated to bring the prolonged seamen's strike of 1792 to a peaceful conclusion. Subsequently he failed to persuade parliament to accept his proposals for a legislative regulation of seamen's pay. He also tried, but again failed, to persuade the northern coal-owners to establish a welfare and pension fund for the coalfield, to be financed from small deductions from miners' wages and a levy on coal to be raised; this proposal was made during the serious miners' strikes of 1831–2, and it is interesting to note that his principal opponent was the radical Lord Durham, who described Burdon in a letter to the Home Office at the time as 'that stupid old man'. This was an illuminating encounter[40a], for Durham was perhaps the most influential radical politician of that time. Political radicalism did not always march in step with the practical needs of workers, for many contemporary radicals were wedded to orthodox conceptions of political economy, and strenuously opposed trade unions and attempts by organized groups of workers to enforce restrictive practices to secure their jobs. The principal early nineteenth-century radical newspaper in the area, the *Tyne Mercury*, was often to be found in vocal opposition to workers during strikes[40b].

Another local magistrate with a long record of mediation in industrial disputes was the Rev. William Nesfield, J.P., Rector of Brancepeth, who succeeded for example in settling the Wearside seamen's strike of 1815 after a long course of patient negotiations with both strikers and employers. Similarly in 1819 it was the patient and balanced efforts of Thomas Clennell, Chairman of Northumberland Quarter Sessions, which brought the keelman's strike to a peaceful conclusion, despite the violence which had already occurred. In all of these cases, and in many others, the men of influence involved evinced an unmistakable sympathy with workers who sought redress of real grievances and an unmistakable impatience towards recalcitrant or inconsiderate employers.

During the prolonged and extremely well-organized and well-managed seamen's strike of 1815 a Durham county magistrate, John Cartwright, was commissioned by the Home Secretary to provide confidential reports from the scene of the trouble. In these reports Cartwright made it plain that the seamen's grievances were well founded, and in one of them he had this to say of the employers involved[41]:

> I found my way yesterday to a public table at Sunderland, where except myself all were ship-owners. I heard a full discussion of the subject. They openly, to my deep disgust, avowed the base dissimulation with which they were acting and that they intend to observe any terms they may *agree to* only until the present compact association and consequent danger are dispersed. The unprincipled avarice, and want of integrity in this class of men as a body, appears to be one reason for the bias observable in favour of the seamen, perhaps too of *the negligence of the Magistrates.*

In many industrial disputes magistrates made no serious attempt to invoke the legal powers they possessed to act in a repressive capacity, even when backed by substantial military forces. Similarly, in many court cases arising from such incidents they either enforced the law very leniently, in comparison with the period's penal practice generally, or even threw out cases against workers where the evidence was strong. This was of course not entirely a matter of generous sympathies, for most magistrates had the sense to see that the peace and prosperity of the area would not be facilitated by the exercise of severe repression.

This attitude of moderation and conciliation was not of course uniformly shared among the local magistracy, but it appears to have predominated, and it was usually encouraged by the principal aristocratic magnates of the region, such as successive Lords Lieutenant of both Durham and Northumberland who, as the extensive correspondence in the Public Record Office shows, were often scathing in their criticisms of difficult employers and quick to report examples of restraint and moderation among leaders of the workers.

Much the same spirit can be found among the naval and military officers who found themselves, in a little governed society, repeatedly called on to bolster up the civil power. During the seamen's strike of 1792 substantial naval forces were sent to the Tyne to strengthen the hand of authority. Successive commanders of this force were prompt in embarking upon attempts to bring the dispute to a peaceful settlement, and made no secret of their sympathy with the striking seamen. Captain the Hon. Alexander Cochrane succinctly summed up the cause of the dispute for the benefit of his superiors in London: 'The Wages of the seamen of this Port have not been increased for a considerable time back, since which the price of every article of living has increased very much.' He rapidly acquired a poor opinion of many of the ship-owners 'whom I am sorry to say that the sailors have but too much reason to complain of'. He reported to Whitehall that sailors had often been disgracefully cheated by their employers in the recent past, and he threw his weight behind Rowland Burdon's mediation which brought about important concessions to the strikers.

During the miners' strike of 1831 the senior army commander of the northern district came to Tyneside to see the situation for himself; Major General Bouverie was no alarmist, but a cool and sensible observer[42]:

> Upon my arrival here I find the colliers perfectly peacable in their behaviour altho' they are all turn'd out, not a single Colliery in this Neighbourhood being at work, there are a great number of processions and meetings, but everything is conducted in the most orderly manner, and they are extremely civil when met with upon the road.

He also thought that 'if the Pitmen continue refractory, they will be awkward persons to deal with, one pitman being equal to three weavers at the least'.

On the whole the conciliatory attitude of most local men of authority was imitated by the central government. Of all Home Secretaries of the period, perhaps Lord Sidmouth has most incurred the reputation of being a repressive minister. He was certainly much concerned to combat political subversion, but he was by no means harsh in his attitudes to ordinary industrial disputes that arose from genuine grievances. During the 1815 seamen's strike he was worried about the strikers' patently illegal and forcible blockading of ports, but when the strike ended he wrote[43]: 'It is now my earnest wish that no Prosecutions may be instituted except among the most prominent offenders, and that, as the law is no longer violated, that Consideration and Liberality may be manifested by the Ship-owners, which is due to British Seamen.' In other letters he was scathing on the subject of many of the employers, and made it clear that by 'most prominent offenders' he meant men whose responsibility for violence could be proved. His attitude was the same during the strike of keelmen which coincided with the agitation after Peterloo; he urged that 'when the Keelmen shall have ceased to transgress the Law, their Complaints shall be listened to with attention and indulgence, and if well founded, the causes of them should, of course, be removed'. In the next year after similar trouble he recorded his 'satisfaction that the Coal-Owners have now shewn themselves sensible of the propriety and justice of keeping faith with the keelmen'.

There were magistrates, such as Nicholas Fairles of South Shields, who for many years took a much stronger line against workers during strikes; in his case he paid for his principles with his life for in his seventies he was murdered during the miners' strikes of 1832. There were also employers who strenuously opposed any concessions to organized pressure from workers, feeling that such matters involved not just a concession on wages or conditions but the negation of that due subordination which was a vital element in the social order. During the 1792 seamen's strike one employer, Thomas Powditch, declared trenchantly that[44] 'it is my opinion that Tampering with a Mob, treating with Rioters, or offering terms to People illegally assembled for the purpose of extorting high wages from their employers, are crimes little inferior in magnitude to rioting itself'. During the great miners' strike of 1831 one coal-owner, George Sowerby, did agree to make substantial concessions, but there came a point when he would yield no more, and he began to recruit blacklegs[45]:

> Conceiving that no Owner of a Colliery ought so far to degrade himself as to permit his hired Servants to dictate to him not only the men whom he shall employ but the manner in which he is to conduct his business, I have, as the only alternative left, engaged a number of Lead Miners from Weardale.

Certainly, however, from the mixed and varied nature of the attitudes displayed by men of property and influence, it is plain that there was no very united front here.

As for the leaders of the men involved in the numerous strikes and disputes which occurred during this period, it could fairly be said that many of them displayed remarkable powers of leadership. They had to operate in an unequal society in which the enlistment of sympathy from uncommitted public opinion, and especially the sympathy of men of influence, was of cardinal importance. To have indulged in the rhetoric of social conflict might have given satisfaction to politically militant groups among the workers and elsewhere, who seem always to have been a small but noisy minority, but such conduct would have been a clear recipe for failure in the conduct of most industrial disputes during this period. Workers' leaders usually had the common sense to adapt their tactics to the situation actually facing them and to have realized that a public image of sweet reasonableness was the best course to follow. Time and again strike leaders clamped down on such activities as obtrusive violence which might alienate public opinion and might force official authority to exert its strength against the strikers. We cannot see into men's minds at this distance removed in time, but there seems no reason to doubt that the reluctance to provoke bitter conflict was sincere as well as tactically advantageous. Declarations of patriotism, loyalty, veneration for national institutions and abhorrence of violence were frequently found on the lips of workers' leaders during this period. In practice these attitudes were not found incompatible with a good deal of illegal activity during industrial disputes, including the blockading of major ports for weeks on end and a good deal of back-street intimidation of blacklegs or disobedient strikers; it was usual for such activities to be organized as unobtrusively as possible. Defiance of official authority was very rare; much more common was the resort to attempts to elicit sympathy or support from magistrates, army and navy officers and others whose effective hostility could be disastrous but whose countenance could be a potent ally.

Co-operation between different groups of workers in mutual support was not very common. For example, although the Tyneside seamen sent in 1826 a donation of £50 to 'the artisans at Bradford', their relations with groups of workers in closer proximity showed little solidarity. Three groups of workers who early showed that they could each act coherently—the miners, the keelmen and the seamen of the colliers—could act to cut the coal trade; all three were repeatedly involved in industrial disputes during this period, but there was little or no sign of joint action between them.

The foregoing argument can perhaps be summed up in a brief account of industrial troubles on Tyneside during a period of particular stress, when major strikes coincided with political excitement over the Reform Act, and the onset of the first great cholera epidemic to hit the area. On 1 March 1831 Lord John Russell introduced into the House of Commons the first form of the Whig government's Reform Bill. The annual bonds of the North East pitmen expired on 5 April, and they refused to enter into new bonds unless their grievances were remedied. A mass meeting on the Black Fell, in North Durham, on 6 April, formulated the men's demands, which were uniformly concerned with conditions of work and had no wider political content at all. The strike which followed was marked by sporadic outbreaks of violence, against the strong urgings of the leaders of the men's new union. The strikers remained solid, and in June the employers gave way, offering important concessions. Boys were not to work more than 12 hours a day, strangers were not to be employed if local miners were out of work, and the position of the union was at least tacitly recognized.

Meanwhile the prolonged stoppage of the collieries had thrown out of work many seamen from the collier fleet. There was no disposition on the part of the seamen's leaders to ally with the miners. Instead they negotiated a treaty with the local magistrates whereby the Mayor of Newcastle instituted a semi-official subscription in the area for the relief of distressed seamen, this fund to be handed over to the seamen's union, the Loyal Standard Seamen's Association, for distribution. In return the seamen would remain quiet during the coal strike. The Home Office was kept fully informed of these transactions. At the end of May one of the mayor's subordinates told him[46]:

> Five of the Seamen deputed by their Body waited upon me at my house this morning, to ascertain the probable amount of the subscription entered into at Newcastle for their Relief, and when they might expect to get any part thereof, as they say their wants are very urgent—I made them acquainted with every particular as you desired me.'

The Duke of Northumberland informed the Home Secretary that 'the seamen of the port are behaving in a very creditable manner'.

During the summer the miners' leaders, led by Tommy Hepburn, had cause to congratulate themselves on the success of the 1831 strike but cause for worry as to whether or not they could restrain their more excited followers from embarking on precarious attempts to go still further. For example, at a mass meeting held near Sunderland in August, Hepburn[47] 'recommended order, sobriety, and attention to their religious duties, as the best means they could adopt to preserve the advantages they had gained, and to keep up in the public mind that favourable feeling which had been so generally exhibited towards them during the strike'. The meeting had been nominally called to discuss the recently enacted Reform Act but 'the topic least commented on was that which they had met chiefly to discuss'.

The hold of the weak union and its moderate leadership was not at all firm, and 1832 was marked by renewed demands from miners for further concessions, accompanied by further outbreaks of violence. At Hetton, after the colliery-owners had resorted to the eviction of strikers from tied houses, and the employment of blacklegs, one of the blacklegs was murdered. On Whit Monday, 1832 an elderly magistrate was murdered by two pitmen. Such events alienated public opinion and assured the coal-owners of adequate support if they acted against the union. Some employers had continued to try to work for a peaceful solution. The Whig coal-owner James Losh, for example, confided to his diary on 15 April, before the escalation of violence[48]: 'this morning I met our pitmen and tho' we did not come to any absolute agreement, I succeeded in convincing a great many of them of the danger and folly of their conduct, and I am not without hope that we shall settle our differences amicably.' The murders and other violence of the next 2 months put such conciliatory courses out of court. The coal-owners had made considerable concessions in 1831, and they found that this had merely brought renewed demands, sporadic further strikes and violence. They were now determined to fight and break the infant union, and the violence which occurred in the summer of 1832 greatly strengthened their hands. Hepburn and the other moderate leaders could not vindicate their authority and saw no way out of their difficulties. In August Hepburn with Birkbeck, another miners' leader, approached James Losh to see if he could suggest any way of composing the troubles. From June support for the union had steadily declined, and before the end of the summer the strike and with it the union had collapsed.

The end of the 1832 strike saw the flow of coal fully restored and a buoyant market. Now, however, Henry Woodroffe and the other leaders of the seamen's union were in a strong position. They refused to man the collier fleet unless their followers were given a substantial pay increase. Woodroffe, who had much experience in dealing with men of influence—he had, for example, been one of the carefully primed witnesses to appear before the select committee which preceded the repeal of the Combination Laws in 1824—played his cards very well. He devoted considerable care to conciliating men of influence, including the senior naval officer on the spot, who could have acted effectively against the seamen, but instead held his hand and sent reports in support of the striking seamen to London. Woodroffe was at pains to explain away minor outbreaks of violence which took place. His success can be judged from part of a letter from Commander Glascock, R.N., in reply to an Admiralty instruction warning him against involving himself with the union leaders:

The propriety of their conduct was too manifest, and their general demeanour too respectful, to refuse them a hearing, which took place in the presence of the commissioned officers of His Majesty's Sloop, *Orestes.* . . . That the seamen have some reasonable grounds for complaints there can be no question, and this is admitted by some of the most respectable and influential ship-owners of North Shields.

The local authorities took no action to break the seamen's strike, whereas the increased disorder and violence on the coalfield in previous months had induced them to supply troops to support evictions from colliery houses and to protect blackleg miners. The seamen obtained the wage increase they demanded in 1832, and for the time being the area reverted to its normal state of relative tranquillity.

This complex chain of events illustrates some of the intricacies of social relationships during this period, and the presence of elements both of conflict and of cohesion.

Poverty and its relief

A factor of similar importance was the way in which society approached the problem of poverty and associated difficulties. This has been the centre of very considerable historical attention and controversy; indeed, historians have tended to attribute to this subject a higher degree of importance than it generally received at the time, or indeed has in practice normally received at any period. Nevertheless the question of the treatment of poverty is an interesting one and again throws light on important general characteristics of that society.

Before the Poor Law Amendment Act of 1834 official poor relief was in most cases on a parochial basis. In the more remote areas of the region the parishes were so large, the population so scanty and scattered, with poor roads and little in the way of retail machinery, that poor relief was administered by individual townships within parishes; this procedure had been authorized by an Act of 1673, but no effective means were found to implement this until the matter was taken up by an energetic Clerk of the Peace of Northumberland, John Davison, in the years after 1771, an illuminating instance of government's limited effectiveness in earlier times[49].

For the most part the old poor law was an essentially local operation based on local knowledge of the resources available and the demands to be made upon them. Relief practices varied from parish to parish and from time to time. Most parishes in North East England depended for most of the time on a simple system of out-relief, those in need being given doles in cash or kind from parish rate income. In the thinly populated rural areas the poor law was normally light in terms of both cost and administrative duties.

For the impotent poor for whom some kind of residential accommodation was needed, parishes varied greatly in their practice. Some erected poor houses of their own, others sent their poor to accommodation in other parishes, paying for their maintenance there. Others still contracted with a private contractor to take care of the poor in return for agreed payments, an arrangement which might save a great deal of trouble to the parish but which guaranteed neither decent treatment to the poor nor any very great savings to the ratepayer.

The major problem areas of the old poor law as for the post-1834 system arose in the industrial areas and the growing towns. Many of these towns, Sunderland, South Shields or Newcastle, for example, covered or came to cover the territory of more than one parish. It was common for the major social problems to accumulate within one poor area, where the parochial authorities might be faced with grave problems, while adjacent areas even of the same town were under no obligation whatever to help. Parochial authorities were always susceptible to the influence of the ratepayers whose money they expended; it was normal in these small-scale administrative units for those whose money was spent to be personally acquainted with those who received relief. This local intimacy could often be a recipe for generous treatment where individual cases excited local sympathy, but direct knowledge of the likely recipients was not always conducive to a more liberal attitude.

In the towns of the early nineteenth century there was still a good deal of diversity in poor law administration. Certainly the old poor law was not always benign, and some of the changes proposed in 1834 had a long history in local poor law administration. At Sunderland, for example, the town built its first poor house in 1744—by public subscription rather than by the levying of a rate for the purpose. The house was enlarged in 1779 but was plainly not a pleasant place to live in[50]: 'The sexes were separated, even man and wife, but the paupers were huddled together and very badly fed.' Adjacent urban parishes could differ significantly in their attitude towards their poor. St Nicholas Parish, Newcastle, opened a new poor house in 1803, which in the 1820s attracted the following comment from Eneas Mackenzie[51]:

> The out-door paupers, who could clean, sew or attend the sick, generally contrive to exist upon the most miserable pittance rather than go into the house, which certainly possesses few attractions, even for those who are steeped in poverty and acquainted with misfortune.'

A few hundred yards away the poor house of the parish of All Saints, though occupying much older premises, was lighter, better ventilated and administered on a looser rein[52]: 'The food is of the best, and those who prefer it may have good table-beer for supper instead of milk.'

The region presents a good deal of evidence for attempts to tighten up on the administration of the poor law long before the 1834 Act prescribed changes on a national basis. While as we have seen the regional economy in general showed a strong expansion, this was compatible with temporary set-backs, which could sometimes be severe. Economic depression produced clearly intelligible reactions on the poor law administration in affected areas. Depression brought increased unemployment and distress, which involved steep increases in poor rates at times when many ratepayers found it least easy to meet such demands. Many ratepayers were by no means rich, and they could often be badly affected by the depression themselves. In addition, as the early nineteenth century wore on, changes in attitudes towards poverty and its alleviation did not always lead to increased generosity, however well meaning they may have been. The wisdom of allowing ready access to poor relief was widely questioned; sometimes of course this could simply be a self-interested defensive reaction by ratepayers, but that was by no means always the case. That stout radical, Thomas Bewick, for example, possessed trenchant views on this topic[53]:

> All men ought to provide for the necessities of old age, & be made sensible of the manly pleasures of being independent—it is degrading and in most cases disgraceful to those who look to parish assistance after a life spent in laziness & mismanagement . . . if savings banks & benefit societies were encouraged by every possible means, there would be little occasion for poor Laws, except as a provision for helpless children & the lame & the blind—By such means as these, perhaps this national evil might be done away.

Bewick's views were exactly echoed by Sir John Walsham, himself a man with sympathy for the poor, when he came to the region as a senior poor law administrator in the mid-1830s.

Especially in the urban areas, though not only there, the early decades of the nineteenth century saw attempts to reduce the burden imposed by increasing poor rates, and at the same time by limiting access to relief to use the system as an inducement to thrift and self-help among working families. This reaction tended to be more strenuous and more obvious in places where a single parish became the centre of the social problems of a growing town, as was the case with both Gateshead and Sunderland in the years around 1820. In both cases industrial expansion had already occurred, and increasing population meant eventually larger numbers of elderly and infirm people to cope with, as well as the victims of the poor housing and sanitation conditions already mentioned.

At Gateshead the amount levied from poor rates rose from £568 in 1780 to £4,500 in 1820. This swingeing increase in 40 years not unnaturally resulted in an outcry from the ratepayers[54]. In April 1820 a parish vestry meeting resolved that 'on account of the enormous increase of the expenditure of the Parish it is highly expedient that a system of strict economy be appointed in the disposition of the funds, and particularly in the relief of the poor'. In the summer of 1821 strict new rules for relief were devised, with the result that expenditure in 1822 dropped to £3,040:

> . . .partly owing to the strict investigation that takes place previous to granting any relief, which, while it does not prevent those from applying who are really objects of parochial aid, prevents applications from the idle and profligate, whose wants principally arise from their own indolence and improvident habits.

One device for which particular effectiveness was claimed applied to the able-bodied male applicants for relief. Previously they had been in practice simply allowed relief; now they were offered relief in return for performing a task of stone-breaking; this was said to have resulted in a large drop in the number of applications.

In Sunderland parish, the centre of Wearside's social problems, increased costs had produced a similar ratepayers' revolt a few years earlier. The parish vestry there had ordered the publication of a printed list of all in receipt of poor relief[55]:

> . . . with the object of awakening a decent and becoming pride, to stimulate industry, to create a disposition to economy as regards the future, in opposition to a *lazy and despicable habit*—that of existing on the industry of more provident neighbours . . . undistinguishing benevolence offers a premium to indolence, prodigality and vice.

Ratepayers were invited to scrutinize this list and 'to send them the names of any paupers having means not divulged, but they need not sign their own names'.

These are only two examples of a number of instances in which parochial authorities tightened up their arrangements at this time. There still remained, however, a considerable amount of flexibility in the working of the old poor law, and parishes had very much a free hand to suit their policies to individual cases. Among items of expenditure by Sunderland parish, for instance, were a gift of 10*s.* to the wife of an unemployed rope-maker to allow her to make pies which she would sell to help support her family, £2 given to another woman to enable her to open a small shop in which she intended to sell tripe, haggis and similar items, and 15*s.* given to a man so that he could buy a pony for his cart after the previous animal died. Similar lists could be compiled from the records of many parishes. Such gifts—and loans for similar purposes which were also common— were not of course instances of simple altruism, for to provide these sums might well protect the parish from more expensive claims from the individuals concerned. At least, however, such devices enabled parochial authorities to meet direct individual needs, which later welfare arrangements were not always able to do.

The effects of the 1834 Poor Law Amendment Act were not very profound in this region, at least until the second half of the nineteenth century. The administrative changes involved were introduced with much less trouble than that experienced in some other areas of industrial expansion. For this there were three main reasons. In the first place the timing of the changes was significant; unlike the experience of Lancashire and Yorkshire the new Poor Law Unions appeared at a time of prosperity. The Northumberland and Durham unions were mostly created in the mid-1830s, while economic depression did not hit the region severely until the early 1840s, and even then the difficulties were not as intense as in some other areas, where the new poor law often coincided with serious unemployment, which made the fears provoked by the new law especially strong. A second reason for the relative ease of acceptance in the North East was the dexterity with which it was introduced[56]. Sir John Walsham, Bt, the Assistant Commissioner for the region in these early years after 1834, was a man who combined high rank and genial disposition with a genuine concern for the poor. He also possessed very useful local contacts, being closely connected by marriage with a leading member of the local gentry who was himself very influential in the region.

The third reason for the law's ready acceptance was that in practice the changes did not make a great deal of difference. Local oligarchies still retained effective control of the new boards of poor law guardians as they had of the previous parishes. Indeed parishes still retained important functions under the new system, especially as rating units, and for many years after 1834 parishes still retained the major responsibility for finding the money which went to sustain their own poor. Moreover the new local authorities retained a high degree of local autonomy in the management of their own affairs, while the new central Poor Law Commission found it extremely difficult to enforce its authority upon recalcitrant boards of guardians. There is a great deal of evidence indeed to suggest that in a number of ways the effect of the 1834 Act in the region was to increase the effectiveness of the poor law machinery[57]. Certainly medical relief to the poor was placed on a more systematic and organized basis than it had been before, though it remained far from perfect. Arrangements for the treatment of vagrants were in most places improved and were significantly more effective by the early 1840s than they had been earlier. Boards of guardians tended in practice to operate workhouse dietaries on a more generous scale than that which they solemnly proffered for the Poor Law Commission's approval—workhouse accounts show the purchase of substantial quantities of items never mentioned in the official dietary; for example, at South Shields the workhouse in 1836–8 was being supplied with two half-barrels of beer a week, supplemented by an extra firkin in 1838. Under Walsham's benign administration, such breaches of the supposed rules were winked at, provided the local authorities proved reasonably competent. Out-door relief to the able-bodied continued to be the usual way of giving relief to the unemployed.

However, the new system was not immune to some of the pressures on the old. The relationship between poor law administration and the health of the local economy continued to be close, and ratepayers no different after 1834 than before. When depression and unemployment did come to the region in the early 1840s, the reaction was to greet the rising spiral of demand on rate income with a distinct tightening up of expenditure. Many of the 'extras' disappeared from workhouse accounts, and the able-bodied applicants for relief received much less generous treatment. Local boards stiffened their already strong resistance to the attempts of the Poor Law Commission to make them pay decent salaries to officials. Even so, the post-1834 workhouses of the region do not seem to have been the 'Bastilles' of contemporary polemic. At Hexham a workhouse of c. 1840 can still be seen as part of a hospital's administrative offices; it was well built of sound materials and seems to have been a distinct improvement on its predecessors in the district.

When applied in a rough world with but very limited resources and skills in administration, the poor law did not succeed in meeting all needs or even in producing anything like uniformity between various districts. Its impact on the poor also varied from place to place and from time to time. Two examples may illustrate the poor law at work in the region soon after the changes of 1834.

Elizabeth Graham cut a tragic figure in the Newcastle of the 1820s and 1830s. A Scots woman, and by then getting on in years, she had no fixed home, and no fixed source of income. She lived in a succession of poor lodging houses and scraped a precarious living by selling tapes and ribbons on the streets when she could. She was a frequent applicant to Newcastle poor law officials, and no stranger to the Mendicity Institute, a privately supported charitable institution for the support of tramps and vagrants. In August 1830 she was before the Newcastle magistrates on a charge of disorderly conduct, being discharged on payment of small costs. On the evening of Sunday, 8 July 1838 her landlady came home drunk, and after a quarrel she ejected Graham from the house, despite the fact that she was feeling very ill. She made her way to the Newcastle workhouse, where an official refused to help her on the grounds that she was a vagrant and should therefore apply to the Mendicity Institute for help. The Keeper of that Institute refused to help her either, on the grounds that he knew her to have lived in Newcastle for a long time and that his orders positively forbade him to admit to the Institute any Newcastle resident. He added, for the benefit of a witness accompanying the woman, 'We have often been troubled with her.' She now returned to the workhouse, where she was still denied admission but was offered a loaf of bread which she refused. A little while after this she was found in the outhouses of a house in Westgate Road, Newcastle, and a sympathetic policeman tried to gain admission to the workhouse for her but failed. She was therefore given a bed in a police cell, and she died there during the night of 9–10 July, having apparently been much more gravely ill than either she herself or any of the other participants had realized. When these facts became known there was a strong public outcry; the coroner's jury severely criticized the local poor law administration and donated their own fees to the policeman who had at least tried to help. Sir John Walsham came to Newcastle to take part in a full enquiry. The poor law official involved was invited to resign; he refused and was then dismissed, for his breach of the general poor law rule that relief must not be denied to urgent cases. He had been seriously and tragically in the wrong, but those acquainted with the shadowy world of the very poor, and the unstable, and the criminal, of the Newcastle of the 1830s—and of both earlier and later periods—will not readily believe that the task of those who had to cope with that world was either particularly easy or particularly pleasant. At the beginning of Victoria's reign, with virtually no profession of social administration, virtually no facilities for training and poor pay, it was not surprising that some officials failed.

David Maddison posed a problem which was in some ways similar. He had been a respected schoolmaster before becoming an alcoholic. His mind was seriously affected, and in the late 1830s he spent a period in a lunatic asylum. His wife also took to drink, though not to the same dangerous extent. He refused to enter the workhouse of the Castle Ward Poor Law Union, north west of Newcastle, where he lived, nor would he accept the light work offered him by local farmers, who remembered him in better days. He wrote a series of angry letters, plainly deteriorating in both coherence and legibility, to both the Poor Law Commission and the Home Office. As was normal, when these complaints reached the Poor Law Commission that central authority asked its regional representative to make a full report on the case. On the first day of 1840 Walsham, the regional Assistant Commissioner, replied with a very full account of how this difficult case had been tackled. Walsham's brother-in-law, Matthew Bell, county magistrate, M.P. for South Northumberland, landowner, coal-owner, master of foxhounds, commander of a yeomanry regiment, lived in the area and at Walsham's request Bell provided the Maddisons with a cottage on his estate, rent-free and with a free supply of coal. In addition Bell provided Mrs Maddison with a job on condition that she refrained from drinking. The board of guardians had given the case long consideration and had decided against granting outdoor relief in cash to Maddison, solely on the grounds that to do so would be to place in his hands the means to drink himself into an asylum again. Instead the guardians granted relief to Mrs Maddison in the form of food and clothing, again on condition that she kept off the bottle. Walsham had himself talked with Maddison on a number of occasions and wryly added that 'he even levies the tribute of an occasional half-crown from the Assistant Commissioner himself'. When Walsham wrote this letter he regarded the situation of this couple as reasonably stable for the time being. Here a great deal of care had been applied in a difficult case by the responsible authorities. The solution arrived at was not perfect, but it is difficult to see that much more could have been done.

These cases are more significant in illuminating a variety of aspects of contemporary society than in their ability to represent the mass of poor law cases. Both were distinctly unusual, and the vast majority of poor law cases leave little trace in the historical record. Both before and after 1834 the great majority of poor law cases, and the bulk of poor law expenditure, consisted in the giving of doles in cash or kind to the non-able-bodied poor. The aged and infirm, orphaned and abandoned children, these provided far and away the bulk of the work of the poor law system. Union workhouses normally contained very few able-bodied people, the young, the old and the physically or mentally infirm providing the great majority of their inmates.

By about 1850 there were distinct signs of a greater degree of regulation and a more sophisticated administrative machinery entering the poor law system. District auditors appeared on the scene in 1844 and brought some tightening of financial practices. The central authority increasingly insisted on the regular submission of routine reports using prescribed printed forms—in earlier years Walsham's reports to his official superiors were often rambling letters including some illuminating digressions. It is not clear that this greater administrative zeal was accompanied by an equally marked increase of efficiency either locally or nationally. There was probably some loss of flexibility and autonomy at local level, but this should not be exaggerated. Boards of guardians in practice retained a high degree of autonomy in the ways in which they chose to handle local affairs, and a high degree of dexterity in frustrating attempts by central authorities to impose uniformity in relief attitudes and practices.

To concentrate on the official machinery of the poor law in the late eighteenth and nineteenth centuries would give only a very partial impression of the ways in which that society handled social problems. We have already seen some of the limitations which the available resources and contemporary attitudes placed on activities by government agencies, such as the poor law. In a period of limited government, the energies of society were predominantly expressed in private and unofficial forms, and this applied to the relief of poverty as to other matters. The development of unofficial philanthropy in the late eighteenth and early nineteenth centuries is a matter of considerable importance, not only for its contemporary significance but also because some of the agencies created during this period were to provide part of the essential foundation for the welfare services of twentieth-century Britain.

This aspect of the period can be conveniently considered under three headings: individual charitable enterprise, the mobilization of charitable funds to meet temporary needs, and the establishment of long-term charities.

Charitable enterprises

Paternalistic charity by many members of the wealthy ruling minorities was commonplace. Such activity was an expected accompaniment of high rank and extensive possessions. It was to be found in many different contexts. Here, for instance, is part of the epitaph on William Colling, Esq., a Durham landowner, in St Michael's, Heighington; he died in 1842:

> In this village and neighbourhood his exemplary regard to the claims of helpless age, of orphan destitution, of struggling industry, and faithful service will long be gratefully remembered.
>
> Nor can it be forgotten how constantly the cheerfulness of habitual benevolence, and of a conscience void of offence, which shone forth in his countenance and brightened his path in life shed its kindly influence on others, endeared him to his friends and the poor, and deepened the regret universally felt at his loss.

It is possible to argue that such activity merely represents an insidious resort to charity as a device of social control, and no doubt the motives which underlay such benevolence could sometimes be mixed. However, the more usual cause seems to have been a sense of what was due and right in society, a society in which rank, wealth and privilege were normally accorded respect, but which acquired in return important social responsibilities also. This spirit was expressed in his autobiography by Thomas Bewick, who was certainly on the left of the contemporary political spectrum. He was recalling rural life on Tyneside in the years around 1800[58]:

> These cottagers (at least those of them I knew) were of an honest & independent character while, at the same time, they held the neighbouring Gentry in the greatest estimation & respect, & these again in return did not overlook them but were interested in knowing that they were happy & well.

The surviving evidence readily provides very many examples of paternalistic charity, but perhaps a few may suffice to illustrate the variety and scope of this feature of society. It was normal for landowners to give rent remissions in times of agricultural depression, but sometimes they went much further than this. In January 1767, during a hard winter, Ralph Clavering of Callaly Castle bought up quantities of flour, meal and corn and sold them to poor people in the district at prices which they considered 'very reasonable' at a time of high food prices; he apportioned the supplies in accordance with family size. This was not an unusual event. In 1771 because of 13 weeks of snow around Easter, and a potentially disastrous shortage of fodder, Lord Ravensworth ordered his agent to distribute a stack of hay to the poor in the district who kept animals and to sell large quantities to local farmers at a price of £2 per ton at a time when the market price[59] had shot up to £6.10s. The Third Marquess of Londonderry has not until recently received a kindly notice from history; it is now clear that by contemporary standards he was a paternalistic proprietor both in Durham and on his Irish estates[60].

Nor was it all the case that his kind of philanthropy was only to be found in the more coherent ranges of rural society, for urban philanthropy is every bit as much in evidence. During the second quarter of the nineteenth century the charitable activity of Dr Thomas Winterbottom in South Shields illustrates an urban situation. He inherited a substantial fortune, and with it he demonstrated that paternalism was by no means only the prerogative of an established landed aristocracy. In 1839 he set aside a fund of £2,300 to provide pensions for retired master mariners, and as an afterthought spent a further £400 in providing gardens for them. Another sum of £5,000 was applied to provide relief to widows of merchant seamen. A fund of £150 was invested to provide annual presents on New Years Day to loyal unmarried female servants in South Shields—the presents graduated according to length of service. £403 was invested to provide annual gifts for retired boatmen from the Tyne. Another Winterbottom charity provided annual prizes for the best ploughmen and ploughboys in North East Durham. A fund of £200 was invested to provide poor people in South Shields with free coal at Christmas. In 1837 he founded a marine school in South Shields; he gave continuing support including financial aid to the Tyne seamen's union led by Henry Woodroffe and sponsored friendly societies and a savings bank. He was of course unusually generous, but he was certainly not alone in his efforts to help those in need in his home area. There was also a great deal of mutual help to be observed among those who were not particularly wealthy. A Newcastle bookbinder, Gilbert Gray, was one of these cases[61]:

> I have often discovered that he did not overlook ingenious Mechanics, whose misfortunes, perhaps mismanagement, has led them to a lodging in Newgate —to these he directed his compassionate eye, & to the deserving (in his estimation) he paid the debt & set them at liberty—he felt hurt at seeing the hands of an ingenious man tied up in a prison, where they were of no use, either to themselves or the community.

Bewick[61] mentions other similar cases too. During the later eighteenth and nineteenth centuries there was a development of business and professional groups in local centres—in 1829 Newcastle and Gateshead between them had 61 solicitors and 53 doctors—many of whom played significant roles not only in the oligarchies which dominated the towns but also in the organization and support of charitable activities. With the growth of urban populations, while individual philanthropy continued common and important, a greater part came to be played by organized charitable activity organized by substantial local groups. Part of this effort was directed in a variety of ways to the organization of corporate local charitable reactions to temporary pressing needs.

In January 1805, five boats, carrying 19 men, were lost in a storm off the Northumberland coast. A local collection for the relief of the dependents of the lost men raised £1,701, mainly from propertied groups on Tyneside. In addition to local tragedies of this kind, hard winters normally provoked local collections of money with the twin purposes of setting up public works schemes to curb seasonal unemployment and of providing direct relief to other sufferers. For example, the Sunderland collection in 1816—one of the many such collections during that bitter winter—raised £2,437. A similar fund was raised there 3 years later, and the Home Secretary, Lord Sidmouth, wrote to Sunderland to express his warm approval of the methods made by public subscription 'for the purpose of finding Employment for poor Persons who have been deprived of it, in consequence of the peculiar Circumstances and Pressure of the Times.' In addition to such public subscriptions, and the establishment of soup kitchens, it was normal practice for local firms to give appropriate gifts in kind—collieries would donate coal for the poor, while gifts of food from farming or fishing interests were equally common. Just as it was an expected role for the landowner to dispense paternalistic charity, so it was for the urban factory or bank. From the time of the establishment of the branch Bank of England in Newcastle, for instance, its correspondence records that in common with all of the other local banks, it was regularly included among the subscribers to a wide range of local charities, in addition to the use of its staff in the unpaid administration of philanthropic societies.

The kind of corporate activity which could be rallied to meet hard times was also employed to meet the need for general celebration. An event such as the coronation of Queen Victoria in June 1838 was greeted by junkettings of various kinds all over the region, with funds being subscribed everywhere to allow the poor to participate. At Newcastle:

> The poor in the various workhouses, and even the prisoners in the gaol, have been provided with ample means of joining in the festivities, and the inmates of the hospitals were presented with five shillings each, for the same purpose.

At Gateshead:

> Upwards of 400 persons, of all ages and of both sexes, were afterwards entertained at dinner in a large tent, fixed in the yard of Gateshead workhouse. The supply of roast beef and plum pudding, and ale, was most profuse; and the guests were waited on by the members of the town council and the board of guardians, the town clerk, the churchwardens and overseers, and other gentlemen; and highly delighted they were with the good fare set before them, and the courtesy which they experienced. An old lady—a venerable and mettlesome octogenarian—officiated as queen on the occasion, and was most stylishly attired for her high office. At the close of the feast, sixpence each was given to the company assembled.

At North Shields there was a distribution of meat, bread and money to 2,500 recipients, and a dinner for 900 old seamen. At Sunderland, among other activities, 1,000 families were given 3 lb of meat and 3 lb of bread each.

Similar activities marked this event all over the region, with the variety which the local rejoicings took demonstrating the spontaneity of this kind of corporate local effort. Royal marriages or births, successful wars and other similar occasions all produced similar rounds of local celebrations, with provision made by voluntary subscriptions for the poor to participate in them.

In addition to such essentially temporary activities, the economic growth of the late eighteenth and early nineteenth centuries was paralleled by the development of an intricate system of voluntary philanthropic institutions of a long-term kind. There is no reason to suppose that the coincidence should be read to indicate that the process of industrialization necessarily caused a proliferation of charitable institutions. A much more likely explanation is that the spread of humanitarian feelings which marked this period sprang from intellectual roots in the enlightenment of the eighteenth century similar to those which sparked off the energy and ingenuity applied to economic development. In one way, however, there existed an unmistakable link between the process of industrial development and the provision of wider philanthropic agencies. It seems highly unlikely that any such substantial increase in welfare provision could have taken place except in the context of a society which was on the whole growing markedly richer. The provision of extended welfare services and more genuine care and consideration for the poorer and weaker sectors of society are unlikely to occur in a context which the resources of society are not increasing. The connection between expanding economic resources and the will and ability to finance benevolence to those in need is supported by a great deal of evidence from modern British history; there is also much to support the view that in times of economic recession it is usually the weak and the poor who suffer most, even if they are not the only victims.

The range of charitable organizations which grew in the century before 1850 was quite unprecedented in its size and scope. For the most part these institutions were essentially local, financed by local resources, administered by those who provided the funds and designed to meet needs recognized within the local community. There were some exceptions; for example the local Ship-wrecked Mariners' Society was, long before the end of the eighteenth century, part of a network of similar societies covering the coasts of Britain and providing reciprocal facilities for seamen from any port who were wrecked or stranded in this area. Largely because of the local basis of these institutions, it would be impossible to list here the varied institutions which came into being during this period, but perhaps those of Newcastle will serve as a sufficient example. Newcastle is the best case to choose, because there was in the world of philanthropy a great deal of emulation and borrowing of ideas. Within this region it was the regional centre of Newcastle which provided much of the inspiration for other places in Northumberland and Durham, while Newcastle itself was not above borrowing philanthropic ideas from elsewhere. (Some major sources for these Newcastle charities are listed under reference 62.)

The emergence of hospitals

The Newcastle Infirmary, ancestor of the present Royal Victoria Infirmary, was founded in 1751 in imitation of a slightly earlier foundation at Northampton, the initiative coming from a group of men prominent in Newcastle's commercial and social life. They launched a public subscription which proved a consider-able success and when the Infirmary's first buildings were opened in 1752, some £3,000 had been spent on them. The Infirmary was rebuilt and substantially enlarged in 1802, work financed by an appeal which provided £5,329, more than £2,000 of this coming from the handful of peers and baronets who were connected closely with the area. A further appeal in 1817 added 'warm baths, on an approved pattern'.

The Infirmary fulfilled two main functions 'for the sick and lame poor of the counties of Newcastle, Durham and Northumberland'. A 24-hour casualty service was provided, staffed by the town's resident doctors serving on a voluntary rota. In addition to these emergency facilities, the Infirmary pro-vided a range of hospital facilities for both in-patients and out-patients. While the casualty service operated without formality for those in urgent need, for the Infirmary's other functions patients must be armed with a presentation letter from a subscriber to the institution's funds. In the 1820s for example an annual subscription of 2 guineas conferred the right to introduce one in-patient or two out-patients during the year, presentation rights rising with subscriptions *pro rata*. Introductions were usually not very difficult to obtain, for many institutions or societies made block subscriptions to obtain ready access for their members to these medical facilities. Friendly societies and trade unions acted in this way; Newcastle's town council made a large annual donation in return for which the mayor, or any two aldermen, could issue a presentation letter to Newcastle applicants. Absentee subscribers often entrusted their presentations to the hospital staff. In 1825-6 the Infirmary spent just under £3,000 in running expenses, almost all of this coming from voluntary subscriptions, and claimed that 1,447 patients were, during the year, 'restored to their friends and the community wholly freed from their complaints'.

In 1778 the Infirmary's services were supplemented by the creation of the Newcastle Dispensary, essentially an imitation of the Infirmary for less serious medical needs of the poor. The Dispensary provided an emergency service without formality for 'slight casualties', and also a consulting and treatment service based on the presentation system, and including the free supply of medicines prescribed for patients; an annual subscription of a guinea entitled a subscriber to present five patients a year. In the late 1820s, when Newcastle had a population of some 40,000 the Dispensary would expect to deal with some 5,000 cases a year, while during the first quarter of the nineteenth century it provided about 20,000 free vaccinations against smallpox. Most of the Dispensary's work was with out-patients, but its voluntary medical officers also operated a system of home visits.

From 1760 onwards Newcastle possessed two charitable institutions for maternity cases. The Lying-in Hospital for in-patients moved in 1826 to very fine new premises (now the B.B.C.'s Broadcasting House) designed by the town's leading architect, John Dobson. Money for this came from a variety of sources, most of it in donations from men of property in the area; the Newcastle Music Festival of October 1824 brought £160 to the funds, the preaching of two special sermons brought collections of £52 and £61, while Newcastle Council gave £100 and Newcastle Trinity House £30. The Charity for Poor Married Women provided midwifery services in the homes of mothers who could not afford such aid. Unmarried mothers were regularly excluded from these facilities and commonly relied on the official system of poor relief; during the nineteenth century, however, a number of special institutions for unmarried mothers were established in the area, though they operated agencies for moral rehabilitation as much as centres for medical and social help.

In 1814 a group of local men of influence, including the Bishop of Durham and the Duke of Northumberland, provided funds for the foundation of a Lock Hospital or specialized institution for prostitutes, who were normally excluded from more respectable charities. A dozen years later a local historian commented that the work of this institution, which provided a refuge, medical care and opportunities for entry to a rehabilitation centre in Edinburgh, was handicapped by the rise of 'false delicacy' which hindered discussion of its interests. A few years later the work involved was transferred to a special section of the Infirmary, kept separate from its ordinary wards, and this practice prevailed long after 1850.

New welfare agencies proliferated as special needs received special attention. Early in 1838 a group of leading citizens met to found a Newcastle asylum for the care of the blind, and all went well until a few months later a serious row developed on sectarian lines about the appointment of a chaplain. As a result there were for a short period two blind asylums, but very soon the Anglican group concentrated on the provision of specialized care for the deaf and dumb, while the non-conformist institution remained the region's principal institution for the care of the blind. In both cases it became increasingly common for poor law authorities to entrust blind or deaf and dumb cases in their care to these voluntary institutions, paying from the poor rate an allowance for their maintenance.

A specialized Eye Infirmary opened its doors on 23 March 1822 and moved to better premises two years later. There every Monday, Tuesday, Thursday and Saturday doctors held a clinic for poor people suffering from eye defects.

A great deal of charitable activity was concerned with the provision of clothing and footwear to the poor. Much keen work and a good deal of money also went into the provision of religious instruction and consolation for the poor, welfare work which seemed of great importance to many contemporaries, though it may arouse less enthusiasm in the modern observer; in these devout causes thousands of pounds and a large amount of voluntary effort were annually expended in Newcastle alone.

These philanthropic endeavours did not transform North East England into an idyllic residence for society's weaker and poorer groups, but they provide evidence of the wider percolation of humanitarian views. Provision for the care of the poor was substantially improved in ways which had not existed before, by voluntary efforts. Beginning in a world which saw much cruelty and lack of concern the creation of these institutions marks an early stage in the evolution of society's welfare institutions. In the late eighteenth and early nineteenth centuries unofficial philanthropy expended much greater resources of energy and money in welfare work than the official poor law possessed, and the provision of new ideas and new facilities was overwhelmingly the work of private philanthropy and not official administration.

There was a considerable connection between the two spheres, however. In practice poor law agencies, both before and after 1834, were controlled by the same local dominant minorities which operated and controlled the local charities, while as we have seen official agencies frequently resorted to voluntary institutions for the care of specialized categories of poor people. Some of the principal welfare facilities in our own towns reflect the twin agencies of welfare provision characteristic of nineteenth-century society. In Newcastle, if the General Hospital represents the development of the official workhouse hospital, the Royal Victoria Infirmary is the lineal descendant of the voluntary

Infirmary of 1751; at South Shields the General Hospital represents the old workhouse hospital, the Ingham Infirmary a local voluntary foundation, and similar conjunctions exist in other places within the region.

Education

One area of importance in which voluntary activity also far outstripped official action during this period was education, a matter of some importance especially in a region of increasing technical progress. Charity schools proliferated in the late eighteenth and even more in the early nineteenth centuries. Many parochial schools were either begun or reformed and expanded during this period. A typical example was that in the parish of St Nicholas, Newcastle. In the 1820s this school educated 400 boys and 150 girls; fees amounted to 1*d.* per week, the school making ends meet by subscriptions and donations from sympathizers of means. Like very many of these schools, this operated on a monitorial system, with the teacher imparting the lesson to a small group of older and gifted pupils who then passed it on to larger classes.

King George III's jubilee in 1810, and the aged monarch's expressed and well publicized wish that every child in his dominions should be enabled to read his Bible, led to the foundation by public subscription of Jubilee schools in many places, including Newcastle and North Shields. By the late 1820s the Newcastle Jubilee Schools provided free education for nearly 500 boys and more than 200 girls, costs being met by donations and subscriptions. These schools also operated on the monitorial system, not just because it was economical but because it was widely regarded as embodying the best in current educational techniques. Here is an account of these schools by a prominent local radical politician[63]; their success

> . . . must soon bring into disrepute the old stupefying practice of fixing the trembling pupil in his seat, where he dozes over his hated task . . . It is a curious and pleasing spectacle, to see above 400 boys, in one room, actively and cheerfully engaged in acquiring the elements of education, while their movements are conducted with the regularity and celerity of disciplined troops. . . . Some of the boys in the upper classes display an acuteness and rapidity of thought almost incredible.

This close observer also highly approved of the system of ranking pupils in such grades as monitors general and monitors of classes, and of the singling out of the brightest pupils into an 'order of merit', for whom a special library was created by public subscription. He very much disliked, however, the institution of completely free education, which he feared '. . . must tend to blunt the delicate pride of both parents and children, to familiarize the mind to dependence on charitable institutions, and to prepare it for the degradation of pauperism. The demanding of a small weekly sum from the parents is evidently gratifying to their feelings.'

We must not expect the philanthropic agencies of the period to conform to much later concepts of how society should work. British society in the late eighteenth and early nineteenth centuries was profoundly unequal—as indeed it always had been. The presentation system in vogue for many major charitable institutions, and the control of such bodies by those who provided the money which created and supported them, were simply a reflection of the nature of contemporary society. Patients in medical institutions were under strict injunctions to offer thanks both to God and to the patron who had presented them, while a neglect of such simple duties might be met by exclusion from the charity's facilities in future. As in social relationships generally there was no general acceptance of egalitarian ideas; facilities were provided on an increasing scale, but a proper sense of appreciation and gratitude for such benevolence was certainly expected.

Here for example is a passage from the Newcastle Infirmary statutes of 1801:

> You are to attend the Infirmary every (-day) at eleven o'clock in the forenoon, during the continuance of your disorder and you are every time to bring back all the medicines which you have not taken, and all your bottles, phials, and galleypots, well cleaned and washed. You are not to presume to loiter about the Infirmary or places adjacent, but come directly into the place appointed to receive you, and as soon as your business is despatched you must return home. When you have had notice to be discharged you shall appear at the Infirmary on the Thursday following at eleven o'clock in the forenoon to return thanks to the gentlemen of the house committee, for the benefit you have received from the charity.

Such minatory instructions were not, however, unknown even in twentieth-century welfare institutions.

The rules of the Ravensworth Almshouses of 1836 included this clause:

> Persons admitted into the Ravensworth Almshouses are to consider themselves as residents only upon sufferance, and that they may be dismissed by the Lady Ravensworth, or any person deputed by Her Ladyship for any offence, or reason, that Her Ladyship may deem sufficient; and it is to be understood that drunkenness, dishonesty, want of cleanliness, quarrelling, meddling with or slandering their neighbours will be considered sufficient reasons for dismissal.

A few years later a meeting of the local Shipwrecked Mariners' Society showed that contemporary charity could appear distinctly smug. A local radical newspaper recorded how, after arranging for the collecting and application of considerable sums of money on behalf of one of the most regularly endangered groups of workers, the members of this philanthropic society 'sat down to a sumptuous dinner at the George Inn, and spent an evening of the most gratifying kind—happily engrafting upon the social enjoyments of the passing hour, a determination to relieve the distresses and promote the comforts of their less fortunate fellow-creatures'.

Friendly societies and savings banks

These varied charitable activities of the propertied groups within the region's society were paralleled by the proliferation of 'self-help' agencies among the workers themselves. Savings banks and friendly societies were among the major manifestations of this spirit, and in both cases the development of such institutions was actively encouraged and helped by richer sections of society. In the late eighteenth and early nineteenth centuries the aristocratic parliament legislated to provide a legal framework for both friendly societies and savings banks, and many local examples exist to show how wealthier groups promoted and encouraged such manifestations of a healthy spirit of thrift and independence.

The first savings bank within the region was founded by the Rev Charles Thorp at Ryton-on-Tyne soon after his presentation to the living there in 1807[64]. By 1815 the managers of this bank included Thorp himself, the Earl of Strathmore, and five of the leading local gentry; deposits in this bank's funds were limited to between 2s. and a maximum of £25, in order to ensure that this protected, interest-bearing facility was as far as possible confined to the workers for whom it was intended, a common practice. The Tynedale Ward Bank for Savings was founded at a Hexham meeting of 'Magistrates and other Gentlemen of Tynedale Ward' in 1817, with an eloquent plea:

> Let it be seriously considered, that in the very humblest class of life, the young and the single must, at times, have more money than they have immediate occasion for. They have at the time no opportunity of applying it profitably; and the sum is too small to seem worthwhile to save. This exposes the inexperienced, and yet virtuous, to temptations, which would otherwise not have occurred; and hence is contracted the taste for dissipation, and the dislike to labour. Here is the foundation laid for a long train of sad consequences, idleness, resort to public houses, drunkenness, bad company, crimes and ultimately punishment. How many poor creatures, who, from the beginning, have come to an untimely end, would have been happy and respectable heads of families, had the opportunity been afforded them of depositing the first money they possessed above their immediate wants in a *Bank for Savings?*

Peers, baronets, bishops, archdeacons, rectors, gentry and leading townsfolk appeared prominently among those who helped to create and administer savings banks, and the sums deposited in these banks by frugal workers were often substantial. Deposits totalling £3,000 or £4,000 a year were to be found in local savings banks in such places as Bishop Auckland and Washington in the 1820s, by which time virtually the whole of the region was covered by a network of similar banks for the benefit of small savers. The Newcastle Savings Bank was the biggest of these and its record of deposits was impressive. Established at the beginning of 1818, with the encouragement and help of the town's dominant official and commercial oligarchies, by 1826 it held small savings accounts amounting to very nearly £200,000, with over 3,500 individual depositors.

Friendly societies also multiplied at a very impressive rate during the late eighteenth and early nineteenth century. By the mid-1820s, for example, there were[65]

> . . . in Newcastle and Gateshead, about 165 Benefit Societies, which, altogether comprise not less than 10,000 members, who reside in the town and surrounding villages, and pay monthly contributions to their respective funds; from which they are allowed, in case of sickness of infirmity, from six to eight shillings per week, for two or three months; but, if they should be disabled by a lingering disorder, or superannuated, their weekly allowance is reduced to 2s. or 2s.6d., for life. Forty or fifty shillings generally are allowed for funeral expenses, and widows have each a legacy of from £5 to £10. No fewer than 117 of these provident societies have deposits in the Savings' Bank which, in November, 1826, amounted collectively to £31,161.14s.10d. Many of them have also money vested in the hands of the corporation, for which they receive four per cent interest.

There were in fact more than 165 societies, for the list given in this source does not include either the 50 or so 'annual benefit societies' which operated on an annual basis, giving small welfare benefits and distributing the bulk of their resources by drawing lots among members, or a considerable number of very small local societies. Friendly society benefits were also provided by a variety of other institutions, such as masonic lodges and trade unions; in 1826 the Tyne seaman's union paid out more than £1,000 in sickness and unemployment benefit, £315 in shipwreck relief, £171 in death grants and nearly £70 in advances on wages, as well as subscriptions of 25 guineas to obtain members' ready entry to infirmary and dispensary facilities[66]. At other places the network of coverage by friendly societies existed on a smaller scale. In 1817, for example, the Bishop Auckland Savings Bank (trustees, the Bishop of Durham, Earl of Strathmore, Earl of Darlington and Viscount Barrington) held £1,224 deposited by three local friendly societies. In a variety of ways members of local dominant minorities were found to help and support friendly societies as well as savings banks. In the remote Northumberland rural village of Ford, for instance, the Ford Insurance Club of the 1830s existed to insure the cows owned by agricultural workers. Local employers were to be responsible for the valuation of the beasts, while the managing committee was dominated by men of greater means than the society's beneficiaries[67]. Although both savings banks and friendly societies were often summed up as 'self-help' institutions, in practice they depended heavily on the countenance and often the active participation of men drawn from social groups above those served by these facilities.

Conclusions

In the workings of society as well as the development of the regional economy the North East of the late eighteenth and early nineteenth centuries presents a diverse and inconstant character. There remained strong traces of the rough and the cruel and the inconsiderate, which had certainly existed in earlier periods, and a continuous existence of a substantial element of crime and vice. The unforeseeable expansion of industry in various forms brought about an unprecedented increase of population in many areas, involving a serious worsening of social problems such as poor housing and bad sanitation which had existed at earlier periods in many parts of the region. These developments took place in a society in which the formal agencies of central and local government were singularly ill equipped to respond effectively to the emerging problems. There was no widespread belief that in substantial expansion of the resources of government lay the possibility of a significant improvement in social conditions. Where amelioration took place it was commonly the result of completely unofficial exertions, exemplified on the one hand by the spreading religious revival and on the other by the considerable extension of voluntary charitable activity in many forms. The economic, social and political institutions of the region continued to be dominated by propertied minorities who combined unofficial influence with control of the limited official agencies which existed. Instances of conflict and violence frequently occurred, but there were also strong elements of cohesion and mutual sympathy between differing social groups. Neither the workers nor the dominant minorities were at all monolithic in their attitudes and activities, and the evidence does not support the supposition that either capital or labour ever formed anything like a coherent united front. Although substantial economic development had occurred by 1850, for most people within the region life was still lived in locally orientated communities of small or moderate size. To contemporaries in 1850 the extent of the transformation effected since 1760 seemed a very considerable one, however, as indeed it was in comparison with any earlier period. The next half-century was to see much more rapid and much more pervasive changes.

References

1   D. Jones, 'Thomas Campbell Foster and the Rural Labourer: Incendiarism in East Anglia in the 1840s', *Social History*, no. 1, 1976, appendix A (i).
2   Anon., *A Handbook of the 41st Annual Co-operative Congress*, 1909, p. 41.
3   E. Grierson, *Confessions of a Country Magistrate*, 1972, pp. 105–6.
    D. D. Dixon, *Whittingham Vale*, 1895, pp. 295–6.
4   A. Appleton, *Mary Ann Cotton*, 1973, p. 129. *Newcastle Weekly Chronicle*, 29/3/1873.
5   T. Oliver, *A New Picture of Newcastle upon Tyne*, 1831, reprinted 1970, p. 173.

6   J. Collingwood Bruce, *Handbook to Newcastle upon Tyne*, 1889, p. 73.

7   A. Watson, *My Life*, (1937), p. 13.

8   J. Rewcastle, *Newcastle As It Is*, 1854, p. 13.

9   Anon., *The County Borough of Tynemouth*, 1949, p. 56.

10   E. Mackenzie, *A Descriptive and Historical Account of . . . Newcastle upon Tyne*, vol. I, 1827, part 2, pp. 163–4.

11   Rewcastle, op. cit., p. 13.

12   H. A. Mitchell, *A Report of the Proceedings in the Mayor's Chamber, During the Mayoralty of George Shadforth, Esq., 1829–30*, probably 1830.

13   Oliver, op. cit., p. 181.

14   J. Philipson, 'Whisky Smuggling on the Border in the Early Nineteenth Century', *Archaeologia Aeliana*, 4th ser., vol. XXXIX, 1961, pp. 151–63. 'Remains of Illicit Distilleries in Upper Coquetdale', *Archaeologia Aeliana*, 4th ser., vol. XXXVIII, 1960.

15   Rewcastle, op. cit., p. 2.

16   ibid.

17   W. M. Patterson, *Northern Primitive Methodism*, 1909, p. 70.

18a   S. Hillaby, *Memoirs of John Allen: A Sunday School Retrospect*, 1850, p. 72.

  b   P. Stigant, 'Wesleyan Methodism and Working-Class Radicalism in the North, 1792–1821', *Northern History*, vol. VI, 1971, pp. 98–116.

19   Patterson, op. cit.

20   C. J. Hunt, *The Lead Miners of the Northern Pennines*, 1970, p. 221.

21   W. L. Burn, 'Newcastle upon Tyne in the Early Nineteenth Century', *Archaeologia Aeliana*, 4th ser., vol. XXXIV, 1956, p. 8.

22   ibid., p. 3.

23   N. McCord, 'Gateshead Politics in the Age of Reform', *Northern History*, vol. IV, 1969, p. 169.

24   N. McCord, 'The Implementation of the Poor Law Amendment Act of 1834 on Tyneside', *International Review of Social History*, vol. XIV, 1969, pp. 90–108.

   P. Dunkley, 'The "Hungry Forties" and the New Poor Law: A Case Study', *Historical Journal*, vol. XVII, 1974, pp. 329–46.

   P. Mawson, *Poor Law Administration in South Shields, 1830–1930, M.A. Thesis*, Newcastle University, 1971.

   R. Barker, *The Houghton-le-Spring Poor Law Union, M.Litt. Thesis*, Newcastle University, 1974.

   P. A. Wood, *The Sunderland Poor Law Union, M.Litt. Thesis*, Newcastle University, 1976.

25   F. Manders, *A History of Gateshead*, 1973, p. 181.

26   D. B. Reid, *A Report on the State of Newcastle and other Towns*, 1845, p. 136.

27   R. Rawlinson, *Report to the General Board of Health . . . on . . . Inquiry . . . into the . . . Sanitary Condition . . . of Alnwick, etc.*, 1850, p. 76.

28   Barker, op. cit., p. 124.

29   Rawlinson, op. cit., pp. 71–2.

30   W. S. Gilly, *The Peasantry of the Border*, 1842, pp. 14–15.
31   Anon., *Inquiry into the Condition of the Poor of Newcastle upon Tyne*, 1850, especially pp. 40–1.
32a W. H. Maehl, 'Chartism in Northeastern England, 1839', *International Review of Social History*, vol. VIII, 1963.
   b D. J. Rowe, 'Some Aspects of Chartism on Tyneside', *International Review of Social History*, vol. XVI, 1971, pp. 17–39.
33   Rewcastle, op. cit., p. 4.
34   Anon., typescript copy of manuscript held in Newcastle Central Library, *Colliery Manuscripts*, vol. J.
35   M. Phillips, *A History of Banks, Bankers and Banking in Northumberland, Durham and North Yorkshire*, 1894, p. 72.
36   Public Record Office, letters in H.O. 42/153.
37   T. S. Ashton and J. Sykes, *The Coal Industry of the Eighteenth Century*, 1929, p. 127.
38   N. McCord, 'Tyneside Discontents and Peterloo', *Northern History*, vol. II, 1967, pp. 91–111.
39   D. J. Rowe, 'A Trade Union of the North-East Coast Seamen in 1825', *Economic History Review*, 2nd ser., vol. 25, 1972, pp. 81–98.
40a N. McCord and D. E. Brewster, 'Some Labour Troubles of the 1790s in North East England', *International Review of Social History*, vol. XIII, 1968, pp. 366–83.
     N. McCord, 'The Government of Tyneside, 1800–50', *Transactions of the Royal Historical Society*, 5th ser., vol. 20, 1970, pp. 17–18.
   b N. McCord, 'The 1815 Seamen's Strikes in North East England', *Economic History Review*, 2nd ser., vol. XXI, 1968, pp. 127–43.
41   N. McCord, 'The 1815 Seamen's Strikes in North East England', *Economic History Review*, 2nd ser., vol. XXI, 1968, pp. 127–43.
42   Public Record Office, H.O. 40/29, Bouverie/Home Office, 26 April 1831.
43   N. McCord, 'The Government of Tyneside, 1800–50', *Transactions of the Royal Historical Society*, 5th ser., vol. 20, 1970, pp. 17–18.
44   ibid., p. 23.
45   ibid., p. 24.
46   ibid., p. 26.
47   R. Fynes, *The Miners of Northumberland and Durham*, 1873, pp. 24–5.
48   J. Losh, in E. Hughes, ed., *Diaries and Correspondence*, vol. II, Surtees Society, 1963, pp. 141, 213.
49   Parson and White, *Directory of Northumberland and Durham*, etc., vol. II, 1828, p. 146.
50   W. Robinson, *The Story of the Royal Infirmary, Sunderland*, 1934, p. 17.
51   Mackenzie, op. cit., pp. 540–1.
52   ibid., pp. 542–3.
53   T. Bewick, *A Memoir Written by Himself*, 1862, modern edn, Oxford University Press, 1975, p. 33.

54   F. W. D. Manders, *A History of Gateshead*, 1973, pp. 217–218.

55   P. A. Wood, op. cit., pp. 16–18.

56   N. McCord, 'The Implementation of the 1834 Poor Law Amendment on Tyneside', *International Review of Social History*, vol. XIV, 1969, pp. 90–108.

57   ibid.

P. Dunkley, op. cit.

58   Bewick, op. cit., p. 24.

59   Dixon, op. cit., pp. 297–8.

60   A. J. Heesom, 'Entrepreneurial Paternalism: The Third Lord Londonderry and the Coal Trade', *Durham University Journal*, 1974, pp. 238–56.

61   Bewick, op. cit., p. 44.

62a   W. E. Hume, 'The Infirmary, Newcastle upon Tyne, 1751–1951', 1951.

  b   Oliver, op. cit., pp. 57–8.

  c   Newcastle Central Library, reports.

  d   Mackenzie, op. cit.

63   Mackenzie, op. cit.

64   Newcastle Central Library, extensive collection of reports and accounts of savings banks and friendly societies.

65   Parson and White, op. cit., vol. I, pp. lxxxviii–ix.

66   Public Record Office, H.O. 40/21, accounts for 1826.

67   Rules of club, printed at Berwick, 1834.

Part Two
1850–1920

3 The Expanding Economy

During the second half of the nineteenth century, North East England was a principal beneficiary of a remarkable increase of economic activity on a national and an international scale. The total volume of international trade in 1850 has been put at about £800 million; the figure was approaching £3,000 million by 1880 and passed £8,000 million by 1914[1]. Within this tremendous growth the British share was very large, and within the British share a substantial portion was taken by the North East. To a greater extent than ever before the region became involved in a complex and far-reaching pattern of economic activity which provided unprecedented opportunities for growth but also brought an increased dependence on external markets which were not necessarily stable or secure.

Coal industry

The continued growth of the coalfield remained of very great importance. The first half of the nineteenth century had already seen considerable expansion of output, but this was to be far exceeded after 1850. Within this overall expansion, although there were substantial increases in demand from home industry, coal exports represented an ever-increasing share of sales. There was a marked widening in the destinations to which coal was sent, but the core of the export demand remained after 1850 where it had been before, in North Europe, where the development of industrialization and urbanization brought an increased need for coal supplies. Coal shipments from the Tyne give a good indication of these trends[2]. Shipments of coal from this major port reached 4 million tons in 1857 and 10 million tons in 1888. As early as the 1830s and 1840s there had been indications that exports were beginning to loom larger in shipments. In 1831 foreign shipments had represented about 7% of total shipments, and by 1845 the proportion had already reached nearly 31%. This tendency rapidly accelerated and by 1888, when well over 6 million tons of coal were exported from the Tyne alone, the figure reached 63% of all shipments. During these years home demand appeared in contrast relatively stable, rising from 2.2 million tons in 1831 to 2.6 million tons in 1874 and then to 3.7 million tons by 1888. As late as the period 1896–1905 coastal coal shipments had reached a plateau of over 5 million tons a year. The relatively slow growth of the coastal coal trade can probably be attributed to increasing competition from other coalfields together with an increase in rail-borne coal traffic. In 1851 London had received less than a quarter of a million tons of coal by rail, while in 1870 the figure was already 3.75 million tons[3].

The most rapid growth in coal shipments from the North East came in the years 1879–1908. In the early years of the twentieth century the Tyne alone shipped some 17 million tons each year, of which appreciably over two-thirds represented export shipments. A list of the destinations involved would be long and world-wide, but many of them were of little importance. About half of this swollen export trade was destined for France, Germany and Italy, while the Scandinavian countries were the next biggest market. Both Spain and Russia took considerable amounts, which sometimes reached as high as 10% each of total exports in the late nineteenth century. Compared with these major customers, exports to destinations outside Europe were relatively trivial. Within the pattern of coastal shipments London not only remained most important but increased its consumption from about 60% of coastal shipments in the 1870s to about 80% in the first years of the next century.

This enormous increase in output was paralleled by major increases in mining employment, most marked in County Durham. In Northumberland in 1851 farming still employed twice as many people as coal-mining, but by the beginning of the twentieth century mining had far outstripped agriculture as a source of employment. There were nearly 11,000 miners in Northumberland (8.6% of total employment) in 1851; 50 years later the figure was well over 37,000 (more than 15% of total employment). The figures for Durham were even more striking; a rise in numbers of miners from 30,000 in 1851 to 100,000 in 1901 (from 18.5% of total employment to 23% in 1901). No other category of employment came anywhere near this proportion[4].

There were also significant changes in the relative importance of different districts within the coalfield. The rapid growth of the Teesside iron and steel industry increased demands on the coking coal of West Durham, while the expansion of demand for steam coal for use in engines of various kinds, including bunkers for steamships, was also responsible for shifts in the pattern of mining. Towards the end of the nineteenth century there were signs of marked depletion of the hard coking coal of West Durham, and the prospect of higher costs of operation there. At the same time there was a considerable increase in the exploitation of the steam and household coal in some areas of South East Northumberland which had been relatively neglected before. Ashington's population grew from 345 in 1851 to 13,956 in 1901, and Bedlington's from 5,101 to 18,766 during the same period. (The census figures for Ashington are here amended to include those living in Hirst, essentially an extension of the Ashington community.) Coal shipments from the adjacent port of Blyth rose from 235,000 tons in 1880 to 1.8 million tons in 1890 and then shot up to more than 4 million tons by 1914. The notably well-managed Ashington Coal Company sank the Bothal pit 1867, the Carl in 1873 and the Drake in 1887. Ashington Colliery had six shafts concentrated together in one small area. Three substantial new collieries were founded by the company subsequently— Linton in 1896, Woodhorn 2 years later and Ellington in 1910.

A number of major local industries contributed to the growing demand for coal. Iron and steel, shipbuilding and the chemical industry were among these. For example, the Tyneside chemical industry consumed about a quarter of a million tons of coal in 1853, and the figure rose to 300,000 tons in the 1860s[5].

The great expansion of coal shipments was facilitated by one major technical breakthrough. Until mid-century the standard coal-carrying vessel was the wooden sailing collier brig. In 1852, however, the situation was revolutionized by the building at Palmer's Jarrow shipyard of the *John Bowes*. She was iron built and screw propelled, and this one small ship was one of the most important ships to be built in the nineteenth century. There had been iron ships before, and screw-propelled ships before, but the crucial thing about the *John Bowes* was that she gave an unmistakable demonstration of the potential commercial superiority of this advanced type in ordinary trading use. She was in fact the first successful modern cargo ship, the ancestress of many thousands of future vessels. Her example was rapidly imitated. Palmer set about building a fleet of similar vessels, and they showed continual increases in size and efficiency. In 1853 the Gas, Light and Coke Company, a major firm shipping coal to the Thames, decided on a rapid changeover to the new type, and, although there were some teething troubles to be experienced, the number of steam colliers in service rapidly grew. (For losses of early steam colliers see reference 6a and for the Gas, Light and Coke Company see reference 6b.)

There were probably more than 20,000 men employed in the sailing collier fleet when the *John Bowes* appeared. Some of these men, indeed many, must have transferred their services to the growing steam collier fleet, but for others it was not so simple or easy. The rapid increase in the numbers and the coal capacity of the new ships rapidly eroded the competitive position of the sailing colliers, with the result that in the older ships standards of maintenance and repair tended to be cut, with increased danger to ships and crews. One of the new ships could carry between 400 to 750 tons of coal per voyage, depending on size, compared with about 280 tons for a good sailing collier. In 1853 the 13 screw colliers afloat carried between them more than 70,000 tons of coal to London in 123 trips; in the next year a total of 36 carried over 200,000 tons in 384 trips. By 1855 there were about 60 screw colliers based in the Tyne, and the number continued to grow rapidly. One of the new ships, largely independent of weather and with much greater carrying capacity, could make very many more round trips than a sailing vessel, and these opportunities more than cancelled out the much higher original costs of the new ships[7]. The sailing collier fleet was increasingly driven to cut corners in order to try to remain in business, and this was a dangerous game. In 1862, 100 colliers were posted at Lloyd's as wrecks as the result of a large fleet of sailing colliers taking the risk of putting to sea in doubtful weather, and 1865 also saw heavy losses of lives and ships for similar reasons. The once-proud fleet of sailing colliers was now associated with 'bad gear, rotting timbers and inadequate crews', but such economies and risks were unavailing in view of the plain commercial superiority of the iron steam colliers. Another traditional sector of North East society was also hit by these changes. The keelmen who manned the coal-carrying keels or barges were already declining in numbers because of the increased use of loading facilities which could be used without them. The new colliers were associated with expanded and improved docks and coal staiths which needed no keels. The existence of the low-level bridge at Newcastle preserved the livelihood of some of the Tyne keelmen for some years, but with its replacement by a swing bridge in 1876 the whole of the port of Tyne was open to the direct loading of coal and the keelmen shrank to a very small group. The introduction of the advanced steam collier, and the docks and installations associated with them, produced adverse results on the position of the sailing seamen and the keelmen, but the savings in transport costs involved helped to safeguard the continuing expansion of the coalfield, and the very substantial employment which depended directly or indirectly upon that crucial element in the region's economy.

We have seen how in the first half of the nineteenth century some members of the old aristocracy had been among the most prominent of the coal-owners. The Earls of Durham remained active colliery-owners for many years after 1850. Lord Durham's colliery income was over £84,000 in 1856, and, although there were some set-backs in the 1860s, the early 1870s, with somewhat of a boom in coal-using industry until late 1873, saw spectacular increases—£80,163 in 1871, £122,658 in 1872, £380,000 in 1873 and £71,648 in 1874. (For the Lambton and Londonderry involvement in mining see reference 8.) The Lambton family owned ten collieries in 1853, 12 in 1871 and 14 in 1896, as well as operating their own collier fleet. In 1896 there was a major shift in policy, direct exploitation was abandoned and the collieries sold.

The Londonderry interest survived longer. Although the number of collieries owned by Lord Londonderry shrank from 11 in 1853 to seven in 1871 and three by 1919, those retained were major undertakings, and in 1919 the three collieries remaining employed a work force of about 7,000 men. Lord Londonderry also controlled the Londonderry Railway (until 1900), a fleet of colliers and the harbour of Seaham Harbour.

Even where aristocratic interests withdrew from active colliery management income from coal sources continued to be important to them. In 1913 Lord Durham, who had sold all his collieries, still received nearly £60,000 from wayleaves, royalties and railway rents. The Duke of Northumberland leased almost all of his coal-bearing land, but his mineral income amounted to £82,450 in 1918.

However, in the late nineteenth century aristocratic coal-owners were distinctly untypical of coal-owners as a whole, although the form taken by colliery-ownership could vary significantly. One major consortium was provided by John Bowes and Partners, a group of four men coming together originally to exploit the coal of the old Bowes family estates, mainly in County Durham, though the enterprise did not confine its activities to that sphere of operations. The quartet represented an interesting amalgam of the qualities needed for successful coal production. John Bowes himself, owning five-twelfths of the partnership, brought the land and the bulk of the capital as his contribution. His stepfather, William Hutt, with two-twelfths, preserved a majority control for the family and brought political contacts as well as a shrewd family concern. Nicholas Wood, with two-twelfths, was one of the most skilful colliery-viewers of the time; Charles Mark Palmer, with three-twelfths, was to carry out a great deal of the day-to-day management and contributed valuable experience from a family firm with a long record of activity in the commercial side of the coal trade. (The best source for the Bowes interests is in reference 9.)

It was still possible for an individual to rise from the ranks of the workers to a position of wealth, status and influence in the coal industry, even in this period when the size of colliery undertakings, and their capital cost, tended to be higher. Sir George Elliott provides a good example[10]. He was born at Gateshead in 1815, and at the age of 9 years entered the pits as a trapper boy at Penshaw Colliery. By the time he was 20 he was an overman in that colliery—in itself no mean achievement even in this period of expansion. He showed a marked mathematical ability and became a skilled surveyor. At 24 he became the effective manager of the important Monkwearmouth colliery, and in the next year part-owner of a colliery at Washington. His ability and drive led to a further appointment as chief mining engineer to the Londonderry collieries. The spirit in which he carried out his duties can be gauged from a recollection from an employee of the Londonderry Railway[11]: 'In George Elliott's time, and long after, when a workman had a few days overtime we dare not show it in the pay bill. If we did, it was sure to have the pen put through it.' In 1863 Elliott bought the Penshaw colliery in which he had begun his mining career, and his coal-owning interests subsequently extended to North and South Wales, Staffordshire and Nova Scotia. His interests other than coal were diverse, he played, for example, a prominent role in the creation of the transatlantic cable link. Miners' leaders such as Alexander Macdonald and George Halliday agreed that Elliott's growing wealth and prestige were compatible with a continuing active sympathy for the working miner. The irascible Samuel Plimsoll, not a notable friend to Tory ship-owners, was loud in his praise for the skilful and benign management which marked the operations of Elliott's fleet of colliers. Elliott was a stout Conservative in politics; he was M.P. for North Durham 1868–74, and in the latter year was defeated in an extremely rowdy election in which the workmen employed by the various candidates fought in their employers' campaigns. The election was disallowed for the violence which had taken place, and Elliott retained his seat. He became a baronet in 1874, and he was a Durham county magistrate and deputy lieutenant. His success, and it was a notable success, was won by hard work, toughness and a powerful fighting spirit.

Another instance in which the coal industry paved the way to higher things is provided by the Joicey family. James Joicey was the son of a Newcastle engineer who entered the coal industry, though on a relatively small scale. James inherited these modest holdings and expanded them into one of the biggest of the region's coal empires, largely by his purchase in 1896 of Lord Durham's collieries. Here again the rewards of success were considerable, and not merely to be measured in money. Firmly Liberal in politics, if no great radical, he became a baronet in 1893 and a baron in 1906, as well as holding a variety of honorific positions within the region.

It remained true, however, that success in coal-mining could not be regarded as a foregone conclusion. Although by the later nineteenth century knowledge of the region's geology and of mining techniques had certainly improved markedly, personal judgement and managerial skill could still count for a great deal. In many cases the connection between ownership and working of collieries remained close. When in 1852 the North of England Mining Institute was founded, its members read like a list of the nobility, gentry and coal-owners of the coalfield[12]. This institution provided a very useful forum for the discussion and exploration of a wide range of problems affecting the coalfield. Its sumptuous premises in Newcastle express in physical form the high importance of the coalfield to the region and the coal interest's clear awareness of its own importance.

If, however, scientific and technical skills were increasingly employed in mining, the winning of coal continued a business in which commercial skills allied with adequate knowledge were a prerequisite for success. A great deal of money could be won, or lost, in the buying or selling of collieries. Two instances associated with the build-up of the collieries owned by Bolckow and Vaughan, the Teesside iron-masters demonstrate this[13]. In 1872 they paid £70,000 plus an annual rent of £2,000 for the South Medomsley colliery; 10 years earlier the colliery had been offered for sale at £8,000 and had actually been bought by a member of the Bainbridge family for £7,000. Bainbridge had spent some money on the colliery during the next few years, but he realized a handsome profit when he sold it to the Teesside firm. Nicholas Wood was a colliery proprietor in his own right as well as a partner in the Bowes collieries. The Black Boy colliery had been an unsatisfactory enterprise to its previous owner, the banker, Edward Backhouse, and he was glad to dispose of it to Nicholas Wood for £72,000. The new owner's ability as a colliery engineer and manager, and his nose for a bargain, may be gauged by the fact that after his death the colliery was sold to Bolckow and Vaughan for about £½ million.

Another very good example of the continued importance of commercial sense lies in the creation and work of the Horden Coal Company[14]. This company was created to expand coal output from a series of pits along the Durham coast, in association with the North Eastern Railway's plans to build a new railway linking the points concerned, such as Horden, Easington and Blackhall, with shipping facilities at West Hartlepool. In the event this company was to prove a major success, but this was not at all apparent at the time of its creation. The original capital required was £¼ million, but attempts to raise this on the open market were met with a very cool reception from financial opinion. *The Economist, The Statist* and *The Financier* all advised their readers against investing in the enterprise. The company's prospectus itself admitted that there was some risk involved, but *The Financier* (9 February 1900) was not much impressed by this openness, remarking that this 'does not render the investment one which is deserving of support, for the elements of speculation existed in too marked a degree to encourage the public'.

Despite this disappointing reception, the promoters of the company went ahead with the project, raising the overwhelming bulk of the capital themselves, since the offer of shares to the public only brought in some £45,000. Their plans including the sinking of some new collieries, and the reopening in modernized form of some older ones, since they believed that with the application of newer techniques they could make these old pits viable. On both counts the undertaking prospered. One of the new collieries, Horden, sunk between 1900 and 1908, was alone to reach an output of almost 1½ million tons annually. The company's first dividend was 7% paid in 1907, and until nationalization dividends were to average 8%. When the company's collieries reached full capacity the company employed 8,750 men, and the company was involved in the management of communities which were virtually small towns, with good-quality housing by contemporary standards and a wide range of social and welfare facilities. Skilful management was an important element in the firm's success. A variety of profitable ancilliary operations was established; these included a large coking business, and the operation of one of the region's biggest brick works. The water which was a nuisance in the collieries was sold in large quantities to local water undertakings.

The Ashington Coal Company provided a Northumberland equivalent in the possession of able management, notably that provided for many years by Jonathan Priestman, whose services were important not only in the company's commercial affairs, including the ploughing-back of a high proportion of profits in continued expansion and modernization, but also in establishing high standards of operations technically, safety measures and the provision of social amenities.

During the early years of the twentieth century output and employment continued to rise, though in an industry with relatively little mechanization underground productivity did not increase proportionately. In 1911 there were well over 54,000 miners in Northumberland, providing nearly one-fifth of all employment. In Durham the result was even more striking, with more than 152,000 miners in 1911, or not far short of 30% of total employment. The average size of collieries and their cost continued to rise—the Durham coastal collieries of the Horden Coal Company in the years after 1900 were some of the largest in the region. There was an increasing tendency for collieries to accumulate in the hands of successful combines. The later nineteenth century saw the creation of permanent miners' unions in both Durham and Northumberland, and subsequently a considerable increase in contacts and negotiations between management and workers. By the 1870s for instance substantial printed books, giving particulars of agreed wage rates and the effects on them of local customs or conditions, were being published by the coal-owners' associations, while the minutes of the county mining unions also show the development of equivalent sophistication in procedure.

Yet at the coal face much continued as before. Although there were repeated attempts to replace manual labour at the coal face by mechanical devices, the technical difficulties were great, and no substantial progress was to be made until the inter-war period. In operations ancilliary to coal-cutting there was more progress, as for example in the provision of coal conveyors underground and mechanical coal-sorting installations on the surface. A few colliery companies pioneered the use of electrical equipment, but this was not very common; as late as 1910 only 2,055 electric lamps were used in British collieries[15].

It is almost impossible to achieve any concrete appreciation of mining wages for they varied enormously between individuals and between different grades of workers employed by the industry; further complications existed in varying degrees of provision of housing and concessionary coal. Coal-hewers, the cream of the underground work force, tended to be among the best paid workers within the region, but this standing was subject to considerable fluctuation and interruption. The great strike of 1844 had virtually signalled the end of the annual bond of engagement in the mines, and by 1872 colliery hiring was normally on a fortnightly basis[16].

Coal-mining continued to be a very dangerous occupation. The steady flow of small-scale accidents continued to mount to a considerable figure, mining diseases continued to take their toll, and the period was punctuated by a series of major colliery disasters. The larger pits, with the greater numbers involved, made explosions increasingly dangerous; the average loss of life incurred by a colliery explosion had been 2.98 in the 1860s, but 20 years later the average was 6.33[17]. A substantial number of explosions brought much more devastating results. Local mining disasters included New Hartley in 1862 (204 men and boys killed), Pelton in 1866 (24 deaths), Seaham in 1880 (164 deaths), Trimdon Grange in 1882 (74 deaths), Elemore, Durham, in 1886 (28 killed) and West Stanley in 1909 (168 deaths). There were increasing efforts made to try to cut down the tragic losses, and the Mines Acts of 1887 and 1911 marked considerable extensions of legislative interference and state regulation. Some of the worst explosions of the period were so devastating because the dangers of accumulated coal dust for long went unrealized. The West Stanley disaster, among others, seems to have been largely due to this cause. As early as the 1880s coal dust had been a suspected agent of destruction, but it was not until the early twentieth century that large-scale scientific tests demonstrated the reality of these suspicions. It is significant of the ways in which the industry was changing that these tests were organized by a national consortium and financed by coal-owners on a national basis[18].

The coalfield remained at the heart of the expansion of the regional economy, not only because of its direct importance but because of the continuing attraction of ready access to coal supplies to the various coal-using industries. Of these the iron and steel industry was to provide another major growth point of the later nineteenth century.

Iron and steel industry

We have already seen how in earlier years a number of small iron works were established in various parts of Northumberland. None of the more remote installations in this group, such as Redesdale and Hareshaw, were able to generate sustained growth, scarcely surprising in view of their isolated situation. It was only where blast furnace plants were situated in close proximity to iron-using industry that iron manufacture in the northern part of the region could compete with the southern challenge which arose after 1850. Even on Tyneside, iron works either integrated with engineering or shipbuilding enterprises near to them or were in many cases closed down before the end of the century. At Bedlington a major iron works, which had occupied a proud place in the regional industrial development in the first half of the century and combined iron-making with various iron-manufacturing interests, rose to employ some 2,000 workers by mid-century but found growing competition too strong and closed in 1867.

Consett remained an important centre of the industry. The first Derwent Iron Company of the 1840s had built up there installations of considerable size, far and away the biggest iron works of the region at that time, but it had done so on a distinctly precarious financial basis. Its involvement with the ill-fated Northumberland and Durham District Bank brought about a major crisis in 1857, and there followed a period of uncertainty until in 1864 a much stronger company, the Consett Iron Company, came into being. This was followed by a period of considerable growth, despite the remoteness from the supplies of iron ore to be used; Consett is several miles from the Tyne by the most direct route, and 15 miles from the South Shields installations from which it was to draw most of its ore imports in later periods. Even in the third quarter of the nineteenth century there was a heavy dependence on ore from the Cleveland deposits, many miles away. Nevertheless these disadvantages were successfully overcome, and in the latter part of the century the Consett Iron Works were consistently the most profitable iron and steel enterprise within the region[19]. The expansion of iron shipbuilding after the *John Bowes* and her successors had pointed the way proved a major market even after the boom in demand for iron rails slowed down. By 1875 Consett employed 5,000 to 6,000 men and was the country's biggest producer of iron ship plates. As technical developments made the use of imported iron ores vital the Consett company safeguarded its supplies by joining with Krupps and the Spanish Ybarra firm in the creation in 1872 of the Orconera Iron Ore Company, which controlled and exploited large iron ore deposits in Spain. A timely transition to steel brought about continued prosperity. By about 1890 Consett produced some 175,000 tons of steel annually, with ship plates remaining a major interest. The skilful management which was responsible for much of the company's success was demonstrated in other ways too. The firm embarked upon a deliberate policy of vertical integration, with the company involved in the supply of iron ore, iron-making, the ownership of a substantial group of collieries (which provided a profitable surplus of output above the demands of the iron works) and the manufacture of a range of iron and steel products. Its directors included men closely involved in other areas of the regional economy with close links to Consett, such as railways and shipbuilding. In David Dale, managing director from 1869 and chairman from 1884, the company enjoyed the services of an able manager well connected with other related enterprises and a man of note in the development of harmonious industrial relations. There were of course years when recession in the industry brought troubles, as happened elsewhere, but the continued success of Consett as an iron and steel centre was a conspicuous example of the application of commercial acumen. Towards the end of the century, however, there were signs that the future might not be so secure. The company was faced, as other steel-producers in Britain were faced, with a decision as to whether or not to embark upon a costly programme of modernization to equip the works with plant which would enable it to meet increasing overseas competition. In the early years of the century the company employed an American expert in blast furnace design to draw up plans for new furnaces, but in the event these plans were not followed up. Instead of embarking upon a programme of large capital expenditure the company chose a less costly alternative, joining with other major British producers in such arrangements as collusive price-fixing and an arranged division of the available market. There were strong commercial reasons for adopting the less costly alternative, but at a time when there was an overcapacity in the British steel industry the Consett company, like other firms in the industry, continued to operate plant which was increasingly out of date by international standards. This was not the case with all of the company's interests. The highly profitable collieries saw considerable investment in modernization, including the extensive use of electrical power before 1914.

The continued growth at Consett was remarkable enough, but it was far outstripped by developments further south, in the prodigious growth of the iron and steel industry in the Teesside area, a story which has been well analysed by Dr. I. Bullock (see reference 20), whose account is followed largely here.

We have already looked at the early growth at Middlesbrough and the Hartlepools brought about by the penetration of the early railways into the colliery areas to the west. These had been important developments but their impact upon Teesside itself had been limited, as the figures of the 1851 census showed. Of the 96,000 people living near the lower Tees about 60% were still living in rural villages and other communities of under 2,000 people. The infant West Hartlepool had itself a population under 2,000. Stockton held less than 10,000, as did Hartlepool, Middlesbrough was over the 7,000 mark and Darlington over 11,000. Three decades later the picture was radically transformed, with the area which had held a total of 96,000 in 1851 supporting 310,000 by 1881. The older Hartlepool had increased only to a figure over 12,000, but the other towns had shown an immense growth rate which transformed the area's population distribution—West Hartlepool, 28,000; Darlington, 35,000; Stockton, 41,000; and the infant prodigy Middlesbrough now an impressive 56,000. There had been a very large inward migration in 1851–71, but by the 1870s natural growth had overtaken immigration as the principal factor in continued population increase. Overall, however, more than 100,000 people had flocked to Teesside in the 30 years between 1851 and 1881 to take advantage of the boom sparked off by the development of the iron and steel industry. If in 1851 farming had employed more people than manufacture, mining and construction industry combined, the situation had been completely transformed 30 years later.

The iron industry in South Durham began some years before the major spurt in development took place, with early reliance being placed on local deposits or iron ore in proximity to collieries. Early blast furnaces were placed inland at places such as Tow Law and Witton Park. In the census of 1841 Tow Law was represented by a single farm; 10 years later the opening of iron works had produced a swollen population of some 2,000 and growth continued there in the following decades. Witton Park saw the erection of blast furnaces by Henry Bolckow and John Vaughan. Bolckow was an immigrant from North Germany, who had worked for some years on Tyneside with Christian Allhusen in the latter's corn trade enterprise. Bolckow left Tyneside in 1840 to go into business on his own account, having accumulated a useful sum of available capital of some £20,000[21]. He entered into partnership with Vaughan, who contributed technical skills in the iron trade as well as further capital, and the partners set up blast furnaces at Witton Park and a small forge iron works at Middlesbrough, encouraged in the latter undertaking by the enterprising proprietors of the site of the growing town, who were anxious to promote further growth by the settlement of new works there. There were vicissitudes in these early years, with a bad patch in the recession years of 1847–8, but the partnership survived to take the lead in the principal developments of the next decade.

The crucial inducement which now appeared was the exploitation of the substantial deposits of iron ore in the Cleveland Hills just to the south. The presence of iron ore there was not a new discovery, and there had been in fact small-scale ore-mining in the district since the 1830s. In 1850, however, the situation was transformed by Vaughan's appreciation of the significance of the main seam of iron ore, recognized at Eston in that year. At once an expansion of mining was put in hand, and in 1851 the Cleveland mines produced 188,000 tons. At first Bolckow and Vaughan sent Cleveland ore by rail to the blast furnaces at Witton Park and then returned the iron to Middlesbrough for working; however, this was obviously not a good arrangement, and in 1851 work was begun on the erection of three blast furnaces at Middlesbrough. They were completed in 1852, and six more were in blast at Eston by 1853. By the next year Teesside had nine smelting works, with 29 furnaces in blast. Darlington had one important iron works, but the overwhelming majority were along the lower Tees.

The new ore supply, with its ready accessibility at low cost, completed a trinity of advantages which underlay these new developments. The early 1850s were in general a period of low iron prices, but the ready availability of low-cost ore supplies, together with cheap Durham coal and proximity to good shipping points, placed the Teeside iron interests in a good competitive position. Teesside growth, as with the contemporary iron works at Consett, depended largely on the cheap mass production of relatively low-grade iron products such as rails and ship plates. Iron prices remained low and fairly stable till the early 1870s, and the pricing advantages which the exploitation of the Cleveland ores brought to Teesside were maintained by the continued technological progress, especially in furnace design, which enabled Teesside plants to remain in a very strong competitive position. By 1861 Teesside, which had not a single furnace in blast in 1850, produced 11% of the national output of iron, and the figure was 19% by 1871. When the period of rapid growth was interrupted by a serious recession in late 1873, this reflected difficulties for the British iron industry as a whole rather than any local weaknesses on Teesside.

Export markets played an important part in the rapid growth of the Teesside iron industry. Even in the high-tariff German market the cheapness of Teesside iron products could in those years effect a substantial penetration. In 1871 Middlesbrough alone shipped 270,000 tons of pig iron to foreign markets, as well as supplying 214,000 by coastal shipping to other areas of Britain, with Scotland a prominent customer. The sharp recession in the 1870s brought a number of casualties among the weaker firms in the Teesside iron industry. The Erimus Iron Works failed in 1874, Swan Coates, the Lackenby Iron Works and Tom Vaughan in 1875 and Hopkins Gilkes and Company in 1879. However, the stronger companies weathered the depression and saw further expansion from the later 1870s. Export markets continued important, with Middlesbrough exporting 430,000 tons of iron in 1881, by which time coastal shipments had risen to 501,000 tons. The main foreign customers were Germany and the U.S.A., with Scotland the principal domestic market. By 1881 Teesside had 27 smelting plants, operating a total of 99 blast furnaces; annual output was up to well over 2 million tons of pig iron, valued at well over £4 million.

Although Cleveland ore had been the basis for early expansion, its primacy was not unchallenged. The Cleveland ores were unsuitable for some processes, especially the Bessemer steel-making process. As steel began to replace iron for many purposes, this became a serious disadvantage, and the import of suitable ores into Teesside grew. Already in 1861 the district had imported 60,000 tons and the figure rose to 260,000 tons in 1871 and 840,000 tons by 1881. Early imports were drawn largely from deposits in Cumberland and Lancashire, but the suitable British ores were costly and available in only limited quantities; during the 1870s imports from Spain began to predominate and by then Teesside was making about $\frac{1}{2}$ million tons of steel a year, virtually all with Spanish ore.

In addition to shipments coastal and foreign, about half of the pig iron made on Teesside was worked locally, mostly in making wrought iron for a variety of industrial purposes. Wrought-iron-making had also begun on a small scale in earlier years; Bolckow and Vaughan had done this at Middlesbrough in the 1840s, using pig iron imported from Scotland. With the tremendous increase in production of pig iron in the 1850s, by 1861 Teesside had five plants for making wrought iron, operating between them 197 puddling furnaces and feeding 35 rolling mills. Rails were a mainstay of local production in these early years; the Darlington Iron Company in the early 1870s made virtually nothing else, and produced about 70,000 tons of rails a year. With railway-building continuing at a high rate in various parts of the world in the 1860s Teesside capacity grew to meet demand; by 1871 there were 24 plants producing wrought iron, with a total of 1,178 puddling furnaces.

The difficulties experienced in the 1870s facilitated changes in production. Although the price of iron rails dropped, there was a much more marked drop in the price of steel rails, from £17.10s. in 1864 to £6.8s. in 1870, at which point the superior advantages of steel were unmistakably plain. Iron rails virtually disappeared as an item of importance in manufacture; between 1872 and 1882 wrought iron rails made at Middlesbrough plunged from 49% to 1% of wrought iron articles made. The market in iron ship plates held up for a little longer, and some Teesside iron works shifted from iron rails to iron plates during the recovery years after 1879. However, here too the future lay with steel, and the price of steel plates, which had been about £20 a ton in 1875, was down to less than £5 a ton by 1894[22]. The discovery in 1879 of the Gilchrist–Thomas process of steelmaking—a process which could use the Cleveland ores—was a useful fillip to increased steel production on Teesside, although in fact the changeover from iron to the making of steel with imported ore was already well under way. During the last decades of the century Teesside produced two main kinds of steel in parallel—acid steel made mainly with Spanish ore, and basic steel depending on the nearby Cleveland deposits.

From the troubled years of the early 1870s three firms had emerged as the most important—Bolckow and Vaughan at Eston, Dorman at Middlesbrough and Bell Brothers at Port Clarence, on the north bank of the Tees opposite Middlesbrough[23]. The pattern of the industry's organization was not, however, a static one, and the later history of the industry was marked by further recessions, notably the bad years of 1902–4. Such fluctuations in the fortunes of the industry were responsible for significant changes in its organization; some firms dropped out of the race, and others continued to grow by skilful management of resources. Bolckow and Vaughan continued to expand their Eston installations but also added to their resources by taking over plant set up originally by other companies both at Eston and at Darlington. Their activities spread into rolling mills and galvanizing, and eventually constructional engineering too. The very large firm of Dorman Long grew up by a series of takeovers. The company began in wrought-iron-making and engineering on a small-scale in Middlesbrough itself, but it then embarked on a series of amalgamations which brought into the fold the Britannia works in 1880, the important Port Clarence interests of Bell Brothers in stages culminating in 1902, the Cleveland wire works in 1899 and the North East Steel Company in 1890. Further takeovers took place during the First World War to make Dorman Long a giant among local enterprises by the inter-war period, a process marked in 1929 when the pioneering firm of Bolckow and Vaughan finally succumbed and became a part of the Dorman Long empire.

In these cases the conglomeration of interests had been created from a basis in iron- and steel-making or early processing. Another development was also important. The shipbuilding firm of Furness Withy at Hartlepool began to develop interests in coal, iron and steel in order to procure more efficient production. In 1898 this firm created the South Durham Steel and Iron Company, which took over a variety of steel plants during the period 1898–1919, to become Dorman Long's main rival in dominating the industry within the Teesside area during the inter-war period.

Other engineering industries

The growth of the iron and steel industry on Teesside during the second half of the nineteenth century had repercussions beyond immediate interests in that industry, for it was a major inducement to iron- and steel-using firms to settle nearby. In 1851 there had been 11 shipbuilding undertakings on Teesside, but their output was insignificant; all were small, rather old-fashioned family firms, engaged in the building and repair of wooden ships of modest size, mostly sailing vessels. The eruption in iron-making brought a drastic change. By 1862 local shipyards built 10,000 tons of iron ships, as against only 5,000 in wood. In 1882 yards in the Teesside area, including the Hartlepools, launched 136,000 tons, all iron built. Moreover the great majority of these vessels were steamers, bringing a further expansion in the district's economy in the manufacture of marine engines; Doxford's entered this trade in 1878 and rapidly built up a flourishing business based on increasing demand, mainly for the production of economical but reliable engines for cargo steamers.

By the 1880s the creation of the Teesside iron industry had sparked off not only shipbuilding and marine engineering but also bridge-building, metal-pipe- and tube-making, and the manufacture of large quantities of railway rolling stock and other equipment. The makers of iron and steel had almost all expanded their interests into manufacturing processes, and in some cases such as Bolckow and Vaughan had established substantial colliery holdings. These were not the only effects. The mushroom growth of Teesside industry required a wide range of ancilliary activities; immense growth in industry required concomitant growth in commercial and financial facilities. Vastly increased trade required new fleets of ships, dock installations, repair yards; Bolckow and Vaughan built up and operated their own fleet of ore carriers, the crews of which formed one element in the firm's total labour force of 10,000. The number of workers involved in transport operations in the area jumped from 2,811 in 1851 to 5,364 only 20 years later. Local agriculture was also markedly affected by the urban and industrial growth, with increased importance allotted to market gardens, milk supply and the growing of fodder for the enormous number of horses employed in booming Teesside.

The growth of various kinds of engineering on Teesside in association with the iron and steel industry was part of a massive expansion in engineering generally within the region. Elsewhere too the forms which engineering enterprises took were in many cases closely related to other economic activities within the region. Firms such as Hawthorn on Tyneside prospered largely because of their ability to meet the needs of the mining and shipbuilding industries. Other enterprises, such as the substantial workshops operated by the North Eastern Railway, served the expanded regional rail network. However, the expanded demand for engineering products was an international one; locomotives from Stephenson's works could be found in many different parts of the world, for instance. Two giants involved in the field of engineering, the Palmer and the Armstrong companies, were also deeply involved in shipbuilding and are sufficiently interesting to deserve more extended discussion later in this chapter.

In central Newcastle the brothers Robert and William Hawthorn had built up an important engineering enterprise by mid-century; in the years after 1850 there was continuing expansion, exemplified by the growth of the work force from 950 in 1850 to 1,300 by 1864[24]. A significant part of this growth was the increasing demand for marine engines. Important changes affected the firm in the years around 1870. Robert Hawthorn died in 1867, and 3 years later William sold out to a new proprietorship. The principal partner in the new management, Benjamin Browne, was a 30-year-old engineer who had been an apprentice in Armstrong's Elswick works and then worked for the Tyne port authority. To find the money needed to buy his way into the Hawthorn firm, he scraped together every penny he could, including heavy bank borrowings, to a total of £60,000. As a partner he brought with him F. C. Marshall, who could supply more expertise in the field of marine engineering as well as a considerable reputation for enforcing high standards of efficiency. Marshall had recently been employed in reorganizing that aspect of the Palmer enterprises at Jarrow, where his reorganization of marine-engine-building had been successful but marked by little consideration for any elements which seemed inefficient. Marshall's terms for joining the new Hawthorn management were stiff—he demanded, and obtained, a salary of £1,000 p.a. plus a quarter of all profits remaining after a 5% dividend on capital.

The new management introduced important changes. Marshall at once set out to repeat in the new firm the methods he had employed at the Palmer Company. There was a rapid purge of workers who did not measure up to his standards of efficiency, which involved the departure of a number of men who had served for long periods under the more indulgent régime of the previous owners. To facilitate the growth of the marine engineering branch of the business a new riverside works was built in 1871-2 at St Peter's, just east of Newcastle, and some £20,000 was spent in new plant both there and in the older Forth Banks works. The major engineering strike of 1871 was an awkward problem at this stage, and it is significant that Marshall, who had worked his way up from the shop floor, was the most intransigent of the engineering employers involved in that prolonged dispute. The subsequent history of the firm was to be much more closely tied to the fortunes of the Tyneside shipbuilding industry.

Engineering firms which did not keep up to date with developments in this fiercely competitive trade could easily find themselves in serious trouble. Two important companies at Gateshead illustrate this point[25]. Hawks Crawshay represented a firm active since very small beginnings as far back as 1747, and in the first half of the nineteenth century had been a progressive company; in 1844 for example they had installed the first Nasmyth steam hammer to be used in the region. A feature of the firm as it developed in the later nineteenth century was the variety of its productions. The following description of the firm's installations was included in an account of local industries in 1889:

> The vast establishment now devoted to the series of industries in which the firm at the present time engage occupies a property extending over forty-seven acres of ground, and about eleven and a half acres of this great area are covered by the boiler works, iron foundry, chain and anchor works, rolling mills for bars, rolling mills for plates, steel works, and other incidental and associated departments. An average force of two thousand hands find employment at the Gateshead Iron Works, but in busy seasons Messrs Hawks Crawshay and Sons give plenty of work to a much more numerous staff even than this. (They) conduct a system of iron-working and engineering industry that embodies in itself ample material for the constitution of half a dozen large and important businesses, each one distinct and complete in itself; and yet the firm have so combined, and, as it were, dovetailed these individual industries as to make one great industry, in which every department has some interest in the successful working of the others.

The firm's products were so diverse as to include bridges, lighthouse equipment and the making of nails. The 'dovetailing' was far from efficient, and the sprawling works contained a high variety of unco-ordinated activities. A conglomeration like this was incapable of meeting competition from better organized and more specialized enterprises, and before the end of the year in which this glowing tribute appeared Hawks Crawshay had collapsed. Although there had been some continued investment in new plant, such as the installation of a Siemens–Martin steel plant on modern lines, there had also been a falling-off in the quality of management during the ministration of the impulsive and eccentric George Crawshay. The company's plant and equipment were auctioned in 1889–90, and there was no bankruptcy, but the firm's sudden failure, with the loss of about 2,000 jobs, was a hard blow to the town's economy.

A similar fate, for similar reasons, overtook Gateshead's second big engineering enterprise, the Park Works of John Abbot and Company. This firm too had a long history, beginning as a small local workship in the later eighteenth century but branching out into extended engineering activities in the first half of the nineteenth century. By 1889 the company employed between 1,500 and 2,000 workers, and like Hawks Crawshay was highly diversified. It made railway engines, water pipes, hydraulic presses, safety lamps and metal tacks. Increasingly hit by more efficient production elsewhere, the firm was in serious trouble by the early years of the twentieth century, and voluntary liquidation followed in 1909.

One eccentric element in the Tyneside engineering trade deserves mention. In September 1866 the firm of Robert Morrison and Company, who operated the Ouseburn Engine Works in East Newcastle, failed and for some years the site lay idle. During recent years there had been a great deal of discussion in the area as to the merits of co-operative production; a principal advocate of this concept was Dr J. H. Rutherford, non-conformist minister, temperance advocate and philanthropist. He took the lead in reopening the Ouseburn works as a workers' co-operative[26]. He and some of his friends provided some of the original capital needed; local co-operative retail societies were persuaded to provide more, and further sums were forthcoming from the co-operative bank which the same interests were also interested in founding at that time. The Ouseburn co-operative set off with a marvellous opportunity in the prolonged engineering strike of 1871 which paralysed most of the local competition, and at first there was no shortage of orders for the new adventure. Most of the directors of the co-operative were drawn from the workforce; wages were similar to those normally paid in the trade, the workers had the 9-hour day for which their fellow engineering workers were fighting in the 1871 strike, and it was agreed that 10% of wages would be deducted and left in the works as share capital. The work produced was regarded as of high quality, but after a few years the undertaking proved a disastrous failure. There seem to have been two main reasons for this. On the one hand the co-operative principle did not suffice to ensure harmonious industrial relations. As one account had it: 'Unexpected labour troubles were the cause of difficulties with the workmen. In some of them a sense of discipline and responsibility was entirely lacking.' The luxury of internal strife could not be safely indulged when, with the end of the 1871 strike, competition for orders became intense again. The second weakness was a flaw in managerial aspects. The works' pricing policy was seriously defective. A number of contracts were entered into at low prices, without any security that coal and iron prices would remain low. When the price of these essential materials rose, the Ouseburn works suffered heavy losses in both 1872 and 1873, co-operative societies refused to put more money into a failing business, and the scheme collapsed. Rutherford and some of his personal friends lost heavily in the adventure, and for the rest of his life Rutherford faced financial problems arising from his involvement here.

This was, however, but one minor eddy in a general tide of expansion in the engineering industry; for example, the 1871 strike, which left some major engineering works unaffected, had involved about 7,500 men on Tyneside. A similar process of growth affected the closely connected shipbuilding industry within the region, with marked expansion on Tyne, Wear and Tees.

Shipbuilding and marine engineering

On the Tyne a series of earlier experiments in iron shipbuilding culminated in 1852 with Palmer's conspicuous success with the *John Bowes* and her successors. Although the Clyde and the Thames took to iron shipbuilding somewhat earlier, it was the North East which soon took the lead in the second half of the nineteenth century. By 1862 there were certainly more than ten shipyards on the Tyne building in iron and employing more than 4,000 workers between them. Despite the relatively substantial involvement in wooden shipbuilding earlier in the century the Tyne saw a rapid changeover to the new techniques, while the Wear changeover to iron was distinctly slower, although the largest yard there, Pile's Yard, was building in iron by the early 1860s. At that time the annual output of yards in the North East was probably about 100,000 tons. By 1889 tonnage built on Tyneside had risen to 280,000, with Wear yards contributing 217,000 tons. At the beginning of the twentieth century more than half of the world's new tonnage was built in Britain and of that total more than half was constructed in the shipyards of the North East. The growth of international trade, and the variety of advances in naval architecture and marine engineering which encouraged re-equipment, provided a demand which rose enormously, though not without marked fluctuations from time to time.

Increasing demand facilitated technical innovation. It was possible for many shipwrights to move from traditional wooden shipbuilding to iron shipbuilding; it took a considerable time for workers in the new forms of construction to become organized in their own craft unions, and in the early stages of expansion in iron shipbuilding workers in the engineering and boiler-making trades were not highly unionized.

While some older shipbuilding companies survived the transition to iron, expansion brought into being a considerable number of new firms to take advantage of new technology and growing markets. Some of these firms were begun with very limited resources. It was said that when Andrew Leslie opened his new Hebburn yard in 1853 his available funds amounted to £198, though he possessed invaluable personal and family connections which gave him adequate access to credit until profits began to accumulate[27]. In 1854 he launched four ships, and a total of 53 in the next 10 years; by 1856 he was in a position to begin a programme of house-building for his workers. Some firms began with more adequate resources. When Wigham Richardson set up his shipyard at Walker in 1860 his father had provided him with £5,000 of initial capital. He too had useful local connections and experience both in shipbuilding and in marine engineering before branching out on his own account[28]. A number of the new yards employed a nucleus of key workers experienced in iron shipbuilding in other shipbuilding centres. Andrew Leslie brought a contingent from Aberdeen, as did Charles Mitchell when he set up his Wallsend yard in 1853. Wigham Richardson's partner, J. D. Christie, brought with him three foremen from Dumbarton.

The demand for merchant and naval vessels associated with the Crimean War helped in the creation of a number of shipyards in the region in the mid-1850s, but shipbuilding remained a very competitive business and much depended on the commercial abilities of owner or manager, and their ability to combine commercial acumen with technical knowledge. It was certainly not enough to be able to build good ships; it was important also to be able to cultivate good relations with both customers and suppliers and to ensure, often with considerable difficulty, a sufficient margin of either money or credit in a trade which entailed heavy expenditure on labour and materials before delivery of a completed vessel to her purchasers.

There was considerable variety in the types of ships in which different North East yards specialized. Some of the biggest success stories emanated both in the nineteenth and the twentieth centuries from firms which concentrated on building a limited range of similar ships in substantial numbers, obtaining repeated orders by establishing a reputation for reasonably cheap but efficient ships. This was the mainstay of the shipyards in the Teesside area, but the same policy worked well for yards on Tyne and Wear too. For example, in the 18 years after 1893 Doxfords of Sunderland built 178 of a more or less standardized turret-deck cargo ship. A Tyneside quip had it that Palmer's yard built their iron colliers by the mile and then chopped off the lengths required. Wigham Richardson emphasized the advantages of such a policy[29]: 'Over and over again during 40 years, I have demonstrated that our principal profits have been made from simple cargo steamers and from repetitions of them.'

This policy was complemented by the careful cultivation of long-term associations with various shipping companies, likely to produce repeated orders for ships designed on similar lines. Readhead was another Tyne yard which concentrated on small- and medium-sized cargo ships and on the sedulous cultivation of long-term associations. In 1878 the yard built its first ship for the

Hain Steamship Company of St Ives; by 1899 the connection had resulted in 35 orders and the total mounted to 87 by 1965[30]. Similar connections produced repeated orders for Readhead from the Runciman and Strick lines. At Hebburn, Leslie developed similar links with a group of shipping companies, including Lamport and Holt, Alfred Holt and Company, and the Booth and Milburn lines; for example, Leslie built 41 ships for Lamport and Holt between 1861 and 1892[31]. The dreadnoughts and the ocean liners tended to receive the bulk of publicity, then and later, but a high proportion of the tonnage launched from North East yards represented the workhorses rather than the greyhounds of the seas.

The development of the oil tanker was also dictated by considerations of cost[32]. The carriage of large quantities of oil in barrels was inefficient in loading and unloading and wasteful in the amounts spent on barrels. The first useful invention in this field was the idea of carrying the oil in large tanks to be carried in ships' holds; James McNabb, a Newcastle ship-broker and ship-owner, suggested this, and the first ship embodying his idea was converted by Hawthorn in 1886. This middle course was, however, already obsolete by then, because in the previous year Henry Swan, then managing Armstrong's Low Walker shipyard, devised the solution of using the ship's hull itself as the oil container. The first embodiment of this concept appeared in 1886 too, and during the next 20 years Tyneside became the biggest centre of tanker building. North East yards built 200 tankers during that period, 21 from the Wear and 32 from the Tees area, but the Tyne built 147, with the Armstrong company taking the lion's share of 96.

Naval shipbuilding was a specialized area in which most yards in the region could not effectively compete. The two Tyneside giants, Armstrong and Palmer, dominated this field, although some other yards obtained minor orders from both British and foreign navies.

Some yards were content to serve varied markets, building either individual ships only or small numbers of expensive specialized vessels rather than a multiplication of standard orders. There was a marked tendency, as the nineteenth century wore on, for the numerous yards to consolidate into larger groupings. For example, 1903 saw a significant rationalization at Wallsend and Walker; Swan Hunter bought up the yards built earlier by the Tyne Pontoons and Dry Dock Company, and Schlesinger, Davis and Company, and also amalgamated with Wigham Richardson's large Neptune yard, to produce a large-scale enterprise capable of tendering successfully for the pending contract for the *Mauretania*, one of the most famous of all Tyne-built ships.

Overseas orders also played an important part in the expansion of North East shipbuilding. Some of the companies were as careful in cultivating foreign connections as in fostering association with British shipping lines. Charles Mitchell nurtured a profitable connection with Russia, operating a shipyard at St Petersburg from 1862 as well as obtaining a number of orders for ships to be built at home. Andrew Leslie also established a strong Russian connection, with

11 of his first 17 ships representing Russian orders[33]. The most intensive fostering of overseas contracts, however, can be seen in the work of Palmer and Armstrong.

In addition to shipbuilding, ship-repairing also expanded. In 1849 the early nineteenth-century shipbuilding firm of Smith migrated from St Peter's, just east of Newcastle, to a site near North Shields in a more convenient part of the essentially unimproved Tyne harbour; the first ship from the new yard was launched in February 1852. The old St Peter's site was left to be inherited by Hawthorn in the early 1870s. In 1886 the Edwards firm from South Shields crossed the Tyne to build a new shipbuilding and ship-repairing yard near to the Smith yard. Increasingly these two yards near the river mouth concentrated on the repairing side of their interests. In 1899 the two companies amalgamated in a stronger Smith's Dock Company, which became one of the largest ship-repairing works in the world. In 1909 the company set up another yard at South Bank, near Middlesbrough, and in future years the firm was to go still further afield.

Marine engineering also expanded in parallel with shipbuilding, with important manufacturers on all three major rivers. The engineering firm of Hawthorn established a very close relationship with Andrew Leslie's Hebburn shipyard, regularly providing engines for ships built there and this connection grew so close that in 1886 the two firms joined together as Hawthorn Leslie. On the Wear the engineering firm of George Clark concentrated on marine work from the mid-1850s, and from a decade later the North East Marine Engineering Company grew up at Sunderland's South Docks. Richardson Westgarth and Company were a similarly specialized company at West Hartlepool[34].

There was a constant increase in the size of shipyard and the numbers employed. In 1851 most North East shipyards employed less than 50 men, and only one boasted of a work force of more than 200; by 1887 one ship-repairing yard, and not the biggest—Wallsend Slipway—employed well over 1,000 men. By 1911 the North East employed at least 50,000 men in shipbuilding, almost half of the national total[35].

Two of the major industrial empires of the nineteenth-century North East, those established by Charles Mark Palmer and William George Armstrong, are particularly interesting, both for their magnitude and because they illustrate some significant aspects of contemporary industrial growth.

Palmer was born into one of Newcastle's mercantile families, prominent in the commercial side of the coal trade. This was a likely breeding ground for commercial skills, though not perhaps for the development of overscrupulous personalities. In 1854 a local banker commenting on the Palmer family firm confirmed that they were certainly successful[36], 'but I do not think that they are much liked being tricky in fulfilling their coal contracts'. During the third quarter of the nineteenth century Charles Palmer worked very hard indeed to build up a personal industrial empire. His membership of the managing partnership of John Bowes and Partners brought him ready access to large quantities of coal at reasonable rates. This connection led him to the significant breakthrough with the *John Bowes* in the early 1850s, which soon saw him established in the iron shipbuilding business, rapidly turning out colliers on his new design. With coal and iron shipbuilding assured the next step was to begin to manufacture his own iron, and by 1857 he had four blast furnaces over the Tyne at Walker. Now an independent supply of iron ore would be useful, and in the aftermath of the crash of the District Bank in 1857 he was able to pick up cheaply substantial iron ore holdings in Cleveland previously held by the failed bank's manager; Palmer promptly negotiated better royalty rates with the landowners concerned before beginning large-scale mining. He built Port Mulgrave on the Yorkshire coast as a small port for the shipping of his ore. Now Palmer-built and Palmer-owned iron colliers could take Bowes coal to London, calling in at Port Mulgrave on the way back to ship a load of iron ore for Palmer's furnaces. By 1863 Palmer owned shipyards on both banks of the Tyne. In August 1863 he staged a characteristic advertising event, by launching four iron steamships simultaneously, two from each side of the river. A similar publicity device was staged in the following year; on 19 December the *S.S. Despatch* was launched and then towed up-river to St Peter's, where she was engined by Hawthorn in sufficient time to return to Palmer's yard under her own steam on 20 December.

Palmer's enterprises continued to expand for many years. In the single year 1883 he built 33 ships. By 1893 he had built 28 warships. There were, however, problems in managing such a broad combination of interests. (Palmer's various interests and activities are referred to in reference 37.) The empire grew in earlier years by the creation of successive separate companies for different functions, with the result that by 1860 Palmer was the principal active manager of the 16 collieries owned by John Bowes and Partners (two of them being recent acquisitions which needed a good deal of care), the Mulgrave Iron Stone company, with its iron ore mines and harbour, the Jarrow Iron Company, with three blast furnaces at Jarrow and two at Walker, Palmer Brothers, with large shipyards on both banks of the Tyne, as well as a sizeable shipping line. In addition Palmer had to be able to find time to cultivate profitable commercial opportunities. In 1860 he obtained a contract to build cable ships for a proposed cable link between Java and Sumatra. In the same year he seized upon a chance to buy at the bargain price of £35,000 a ship he had built earlier; he spent £2,000 in refurbishing her and then disposed of her for £61,000 to the French government. In 1862 he obtained an Italian government contract to build the ships needed to establish a new mail line between Ancona and Alexandria. In 1863 he won a contract to build ten screw steamers at a price of £60,000 each to form the fleet of a proposed Liverpool–New Orleans shipping line. In 1865 there was some reorganization of his interests, which now came together under the umbrella of the Palmer Shipbuilding and Iron Company, but he effectively remained the active manager of them all.

There was also some marked rationalization of the main plant at Jarrow, with F. C. Marshall as one of the principal agents in this. When in 1887 the Institution of Naval Architects visited the Jarrow works they saw a fine example of an integrated production layout; the site was organized with the input of coal and iron ore at the west end, proceeding through blast furnaces and rolling mill to the marine engineering works and shipbuilding slips at the east end.

Commercial and technical success brought appropriate rewards—a fine country mansion and a fine London house, magistracies, deputy lieutenancies of counties, a baronetcy. He dominated the town of Jarrow which had largely been called into being by his installations; he was the town's first mayor, and, when Jarrow received independent parliamentary representation, Palmer had almost a pocket borough.

The later years were less happy[38]. There was a recession in shipbuilding in the late 1880s, and to keep the main works in action the Palmer company entered dangerously low tenders for two of the new battleships to be built for the Royal Navy under the recent Naval Defence Act. The accounts for 1890 and 1891 saw significant losses, and confidence in the company sagged. In order to facilitate recovery and to obtain an injection of new capital, Palmer was forced to yield any active management of the great company which bore his name to new directors. The fortunes of shipbuilding fluctuated thereafter, and the company's fortunes fluctuated with them. There were some good years, but hardly enough to justify the company's adoption of increased shipbuilding capacity in 1911 by buying the Hebburn shipyard which the Stephenson Company had tried its hand at between 1886 and 1908. The future of the Palmer empire was foreshadowed in the signs of weakness which had already appeared in the early 1890s, although the end was delayed by renewed pressure of business during the 1914–18 war.

Armstrong's origins were similar to those of Palmer, for he too sprang from the close-knit Newcastle oligarchy of commercial and professional families. Like Palmer, too, these connections gave him access to the modest amounts of initial capital needed to enable him to begin a career of expansion. In 1847 Armstrong, solicitor turned engineer, established a small factory at Elswick, just to the west of Newcastle, for the manufacture of hydraulic machinery of his own design. He had three partners—Armorer Donkin, George Cruddas and Addison Potter—all of them with a variety of interests already in various aspects of Tyneside business affairs. Each of the three put up £5,000, while Armstrong added £2,000 in cash and an estimated £3,000 in the value of the patents he held[39]. Until his death in 1879 Cruddas acted as a kind of financial director, and his contribution to the firm was second only to that of Armstrong himself, for Cruddas played a key role in establishing the viability and credit-worthiness of the company in its early years. The partners agreed to restrict dividends severely and to plough back profits; in 15 years capital grew from the nominal £20,000 of 1847 to £100,000. The firm early acquired a local reputation for financial integrity in an uncertain world by meeting bills promptly and in cash, keeping borrowing down to an absolute minimum.

There were problems to be surmounted in these early years. Armstrong's early hydraulic machinery was not by any means a never-failing success in operation, and there were some disappointed customers to placate. Armstrong's decision to interest himself in gun design during the Crimean War paid off in the immediate future, with service orders of more than £1 million between 1859 and 1863. However, there then came an abrupt and unexpected stop, and from 1864 orders from the British services totalled only £60,000 during the next 14 years. The firm was, however, financially strong enough to meet this crisis and skilful enough to seek out alternative work in time. In 1867 Armstrong provided the armament for a group of gunboats which Charles Mitchell was building at Walker, and this ushered in a period of close co-operation in warship building and other forms of shipbuilding, which blossomed into a union of the two companies in 1882, and a rationalization of their interests. With the replacement of the old low-level Newcastle bridge by a swing bridge (operated by Armstrong hydraulic machinery) in 1876, it was now possible to build sizeable warships at Elswick itself, in convenient proximity to engine-making and armament plant. The old Walker yard of Charles Mitchell dropped the construction of warships, now to be concentrated at Elswick, and instead confined its activities to merchant tonnage, especially the spate of tanker-building which followed Swan's innovation in that field. The Armstrong Mitchell empire flourished during the next few decades, partly because the state of international relations provided a high level of demand for warships and other armaments. In 1897 the success of the firm in relation to a prominent competitor was shown by the Armstrong takeover of Whitworth's armaments company with a change of name to Armstrong Whitworth.

There were, however, other factors at work which helped to explain the success of the firm, especially in the warship and weapons fields. The receipt of a long string of warship orders from both the Royal Navy and a variety of foreign navies is not to be explained simply in terms of the quality of the product— indeed it can be shown that Armstrong designs were sometimes seriously defective—but rather because of the skilful and determined salesmanship, an absolute prerequisite in the highly competitive international armaments industry of the period.

From the time when the Armstrong company first began, a small team of key managers had been built up; two of the men involved were the Rendel brothers, George and Stuart. George was a competent manager with expert knowledge of engineering and warship design; Stuart was also a good manager but made a major contribution as a successful salesman. From the beginning an important preoccupation was the maintenance of effective contacts with the service agencies at home and abroad who must be the source of warship and gun orders. In 1860 Captain Andrew Noble joined the management team; he had previously served in the Royal Artillery and become a recognized expert on gun design. Noble was to work for the Armstrong firm for more than half a century, and to become wealthy and distinguished in that service. Like the other members of the team, however, he had to work hard to attain this. We see him for instance making a fleeting visit from Elswick to London in March 1898[40]. He arrived in the capital late at night; the earlier part of the following morning was spent in coping with a sheaf of letters and telegrams: at 11.30 he was in attendance on a major customer, appearing at an investiture at the Chinese Embassy: at 12.00 he had an appointment with the Controller of the Royal Navy, at 12.15 with the Navy's Chief Constructor, at 13.00 with an important naval commander-in-chief: he was then due at the Foreign Office at 13.30 and the American Embassy at 14.00: technical matters took him to the Physical Laboratory for much of the afternoon, beginning at 14.30, but he had to see the First Sea Lord at 17.00. At 18.30 he met George Rendel for a business discussion, after dealing with more telegrams. Noble dined at 19.15, and left King's Cross for Newcastle at 20.15. This kind of timetable does not seem to have been very unusual for Armstrong managers. Even at home business must obtrude; guests must include people such as the Spanish Inspector of Armaments, who may well have been in receipt of Armstrong payments, Admiral Lord Charles Beresford, Admiral Fisher, Admiral Beatty, Admiral Togo and a procession of others to be carefully entertained and cossetted by Noble and his wife.

The livelihood of a rapidly increasing work force on Tyneside depended on the skill and the dexterity with which the salesmen operated. Care was taken to ensure that the firm was well informed about Admiralty needs and relationships, and there was a series of appointments which cemented such links. When the Elswick warship-building yard was opened in the early 1880s after the merger with Mitchell, its first head was Sir William White, previously Chief Constructor to the Royal Navy and its principal adviser on warship design. At the Admiralty he received £600 p.a. with only small extra payments; at Elswick he received £2,000 p.a., with handsome extra payments on a basis of tonnage built in the yard. When the Navy wanted White back in 1885 Armstrong relinquished him only on condition that he would continue to act as an Armstrong consultant for the remainder of his contract period. When White finally retired as Chief Constructor in 1902 he was replaced at the Admiralty by Philip Watts from the Elswick yard; when Watts retired in 1912 he was replaced as Chief Constructor by Eustace Tennyson d'Eyncourt, also from Elswick and the nephew of a prominent admiral. It is understandable that the Armstrong company continued to receive during this period a sizeable share of naval orders. In addition the Royal Navy of those palmy days was widely resorted to as a source of help and advice by minor powers seeking some small share of naval glory, and useful Admiralty contacts were often relevant in dealings with foreign navies too.

The principal salesmen for the Armstrong firm were adept in exploiting any kind of contact which might bring the orders which the firm needed to keep afloat. During the American Civil War Stuart Rendel used his friendship with a southern banker to try to obtain gun orders from the Confederate States. He carefully established a personal friendship with an Italian naval attaché, which served as a channel for the receipt of orders for naval guns. Rendel was also well acquainted with G. J. Goschen, a prominent banker and former Liberal First Lord of the Admiralty; when in the later 1870s Goschen represented Britain on the Egyptian Debt Commission this channel was exploited with a view to Egyptian orders. Not everyone approved of Armstrong sales techniques. When in 1870 Sir William Armstrong himself tried to obtain an interview with Hugh Childers, the Liberal First Lord of the Admiralty, his request was turned down; Childers was not, however, a man of any very great tact, as the remainder of his Admiralty experience demonstrated[41].

When the South American republics began to intensify their own naval competition Armstrongs were soon very closely involved. Another ex-Chief Naval Constructor, with Armstrong links, Sir Edward Reed, 'happened conveniently to be in the Chilean capital' when Chile was contemplating the purchase of battleships. In Brazil the Walter brothers, who had been at Charterhouse school with Elswick's d'Eyncourt, were retained as agents and helped to secure a number of important orders. The senior Brazilian naval officer entrusted with warship purchases in Europe was also conveniently enlisted among d'Eyncourt's personal friends. It was known in 1911 that Brazil was contemplating the purchase of a large modern battleship, and d'Eyncourt hastened off to join the Walter brothers in Rio with eight alternative designs for such a ship in his portfolio[42]. At Elswick it had been imagined that a strong selling point would be a proposal to fit the new ship with guns bigger than the 12-inch main armament then carried by many battleships. However, when d'Eyncourt landed in Rio it was to discover that German salesmen were also on the spot and had already persuaded the Brazilian Admiralty of the superior advantages of 12-inch guns; the eight Elswick draft designs were incontinently abandoned overnight, and d'Eyncourt surfaced the next day with a new draft design which would mount more 12-inch guns than any other ship afloat. An intensive sales campaign followed, from which d'Eyncourt returned to Tyneside bearing this fat contract, with its provision of profits—and continued employment—at Elswick for some years. The ship was launched in 1913, a sizeable Brazilian contingent attending the ceremony being brought from London in a special Pullman train, with champagne after tea, followed by a seven-course dinner *en route*.

However, a cloud now loomed on the horizon—economic difficulties in Brazil brought about the cancellation of the contract. Two consequences at once ensued—800 men were laid off at Elswick, and the sales organization was again put into high gear to try to find a new owner for the expensive ship. There was friction between Greece and Turkey; d'Eyncourt was well acquainted with Admiral Sir Douglas Gamble, who had led an important British naval mission to Turkey in 1908 and had useful contacts in Turkish naval circles. Turkey took over the contract, and the battleship *Rio de Janeiro* became the *Sultan Osman I*—with some hurried changes of name plates and similar indicators. Work on the ship was under way again, and the full work force at Elswick was back at work in 1914. During the summer the Royal Navy dropped a hint that there was much to be said for not hurrying the completion of the ship, and the Armstrong firm deliberately held back some of the main armament installation, so that the battleship was still in works hands at Elswick when war broke out in August. The ship was promptly taken over by the Royal Navy, quickly completed and joined the Grand Fleet as *H.M.S. Agincourt*; she was badly overgunned, the installations for loading the big guns were an untried system which did not work very well, and she was a very poor gun platform. She was scrapped as soon as the war was over.

The Armstrong salesmen could not afford to be unduly sensitive as to the methods they used to secure orders; if they failed to secure a warship order, there were many competitors who would be willing to go to considerable lengths to secure it. We have from one source a cryptic note to the effect that[43], 'in April 1883 the company was approached by a gentleman whose relations with Spain enabled him to obtain early information with regard to any future programmes of armament and shipbuilding, and in some degree to influence orders'. It seems highly unlikely that this was an entirely disinterested approach; a few years later the Armstrong company completed two cruisers for the Spanish navy. It is not perhaps surprising that the men at the head of Armstrong, deeply engaged from year to year in this kind of activity, were not overly scrupulous in their care of their own interests; a boardroom row of the early twentieth century demonstrated that the executive directors had been surreptitiously overpaying themselves for years[44].

These Armstrong managers may not have been the most admirable of people, but economic success does not generally go to the meek or the overly scrupulous; on the success of the selling campaigns of these armaments-makers depended not only their own incomes but the livelihood of the majority of the 26,000 or so workers employed by the Armstrong concerns in the years before the First World War. It is unlikely that many of these workers were deeply opposed to the manufacture of engines of war and destruction or that they would have been very disturbed to learn of some of the methods by which the company obtained some of the contracts which kept them at work.

By contemporary standards wages at the Elswick works were good, especially in the skilled trades. Apprenticeships there were eagerly sought after and formed part of the great web of patronage among workers which determined which boys should be admitted to skilled trades in such industries as shipbuilding and engineering. Elswick foremen were men of considerable status in the local community; when the British Association made a much-publicized visit to Elswick in 1886, it was the foremen of the various shops who acted as guides in showing the distinguished visitors around the various installations.

Although an aura of considerable success still surrounded Armstrong in the years before the First World War, there were signs of strain. Andrew Noble was at the head of the firm after Armstrong's death in 1900; he was certainly a hard worker, but he was by now a very old man. The Rendel brothers remained large shareholders but dropped out of active management functions during the 1880s; they were often distinctly critical of later management. There was less harmony at the top than there had been in earlier years. There were attempts before 1914 to maintain progress, and tentative moves into new fields, such as the manufacture of motor cars and aeroplanes, but in 1914 the company still depended heavily on a continued market for warships and other armaments at home and abroad. In 1913 warship-building was significantly extended with the opening of the new Naval Yard at Walker, in time to build the new battleship, *H.M.S. Malaya*. During the 1914-18 war of course, the company had plenty of work. They built 47 warships, armed another 62 and repaired or refitted 521. They produced 1,062 aircraft, but not to their own design. They made 13,000 guns, 12,000 gun carriages and $14\frac{1}{2}$ million shells. The end of the war saw Armstrong in possession of considerable funds but facing a very difficult future in a world which no longer wanted many new warships and immense quantities of arms and munitions.

Turbines and electricity

One specialized branch of engineering on Tyneside in the later nineteenth and the early twentieth centuries was inaugurated by Charles Algernon Parsons, younger son of an Irish earl with strong scientific interests. Parsons served 4 years as a premium apprentice in the Armstrong works at Elswick and then moved in 1884 to the Gateshead firm of Clarke Chapman which had begun life as a manufacturer of marine equipment but was now becoming a major engineering firm. At Gateshead Parsons began a series of experiments on turbines. Disagreements with colleagues brought a break in 1889, and in that year Parsons established his own establishment at Heaton, east of Newcastle. Turbine development took two main lines, their use in ship propulsion and their use for generating electricity. Parson achieved success in both of these lines, demonstrating the superiority of turbines over various types of steam engines then in use for certain kinds of ships and for generating. Marine turbines grew rapidly in size and reliability from the tiny installation in the *Turbinia* of 1897 to the 70,000-h.p. engines of the *Mauretania* of 1907.

Success in the electrical field was even more significant, and there was some irony in the successful development of this rival source of power in a region which had profited so much from the enormous expansion in the use of steam engines in the recent past. Parsons was well known in technical circles on Tyneside, at a time when experimental work was often closely watched by leaders of local industry and commerce. As soon as Parsons had demonstrated the utility of his turbines for generating purpose, he found no difficulty in obtaining adequate local backers to put the new devices into operation. By 1889 Tyneside already had two rival generating companies, although they were able to reach working agreements on pricing and the division of territory. Parsons' success induced further developments. Reyrolles, a small company interested in electrical equipment, moved to Tyneside from London in 1901; at that time its work force totalled only 58, but a considerable future lay ahead for the newcomer. The generating station opened at Carrville on Tyneside in 1904 was the first large modern generating station, and firms such as the large works of the North East Marine Company, which built marine engines nearby, became early examples of large-scale industrial users of electrical power. A Tyneside railway line was electrified 5 years before any London suburban line used electric traction[45]. In a rare fit of municipal enterprise, Tynemouth Corporation erected municipal generating plant in 1901 but 5 years later came to the conclusion that it would be better to buy supplies from major local producers rather than continue independent generation; the municipal power station finally went out of use in 1915[46].

Before 1914 a number of the more progressive colliery companies in the region were actively introducing electrical equipment. The collieries belonging to the Consett Iron Company were one good example in early use of electricity, while by 1912 the Ashington Coal Company's generators were producing more than 5,000 h.p. For many years the North East, and especially Tyneside, was to be in the forefront in both technical and commercial exploitation of electrical power, and a growing capacity in this industry was to provide a very useful and much needed source of income and employment in ensuing years.

Industries in decline

A wide range of industries had shown a tremendous capacity for expansion in the years after 1850. During this period, however, as earlier, massive success on the one hand and an overall pattern of growth were compatible with shrinkage and failure in other areas of the region's economy.

In 1850 the lead-mining interests in the western areas of the region were still prosperous, with lead prices buoyant and increasing output[47]. For example, during the census decade 1851–61 the population of Middleton in Teesdale rose from 1,849 to 2,266 mainly because of further expansion in lead-mining. Growth continued until the 1870s, to be followed by a sudden and catastrophic decline. A minor cause of the trouble was an increase in production costs as more accessible lodes were worked out, but the fundamental cause was a collapse of lead prices due to the availability of large supplies of much cheaper lead from foreign producers. British lead was fetching £21.49 per ton in 1877, but only 8 years later the figure had slumped to £12.25 and showed no sign of recovery. Under the stress of this development, the region's lead-mining activities rapidly declined. There were attempts to keep going by cutting costs and accepting lower standards, but the drop in lead prices was too steep for such expedients to have any significant impact[48]. By the end of the nineteenth century lead-mining in the western dales of the region was virtually dead, and with it a peculiar district culture of mining combined with small hill farms which had played an important part in the region's economy for generations.

The chemical industry on Tyneside also continued to grow in the years after 1850, though here again trouble lay ahead. In 1852 Tyneside employed 3,067 of the national total of 6,326 working in this industry. Tyneside plants consumed annually some 230,000 tons of coal, and by 1860 the figure had risen to about 300,000 tons. In 1852 Tyneside chemical firms produced 23,100 tons of alkali out of a national total of 71,163—Lancashire was a little ahead with 26,343. In the production of soda crystals Tyneside's quota of 42,794 tons out of a national total of 61,044 was far ahead of any rival[49]. By the 1860s more than half of the national production of alkali and bleaching powder was coming from the 24 chemical works along the banks of the Tyne[50]. Not surprisingly the leaders of the local chemical industry included some of the most prominent men in the regional economy. One of these was Christian Allhusen, like Henry Bolckow an immigrant from North Germany, an area with long-standing economic links with the North East. His character was well summed up by a local banker[51]: 'He is considered a first rate man of business, tho' somewhat keen.' Before 1850 he had built up a considerable position in a variety of trades, not only the chemical industry but also commercial interests in corn, coal and iron, in all of which contacts in North Germany were distinctly useful. Like many other local business men, including some of considerable acumen, he burned his fingers badly in the affairs of the ill-fated Northumberland and Durham District Bank, but by September 1858 he had managed to extricate himself from his commitments arising out of that fiasco[52]. Increasingly his chemical interests predominated, and his Newcastle Chemical Works grew to occupy a site of 137 acres and a capital of £600,000[53].

Another magnate of the industry was James Cochran Stevenson, who came to Tyneside in 1844, when his father bought the existing chemical works of Cookson and Cuthbert near South Shields[54]. These now became the Jarrow Chemical Works, and in 1858 Stevenson bought another major chemical concern, the works at Friar's Goose, near Gateshead. In the later years of the century his chemical works on Tyneside employed about 1,400 workers. Although but recently arrived on Tyneside, he took a prominent role in the agitation which brought about the creation of the Tyne Improvement Commission in 1850, and he served on the Commission for many years. He became the proprietor of an important local newspaper, the *Shields Gazette*, in 1848, and used it as a principal organ of publicity against Newcastle's monopoly control of the Tyne; the *Gazette* was one of the most progressive provincial papers for many years[55]. Stevenson sat for many years on the borough council of South Shields; he became Liberal M.P. for the borough in 1868 and held the seat with little difficulty until the end of the century.

The kind of sustained growth in the chemical industry which had supported these careers was not to be maintained. The Tyneside plants had risen on the basis of the Leblanc process; this was, however, an inherently inefficient method of alkali production. For many years technical progress was concentrated on the elaboration of a range of ancilliary equipment, which made possible the profitable use of by-products of the basic system; this, however, added to the very large sums of capital attached to the operations of the basic conception and made a fundamental shift in manufacture even more difficult[56]. From the 1870s a formidable competitor was available in the much more efficient Solvay process, and the competitive position of the Tyneside plants was steadily eroded. In the latter part of the nineteenth century a combination of factors brought about a rapid run-down of the once flourishing Tyneside chemical trade. The reluctance to move away from the basic Leblanc process not only exposed the Tyneside plants to competition from more efficient British producers but also had serious ill effects in the export markets which played an important part in the industry's sales. The Tyneside plants were overtaken by technical developments at the same time as their principal continental markets were developing their own chemical industries on up-to-date lines, so that the position of the Tyneside plants was doubly eroded.

There was also a shift of emphasis within the region, to the detriment of interest and investment in the older Tyneside centre. The ample brine deposits of South East Durham offered a readily accessible raw material for more advanced processes which could outstrip any locational advantages still possessed by Tyneside. In 1885 J. C. Stevenson reorganized his chemical interests in a new limited company and in the following year joined with another leading chemical-manufacturer on Tyneside, Tennant and Company, in acquiring extensive salt or brine royalties at Haverton Hill on Teesside, where the future of the chemical industry in the North East increasingly lay. In 1891 there was a major rationalization of the chemical industry, resulting in the creation of the United Alkali Company, forerunner of Imperial Chemical Industries. Part of the policy of the United Alkali Company was the closure of obsolescent and inefficient plants, and a number of Tyneside chemical works disappeared under this programme. Although some plants, including Allhusen's Newcastle Chemical Works, managed to survive for some time, by 1914 the Tyneside chemical industry had shrunk to relative insignificance.

A group of other local industries can be conveniently considered in conjunction with the chemical industry, with which they had much in common. Soap-making continued to show modest growth, and by the end of the century two Newcastle firms, Taylor and Hedley, were large-scale manufacturers of soap for both household and industrial uses, and Hedley in particular still had a considerable future ahead. A local survey of industry towards the end of the century claimed that Hedley 'rely on *quality* rather than on *advertising*', but from the later 1890s this was to give way to more sophisticated attitudes. The company embarked upon a policy of increased production, based in part on the use of a wider range of imported raw materials, such as the African palm oil used in increasing quantities from 1890. From 1898 the firm began to spend increasing sums on advertising with Fairy soap the first of its products to be energetically pushed in this way[57].

Paper-making was another similar industry long established in the area[58]. By 1862 a total of about 8,000 tons p.a. was being produced by 12 local paper works. The 1860s saw a significant shift in techniques, with the large-scale use of imported esparto grass as a major ingredient. The Ford Mill at Hylton near Sunderland, built in 1864, was the first plant in the world built for this purpose, and by the following year some 18,000 tons of Spanish esparto were imported into the region. The initiative which had brought the Ford Mill into being was also demonstrated in its early management. The plant showed a profit of $21\frac{1}{2}\%$ on capital, but the dividend taken was only $7\frac{1}{2}\%$, the remainder being ploughed back in further innovations, especially in equipment making it possible to recycle the bulk of the chemicals employed and thereby to reduce production costs[59]. About £40,000 had been spent in setting up this pioneer enterprise. The Ford Mill continued in profitable operation for the remainder of this period. A near neighbour on Wearside, the Hendon Paper Works, employed well over 400 workers in the early twentieth century[60]. While achieving a modest prosperity, paper-making always remained one of the lesser local industries.

Pottery and glass-making

Both Sunderland and Newcastle were important centres of pottery manufacture in the years after 1850. In the late 1860s there were 13 substantial potteries on Tyneside, employing about 1,200 people. By the late 1880s the two works belonging to the Maling company themselves employed 1,200 workers in the highly mechanized production of huge quantities of containers and similar cheap articles[61]. Sunderland was another important centre, with considerable expansion in employment and production during the third quarter of the century. The industry was then badly hit by foreign competition, and the late nineteenth and early twentieth centuries saw severe shrinkage in the North East. The two principal potteries in Gateshead closed in 1892 and 1909 respectively[62]. At Sunderland the Ford pottery closed in 1864, the Southwick pottery in 1874 and another pottery at Southwick in 1897; the important Deptford pottery closed in 1918[63]. Although these enterprises were not on any very extensive scale, employing usually about 100 to 200 workers, in the 1860s they had collectively provided about 3,000 jobs, with men and women, boys and girls, all included. Much of the output had been for home consumption, but export trade had developed also. This showed a catastrophic falling-off at the end of the century. Sunderland exported, for instance, 684 crates of earthenware in 1881, 222 in 1891 and 26 in 1900. With free trade a national dogma, and relatively high labour costs, the pottery industry in the North East could not maintain its growth in the face of a considerable increase of cheap foreign imports, as well as competition from other British producers.

By 1850 glass-making was already an important industry on Tyne and Wear, and in 1851 both Swinburne's works at South Shields and Hartley's works at Sunderland made major contributions to the Crystal Palace[64]. The industry demonstrated early examples of strong organization among both employers and workers. By the 1860s a closed shop existed in the blown flint glass works, with the employer bound to take the next name on the union's list when a vacancy occurred, while in a variety of ways a tight union organization ensured the maintenance of what were by contemporary standards good wages. This dominant position was, however, short lived; it is unlikely that without this factor the blown flint glass works could have stood up to the competition of much cheaper mechanized production of pressed glass articles after the introduction of the new process about 1860, but high labour costs encouraged the rapid collapse of the older process.

In sheet glass of various kinds there were early examples of collusion between manufacturers. As early as 1841 a conference of British sheet-glass-manufacturers, including those from North East England as well as firms elsewhere such as Pilkington and Chance, agreed on production quotas to be observed. The position of the Sunderland firm of Hartley was enhanced by their invention of rolled plate glass in 1847, and by the 1860s the making of sheet glass was dominated by a triumvirate of Chance, Pilkington and Hartley working in collusion. During the latter part of the third quarter of the century increasing imports of cheap Belgian glass disturbed this tranquillity. It was a source of regret to the British triumvirate that it was impossible to extend some form of agreed market division to these interlopers because 'there is unfortunately no association of window-glass-manufacturers in Belgium and no understanding of any kind amongst them'.

The Belgians were not able to maintain their scale of competition because of their own increasing costs, but the British cartel came under increasing pressure, as Pilkington began to move steadily ahead of their two partners. The St Helens' firm owned their own collieries and took the lead in improved technology. Gradually the glass works of the North East were squeezed out, with eight closures in Sunderland alone. James Hartley himself died in 1886, and before then the major enterprise he had founded was in serious trouble. His Wear glass works, which in the third quarter of the century had been one of the industry's giants, finally closed its doors only 10 years after its founder's death.

On the Tyne the story was similar. Gradually the local producers were squeezed out by competition from other centres. The Swinburne enterprise became the Tyne Plate Glass Company in 1868, when the plant covered 7 acres and employed about 600 workers. In 1891, however, the company collapsed with heavy liabilities, and by 1900 South Shields possessed only one small pressed glass maker as a survival of what had been one of the area's major interests[65]. Bottle-making had been another standby of the glass industry of the North East; by 1862 about 4 million bottles were being produced annually. Here too competition gradually gained the upper hand. Glass-making did not completely disappear but continued in various parts of the region; for example, the first electric light bulb was blown at Lemington before its unveiling at the Newcastle Literary and Philosophical Society on 3 February 1879, and the region was an early centre of bulb manufacture. However, glass-making never matched in the twentieth century the relative importance it possessed as a source of income and employment by the third quarter of the nineteenth century. One of the reasons for the decline of such industries in comparison with their continued importance in other parts of Britain was the fact that in this region they could not occupy the centre of the stage in the regional economy and could not attract a substantial share of the available capital and interest, because of the superior attractions of such areas as coal, iron and steel, engineering and shipbuilding.

Docks and railways

The experience of the region's economy was therefore a distinctly mixed one. Overall, however, the prevailing trend was one of massive increases in production, trade and employment. The growth in production and trade necessitated a concomitant improvement in transport facilities. On the Tees the Middlesbrough Dock, opened first in 1842, was enlarged three times during the remainder of the century, and many other port facilities were created to meet the needs of the growing Teesside industries. On the Wear successive dock-building schemes produced a total of 210 acres of docks by the early twentieth century, while at the harbour mouth new pier construction and lighthouse construction were substantially completed by 1903.

The most dramatic changes, however, came on the Tyne, where the work of the Tyne Improvement Commission during the second half of the century transformed a dangerous shoal-ridden estuary into a major modern port. In 1847 clearance at low water over the bar at the river mouth could be as little as 6 feet 1 inch—much the same as it had been in 1818. By 1865 river improvements had already made this 15 feet, and by 1875 there was a channel of not less than 20 feet in depth between the harbour mouth and Newcastle quay, enabling sizeable ships to make their way up-river and to serve the expanding industrial areas on both banks. Large new docks were built on both sides of the river, and quays equipped with modern cranes, improved coal-shipping machinery and similar installations also multiplied on both sides of the river. In 1876 the route still further up-river beyond Newcastle was opened by the building of a swing bridge; without this the rapid growth of Armstrong's Elswick complex would have been impossible. In carrying out all this work the Tyne Improvement Commission was helped not only by improved harbour technology but also by the fact that the majority of Tyne commissioners were men deeply involved in the area's industry themselves, with a keen personal interest in ensuring the most efficient and economical shipping facilities. Moreover, much of the money expended in port improvement either came directly from the river dues harvested from the port's growing traffic or was borrowed on the strength of that growing revenue. Lesser ports were also affected. At Seaham Harbour the early years of the twentieth century saw considerable investment in a programme of improvement, with large amounts spent on the building of new breakwaters. Blyth harbour had been difficult, dangerous and of very limited capacity in earlier years; from 1885 a great deal of money was spent in improving the port, a timely exercise in view of the massive increase of coal shipments which lay in the years immediately ahead.

There was also a process of expansion and rationalization in the region's railway network, which had begun life as a patchwork of small local lines. The North Eastern Railway gradually aspired to a monopoly, absorbing the Stockton and Darlington Railway in 1863, the Blyth and Tyne Railway in 1874 and the Londonderry Railway in 1900. By that time the regional domination of the North Eastern Railway was complete, and the company owned not just railways but important docks and coal staiths too. The company was efficiently managed and found no difficulty in raising funds when they were needed; by 1903 the North Eastern Railway had 40,000 shareholders. Like the Tyne Improvement Commission the North Eastern Railway's success was in large measure due to a group of men who directed it and who were closely connected with the principal interests served by the railway. In 1898, for example, the chairman was Sir Joseph Pease, of the Darlington Quaker family with links to many local interests, the deputy chairman was Sir Isaac Lothian Bell, a leading ironmaster, and other directors included members of the Ridley and Grey families of Northumberland, Sir David Dale of the Consett Iron Company, the coal-owner Sir James Joicey, and Sir William Gray, a leading West Hartlepool shipbuilder. With such men at the helm, there was every chance that the North Eastern Railway would provide an efficient service for industry in the North East. The railway had a good record in selling its services and in the application to policy of statistical analysis and other careful planning. The recruitment of able young men to the company's service was a continuous concern, and their resort to educational facilities was encouraged. The North Eastern Railway was early in coming to formal recognition of the railway unions in 1908, and a systematic conciliation machinery for the settling of disputes was devised. When the London and North Eastern Railway came into existence after the 1914–18 war, the North Eastern Railway was clearly the largest, the most efficient, the wealthiest and the most influential of all the components merged into the new grouping.

Railway development in some areas continued to influence the pattern of residence and occupation. Successive extensions in the 1860s and 1880s greatly improved rail links between Newcastle and the coast. This led to the growth of Tynemouth and Whitley Bay as pleasure resorts and also enabled these and other places *en route* to develop as dormitory areas for Newcastle and the industrial belt along the Tyne. The building of the Durham coast line authorized by an Act of 1894 provided, as we have seen, an essential ingredient in the plans for the creation of the Horden Coal Company and the expansion of a group of very large collieries along that coast at places like Horden, Easington and Blackhall; most of this coal was taken by rail to West Harlepool, where modern equipment facilitated a very rapid turn-round rate in the use of coal waggons. There was also some further building of railways into the rural areas, such as the building of the Alnwick–Cornhill line which opened in 1887 and helped in a variety of ways to penetrate what had previously been a large isolated area.

Suburban transport

Suburban transport facilities saw rapid growth, with important social effects. Gateshead's tramways were authorized by an Act of 1880, and the first stretch of track was in use 3 years later. By 1898 there were $6\frac{1}{2}$ miles of tram routes in the town, served by steam locomotives, though these gave way to electricity at the beginning of the new century. Newcastle Corporation obtained powers to run electric trams in 1899, and the first municipal tram appeared in Pilgrim Street at the end of 1901; within 25 years the mileage of tram lines in the city rose to 50. In 1894 Sunderland's horse trams travelled about 265,000 miles and carried 2,300,000 passengers, though there were only 6 miles of track. The mileage had risen to 7 when the first electric tram appeared there in 1900; during their first 9 months the new electric trams ran nearly 400,000 miles and carried $6\frac{1}{4}$ million passengers. By 1905 there were 11 miles of track, and passenger journeys reached an annual total of 14 million in 1914[66]. The first motor buses had arrived on the scene before the 1914–18 war, and by 1914 the Northern General Transport Company had already swallowed up a number of small local companies and operated a fleet of 54 vehicles[67]. However, by 1914 the tram services and the infant bus services only covered relatively small areas adjacent to the main urban centres; elsewhere communities depended on trains; in the very many places which the railways did not touch, and for the very many people who could not readily afford rail tickets, movement was limited to the speed of a man or a horse. Early twentieth-century photographs of mining and rural communities frequently show them with unmade-up main streets, eloquent of the limited transport facilities and the relative isolation which continued to face many communities before the great expansion of buses and motor cars after 1918. In the late nineteenth and twentieth centuries it was not at all unusual for poorer people to walk long distances either for work or for recreation. There was nothing at all out of the ordinary for workers' children to walk from Jarrow to Tynemouth and back for a seaside trip, or for a miners' children to walk from Boldon colliery to the Town Moor Fair at Newcastle, with money which might otherwise have been spent on railway fares retained for more enjoyable purposes.

However, the expansion of the suburban transport facilities which occurred on Tyne, Wear and Tees in the late nineteenth and early twentieth centuries did have important results. Previously a worker either must live very close to his work or must face long walks in all kinds of weather. With the coming of the tram and the extension of suburban trains, together with higher wages for many categories of workers, it was increasingly possible for workers to live at some distance from their place of work. This facilitated the reduction of overcrowding, and the extension of housing into more peripheral areas, where land prices were generally lower.

Banking

The expansion of industry and trade greatly increased the need for a variety of ancilliary activities connected with the commercial and financial aspects of the region's economy. In contrast wth the traumatic experiences of 1847 and 1857 the history of the region's banks in the second half of the nineteenth century was a tranquil one. The more stable and secure institutions which survived continued to provide a great deal of financial support and banking services for expanding local industry. The Newcastle branch of the Bank of England continued as a lynch-pin of local banking activity, and the ranks of the distinguished local private banks were reinforced after 1859 by the arrival of a new banking partnership—Hodgkin, Barnett, Pease, Spence and Company. This new foundation possessed ample resources, a wide range of useful connections within the region and elsewhere, and competent management. We can see the usefulness of local banks in two early examples of this firm at work. During a short but sharp shipbuilding recession in 1866 this bank shored up more than one local shipyard. Wigham Richardson's firm was one of these, and he later recalled[68]: 'There was so little work at Walker that grass grew in the shipyard, and the cartmen requested permission to reap the hay. . . . If it had not been for the kind support of our bankers, and especially of John William Pease, I think we should have lost heart and thrown up the sponge.' A few years later it was the backing of this bank which made possible the reconstruction of the major firm of R. and W. Hawthorn under its new owners and set it on a renewed voyage of expansion.

In the later nineteenth and early twentieth centuries many of the key industrial and mining companies, the main mercantile and shipping houses, and the principal banks of the area, were under the direct control of a relatively small and coherent group of men. On Tyneside, on Wearside and on Teesside this position obtained. Such men were linked together in a variety of ways. There were links of family and marriage connections and a network of personal friendships. There were links of common interest in the intellectual and cultural societies of the main centres. There were links of shared interest in sport and recreation. There were links of shared schooling or apprenticeship—both Armstrong's Elswick and Palmer's Jarrow firms were nurseries of men later to hold key positions in companies in the region and elsewhere. There were for very many of them common connections in the activities of church and chapel. One amusing example of such links—if not perhaps an especially typical one—was created in the years after 1882 by John Wigham Richardson, who with his partner, J. D. Christie, owned the important Neptune shipbuilding yard at Walker[69]. During the winter months he held regular Virgil evenings at his home. A party of friends dined together and then settled down to read and discuss passages of Virgil. When the main works of that poet had been covered,

Horace came next, though we are told that a subsequent proposal to move on to Lucretius 'frightened some of the members'. Those involved included Thomas Hodgkin, a leading Newcastle banker as well as a distinguished historian, W. S. Dalglish, a leading local ship-owner, Benjamin Browne, senior partner in Hawthorns, Benjamin Noble, banker and brother of an Armstrong director, and Theodore Merz, a leading local scientist and an expert in the industrial application of improved scientific techniques.

Similar links which brought together key men in industry, commerce and local administration existed among kindred groups on both Wearside and Teesside. However the gradual emergence of a more sophisticated and inter-locking economy covering much wider areas began to erode the autonomy of the regional economy. The process was well exemplified in the history of local banks in the years around 1900, as one by one the purely regional institutions succumbed to the embraces of national institutions. In 1897 the long-estab-lished local banking firm of Woods and Company was taken over by Barclays Bank, while Lloyds Bank absorbed Hodgkin, Barnett, Pease and Spence in 1893 and the venerable Lambton Bank in 1908.

Agriculture and fishing

Even if the region's agriculture did not play during this period the same crucial role in the development of the regional economy as it had done at all previous periods, it remained important, still providing 1 in 20 of all jobs in Northumberland in 1911, though less than half that in County Durham. The second half of the nineteenth century saw a continuing spread of improved farming techniques; for example, when the Fourth Duke of Northumberland succeeded his brother in 1847 he at once embarked upon an extensive and sustained campaign of estate improvement and modernization which brought the largest landholding in the region, for the first time, into the ranks of markedly improved estates. The continued expansion of urban and industrial demand, coupled with enhanced foreign competition in some major foodstuffs, produced some changes in the region's farming. There was a shift from cultivation towards pasture, and the 1871 census report, for instance, included a number of references to reduced rural population attributed to the substitution of grazing for cultivation. The figures for sales at Newcastle cattle market indicate this shift; in 1852 a total of 38,109 cattle, 250,369 sheep and 34,544 pigs were sold, but 30 years later the figures were 111,705, 302,504 and 41,747. Farms within the region still supplied a large share of these totals, but imports into the region from further afield also provided much of the expansion. By the 1880s there was some import of both cattle and sheep from Denmark and Sweden, while pigs were moved from Aberdeenshire and Northern Ireland. In September 1884 a Durham co-operative society recorded its first sales of frozen New Zealand mutton[70]. Butter was also imported in increasing quantities; one Newcastle merchant house claimed about 1890 that it regularly held stocks of Danish butter worth about £20,000[71].

There were still poorer areas of marginal farming within the region, but also signs of continuing interest in the application of improved and more scientific farming techniques. The College of Science at Newcastle received its first professor of agriculture in 1891, though at first the number of students involved was very small. Northumberland County Council, with a strong farming and landowning representation among its members, set up an experimental farm at Cockle Park, but this was viewed with some suspicion by many practical farmers for some time. In 1905 the Duke of Northumberland, in his annual address to his tenants, was at pains to quiet opposition to the use of rates to finance this enterprise and claimed that the practical contributions of the farm were worth 'an incalculably greater amount than the trifling loss'. The region continued to provide distinguished agricultural improvers among both land-lords and tenant farmers. When Major Browne acquired the Callaly estate in North Northumberland in 1877 he at once embarked upon a campaign to bring his new property up to date, including the rebuilding of many of his farms[72]. In the second half of the nineteenth century one of Britain's most distinguished farmers was Jacob Wilson, who farmed the Woodhorn Farm near Ashington as well as becoming the principal agent to the Earl of Tankerville's estates. He pioneered the application of new techniques such as steam ploughing and was also well known as a successful animal-breeder. He was knighted for services to agriculture in 1889, no mean achievement for a man of his position in Victorian Britain. Despite continued progress in the region's own agriculture, an increasing proportion of the food needed by the swelling urban and industrial population was imported from abroad. This point is brought out clearly by the increased shipments to the Tyne of the following foods between 1863 and 1883—butter from 32,242 cwt to 332,120 cwt, flour from 12,214 sacks to 334,384 sacks, wheat from 87,995 quarters to 224,070 quarters and cheese from 18,911 cwt to 30,160 cwt[73].

The region's fishing industry made its own contribution to the local food supplies. As late as 1870 the Tyne itself still produced considerable quantities of salmon, but pollution was to end that on all three major rivers. The major supply of fish came from the sea. In 1877 William Purdy of North Shields, who owned a number of steam tugs, conceived the idea of using them as trawlers, and by 1909 North Shields was a major fishing port, with 76 steam trawlers based there, and many more visiting the port on a seasonal basis[74]. The region made a notable contribution to the national diet in 1860, when Woodger of Newcastle invented the kipper[75]. By 1910 nearly 20,000 tons of herring were landed at North Shields alone annually, though Norwegian contributions represented part of this total. In the years before the First World War more than 600 herring boats appeared at North Shields. The port's fishing interests normally employed about 2,600 people, but at the height of the summer herring harvest seasonal labour could swell the total at work at North Shields to nearly 6,000[76].

The retail trade

The distribution of the necessary food and other supplies to the greatly increased population involved a considerable expansion of the retail trading sector. The traditional markets of this kind continued to exist for the most part; in Newcastle, for instance, the old provision market in the Bigg Market continued to be held every Thursday and Saturday morning, and by the late 1880s the areas drawn on for eggs to supply this facility were by no means confined to the region but included Ireland, Scotland, Denmark, Germany, France, Italy and Hungary—an illuminating instance of the development of international transport and trade[79]. The new markets built for the city in the early years of Victoria's reign continued as a major retailing centre, especially for meat. In the early 1880s there were 145 slaughter-houses and triperies within Newcastle itself, exemplifying a substantial public health problem as well as an extended food supply; in 1895 the city possessed 73 dairies with a total of 628 cows[78].

There was, however, a large expansion during this period in the number and variety of shops. The wealthier society of the late nineteenth and early twentieth centuries enjoyed retail facilities on a much more extensive and sophisticated scale than at any previous period. In 1898, for example, Newcastle possessed 44 makers of ice cream[79]. The later nineteenth century saw the arrival, especially in Newcastle, the regional capital, of larger shopping establishments such as that operated by the Bainbridge family, which was founded in 1867 and by the early twentieth century had extended to the provision of large department stores in both Newcastle and Leeds[80]. A parallel development was the creation of Fenwick's shop. The firm's founder was a drapery assistant in a Mosley Street shop before branching out on his own[81]. In both of these cases success was achieved by patience and hard work. Even in the later 1890s J. J. Fenwick himself was only drawing some £700 to £800 p.a. from what was then a distinctly prosperous business; his manager–buyer had a salary of £500 p.a. Both of these big stores established and largely financed benevolent institutions for their workers and operated distinctly paternalistic regimes. In 1917 the Bainbridge Store employed 107 people who had been with them for more than 25 years.

An important feature of the expansion of the retail facilities of the region was the development of co-operative stores. By 1875 a return submitted to Parliament, which was not in fact a complete tally, showed that County Durham had 48 co-operative societies with a membership of nearly 40,000. In the previous year their trade had amounted to £1¾ million, and nearly £120,000 had been distributed to members as dividend. Northumberland then had 37 societies with well over 16,000 members; in the previous year their trade had totalled £600,000 and dividend had amounted to nearly £60,000[82]. The mining areas provided a substantial share of the striking growth in co-operative trading. The capital of the Crook society[83a] grew from £67 in 1865 to £16,000 in 1876, with a rise in membership from 40 to about 2,000. By 1915, this society's total sales over fifty years amounted to well over £7½ million, and the 5,025 members then held an average of £30 in the society's funds. The Bishop Auckland society[83b] began in 1860 with £100 contributed by its 118 founder members. By 1910 the society was trading at more than £113,000 p.a., had 15 shops and a membership of 16,774. Both of these societies were essentially societies for mining families, and both provided facilities beyond retail trading. Annual celebrations and regular social gatherings were a regular adjunct to the societies' commercial activities. In 1874, for example, in place of their annual tea party the members of the Crook society determined upon a trip to Sunderland 'if possible when the Channel Fleet are in'. Many local co-operative societies entered the housing business in the later nineteenth century. The Bishop Auckland society first provided some houses for its paid staff in 1888 and then in 1897 began to help members to buy houses; by 1909 it had provided 1,400 mortgages. The Crook society entered the mortgage business in 1899, and by 1914 had advanced nearly £35,000 to members in loans for this purpose. At Wallsend[83c] the co-operative society began to build houses to sell to members in the late 1860s, and such streets as Mutual Street, Equitable Street, Provident Terrace and Rochdale Terrace still stand as examples of the solidly built houses erected under the aegis of this Tyneside society[84].

In the last years of the nineteenth century and the early twentieth century the predominance which the co-operative societies had acquired in many parts of the region, and the position of many small independent shops, were challenged by the arrival on the scene of a variety of chain stores[85]. Between 1895 and 1914 the Duncan firm, beginning in South Shields, gradually extended its sphere till it controlled eight shops in various Tyneside towns. Bulk wholesale buying and keen and careful management were the advantages to be exploited. More notable was the enterprise created by J. W. Brough, who came from a family well established in wholesale provision dealing. Brough made a carefully planned incursion into the mining districts, with a programme designed to undercut the existing co-operative and other stores in supplying a range of necessary goods. Costs were kept to a bare minimum, and the basis of success was the offering of standard kinds of food in sizeable quantities to meet a housewife's needs for periodic replenishing of food in constant use. In the mid-1890s Brough sold sugar in quarter-stones at 5d., when other shops were selling at 2d. or 2½d. per lb. Travelling salesmen toured mining villages and similar communities, canvassing orders, and an extensive system of van deliveries was organized. By 1906 branch depots had been established at Ashington, Bedlington, Gateshead, Crook and Stanley, apart from a number of Newcastle establishments; in the next few years the tentacles were extended to at least nine other centres within the region. Each local branch employed about 30 men; for most of them the first part of each was spent on the road securing orders, mid-week was spent in making up orders, while Friday and Saturday saw delivery and obtaining payment. Business was on a strictly cash basis. Even in areas where co-operative societies had earlier established a strong position they found it difficult to meet this strong and forceful competition.

These are only two examples of a series of chains established within the region during these years. They provided an increasing range of goods and economical shopping for working families and formed one important element in a retail sector which was rapidly growing in size and complexity.

Some of the goods sold in these shops also represented the beginnings of significant changes. The later nineteenth century and the early twentieth century saw much greater interest allotted to advertising by many firms, and the gradual increase of 'convenience foods' and similar items in local shops. This was a small beginning, but already the more prosperous working families need not shy away from such items as tinned goods of certain kinds. In 1903, after a successful spell with Lever Brothers, Angus Watson set up his own tinned goods enterprise on Tyneside, his original home[86]. His first successful line was the sale of tinned Norwegian sardines—with the famous 'Skipper' trade name. He spent what was then the considerable sum of £1,000 on his first sustained advertising campaign in 1907. To 'Skipper' sardines he added 'Sailor' tinned salmon, and the 'My Lady' range of tinned fruit; by 1911 he was spending £40,000 to £50,000 on advertising both in Britain and in America. All of these goods were offered to both retailer and consumer with a 'money back if not satisfied' guarantee. Watson was also a pioneer in industrial relations, with profit-sharing by means of an advanced scheme of share distribution to employees; meticulous records of individual workers were kept, but under the joint supervision of a committee of representatives from both management and workers. The kind of goods which this enterprising firm produced were not the first time tinned goods had been seen in the area by any means, but large-scale production and thorough advertising brought them more into the ambit of many families which would have had little or no experience of such a convenient dietary item before.

Distribution of investment

The arrival of 'Skipper' sardines may be taken as exemplifying the arrival by the early twentieth century of higher standards of income and comfort for a high proportion of the region's population, even if significant areas of continuing poverty did remain. The higher standards of living for the great majority had been brought about largely as the result of the tremendous growth in the region's industrial resources which had taken place since 1850. The increasingly rapid population growth of the decades after 1850 had imposed very severe social strains on a society which was in a number of ways ill equipped to cope with them, as we shall see. Moreover, by the time of the First World War there were some precarious aspects to the region's prodigious economic growth. A very high proportion of the region's income and employment was derived from a small number of major industries, and the crucial importance of coal, iron and steel, engineering, shipbuilding, was only thrown into starker relief by the failure of such interests as lead, glass and chemicals to maintain their earlier importance. There had been an increasing tendency for the region's available capital to be concentrated in a handful of major growth sectors. No doubt there were at the time sound commercial reasons for the kind of investment choices which produced this pattern of concentration, but it meant that by the time of the First World War the regional economy rested to a dangerous extent on a very few supports. The 1914–18 war did nothing to remedy this; indeed it exacerbated the situation. There was not a great deal of new investment within the region in long-term productive capacity, and enhanced production during the war was largely the result of more intensive working of existing plant by, for instance, intensifying shift systems. Any expansion that there was took place in those areas vital to the war effort, which again tended to be the few basic industries of the region. Although the progress made during the late nineteenth and early twentieth centuries had been phenomenal and represented an enormous increase in wealth and employment, major changes in demand could see the regional economy facing bleak prospects as the inter-war period was to show. It is, of course, utterly unreasonable to expect that major investment decisions in late Victorian or Edwardian Britain should have been based upon an appreciation of inter-war conditions. We are not dealing with a period in which parliament, government or for that matter anyone else proffered claims to an overall supervision of the national economy. It was very natural that aspiring industrialists and investors should select for their activities the limited range of interests which proffered the most striking opportunities. There was no factor present which could have effectively stressed the potential long-term advantages of a more diversified basis for the regional economy, and it is in any event not at all clear that a wider diversification would have been a sensible policy in the second half of the nineteenth century in the light of the information available at the time. By 1914, however, the regional eggs were lying in an uncomfortably small number of baskets, and if they should fall the damage would be proportionately great.

Nevertheless, if these dangers lay in the future, the achievements of the regional economy between 1850 and 1920 were phenomenal. In the early twentieth century not only were Northumberland and Durham supporting very many more people than ever before, but the rapid increase in population had been accompanied, not by a general drop in the standard of living but overall by a significant improvement in the standard of living of the overwhelming majority of the region's inhabitants. The unprecedented increase in population and the unforseeable transformation of the regional economy posed difficult problems of social adjustment; by 1920 considerable progress had already been made in coping with the most damaging effects of prodigious growth in a little governed society. Some of the aspects of this process form the subject of the next chapter.

References

1   W. Ashworth, *A Short History of the International Economy*, 3rd edn, 1975, pp. 214–15.

2   N. R. Elliott, 'A Geographical Analysis of the Tyne Coal Trade', *Tijdschrift voor Econ. en Soc. Geografie*, March–April 1968, p. 85 et seq.

3   R. Smith, *Sea-Coal for London*, 1961, p. 283.

4   D. J. Rowe, 'Occupations in Northumberland and Durham', *Northern History*, vol. VIII, 1973, pp. 119–31.

5   Bank of England, Newcastle Branch, correspondence, 10 February 1853.
    D. J. Rowe, 'The Economy of the North-East in the Nineteenth Century', *Northern History*, vol. VI, 1971, p. 130.

6a J. F. Davidson, *From Collier to Battleships*, 1946, p. 40.
  b Smith, op. cit., pp. 286–7.

7   Smith, op. cit., p. 285.
    C. Winchester, *Shipping Wonders of the World*, vol. II, c. 1936, p. 1321.

8   J. Ward, 'Landowners and Mining', in J. Ward and R. Wilson, eds, 'Land and Industry', 1971, pp. 63–116.

9   C. Mountford, *The History of John Bowes and Partners up to 1914*, M.A. Thesis, Durham University, 1967.

10 W. G. Armstrong et al., *The Industrial Resources of Tyne, Wear and Tees*, copy in Newcastle Central Library, inter-leaved with additional material.

11 G. Hardy, *The Londonderry Railway*, 1925, p. 105.

12 Ward, op. cit., p. 84.

13 Bank of England, op. cit., 9 May 1872.

14 Horden Collieries Ltd, *75,000,000 Tons of Coal*, 1946, pp. 3–4.
    National Coal Board, *Horden Colliery*, pp. 1–5.

15 R. A. S. Redmayne, *Men, Mines and Memories*, 1942, p. 154.

16 Durham Coal-Owners' Association, *Wages and Trade Customs, 1874*, 1875, p. 310.

17 Redmayne, op. cit., p. 159.

18 ibid.

19 H. W. Richardson and J. M. Bass, 'The Profitability of Consett Iron Company Before 1914', *Business History*, vol. VII, no. 2, 1965.
    A. S. Wilson, *The Consett Iron Company Limited: A Case Study in Victorian Business History*, M.Phil. Thesis, Durham University, 1973.

20 I. Bullock, 'The Origins of Economic Growth on Teesside, 1851–81', *Northern History*, vol. IX, 1974, pp. 79–95.

21 Bank of England, op. cit., 20 February 1841.

22 R. W. Johnson, *The Making of the Tyne*, 1895, p. 246.

23 J. W. House, *The North East*, 1969, pp. 122–4.

24 Anon., *Historical Sketch of Forth Bank Engine Works*, 1887, p. 14.
   B. C. Browne, *Selected Papers of Benjamin Chapman Browne*, 1918.
25 F. W. D. Manders, *A History of Gateshead*, 1973, pp. 66–70.
26 Browne, op. cit., pp. 166–8.
   W. Maw, *The Story of Rutherford Grammar School*, 1964, pp. 48–9, 56.
27 D. Dougan, *The History of North East Shipbuilding*, 1968, pp. 44–6.
28 J. Wigham Richardson, *Memoirs*, 1911, pp. 125, 71.
29 ibid., pp. 143–4.
30 R. P. Kent, 'A Trip Down the River Tyne', *Tyne Industrial Archaeology Group Newsletter*, no. 13, March 1975, p. 4.
31 Dougan, op. cit., pp. 44–6.
32 ibid., p. 77.
33 ibid., p. 46.
34 House, op. cit., p. 170.
35 Dougan, op. cit., pp. 237, 233.
36 Bank of England, op. cit., 22 March 1854.
37 Bank of England, Newcastle Branch Correspondence, *passim*.
38 Dougan, op. cit., p. 119 et seq.
39 A. Cochrane, *The Early History of Elswick*, 1909.
   D. Dougan, *The Great Gun Maker*, 1971.
   J. D. Scott, *Vickers: A History*, 1962.
40 M. D. Noble, *A Long Life*, 1925, p. 82.
41 N. McCord, 'A Naval Scandal of 1871: The Loss of H.M.S. Megaera', *Mariners' Mirror*, vol. 57, 1971, pp. 115–34.
42 R. Hough, *The Big Battleship*, 1966.
43 F. Manning, *The Life of Sir William White*, 1923, p. 140.
44 Dougan, op. cit., pp. 93–4.
45 R. Bell, *Twenty-five Years of the North Eastern Railway*, pp. 28–9.
   R. A. S. Hennessey, *The Electric Revolution*, 1972.
46 Anon., *County Borough of Tynemouth, 1849–1949*, 1949, p. 90.
47 C. J. Hunt, *The Lead Miners of the Northern Pennines*, 1970.
   L. Turnbull, *The History of Lead Mining in the North East of England*, 1975.
48 Hunt, op. cit., p. 41.
49 Bank of England, op. cit., 10 February 1853.
50 W. A. Campbell, 'The Newcastle Chemical Society and its Illustrious Child', *Chemistry and Industry*, 1968, p. 1463.
   W. A. Campbell, *The Old Tyneside Chemical Trade*, 1964.
   W. A. Campbell, *A Century of Chemistry on Tyneside, 1868–1968*, 1969.
51 Bank of England, op. cit., 3 July 1856.
52 Bank of England, op. cit., 20 May 1858, 11 September 1858.
53 J. Collingwood Bruce, *Handbook to Newcastle upon Tyne*, 1889, pp. 135–6.
54 Johnson, op. cit., pp. 156–8.

55 M. Milne, *Newspapers of Northumberland and Durham*, 1971, pp. 54–5.
56 Campbell, op. cit.
57 Anon., *A Descriptive Account of Newcastle*, c. 1894, p. 88.
    Newcastle Central Library, ephemera published by Hedley.
58 C. F. Maidwell, *A Short History of Paper Making in the North East*, 1959.
59 Bank of England, op. cit., 26 May 1868.
60 W. C. Mitchell, *History of Sunderland*, 1919, pp. 157–8.
61 Collingwood Bruce, op. cit., p. 139.
    R. C. Bell, *Tyneside Pottery*, 1971, p. 6.
62 Manders, op. cit., p. 65.
63 Mitchell, op. cit., p. 149.
64 Viscountess Ridley, 'The History of Glass-making on the Tyne and Wear', *Archaeologia Aeliana*, 4th ser., vol. XL, 1962, pp. 154–62.
65 G. B. Hodgson, *The Borough of South Shields*, 1907, p. 364.
66 S. A. Staddon, *Sunderland Corporation Transport*, 1973.
67 B. C. Kennedy and P. J. Marshall, *British Bus Fleets, No. 10, North Eastern Area*, c. 1965, pp. 18–25.
68 Wigham Richardson, op. cit., p. 205.
69 ibid., pp. 253–4.
70 E. Lloyd, *History of the Crook Co-operative Society*, 1916, p. 188.
71 Anon., *A Descriptive Account of Newcastle*, c. 1894, p. 135.
72 D. D. Dixon, *Whittingham Vale*, 1895, p. 139.
73 Anon., *Notes on the Leading Industries of the River Tyne*, 1886, p. 8.
74 W. Wood, *North Sea Fishers and Fighters*, 1911.
    Anon., *The Fishing Port of North Shields*, c. 1911.
75 *The Fishing Port of North Shields*, p. 11.
76 Newcastle Chamber of Commerce, *Year Book and Commercial Review*, 1911, p. 23.
77 Collingwood Bruce, op. cit., p. 43.
78 H. E. Armstrong, *Report on Recently Increased Death Rate of the City*, 1883, p. 10.
    H. E. Armstrong, *Report on the Milk Supply*, 1895, p. 6.
79 *Report by the Medical Officer of Health on the Manufacture of Ice Creams*, 1898, p. 3.
80 *Report of the Proceedings of the Business Jubilee of Alderman G. B. Bainbridge, J.P.*, 1917.
81 R. Pound, *The Fenwick Story*, 1972.
82 *Newcastle Weekly Chronicle*, 30 June 1877.
83a Lloyd, op. cit.
  b T. Readshaw, *History of the Bishop Auckland Industrial Co-operative Society*, 1910.
  c Anon., *Jubilee History and Handbook, Wallsend Industrial Co-operative Society*, 1912.

84 *Jubilee History and Handbook, Wallsend Industrial Co-operative Society*, 1912, pp. 56-7, 61-2, 77.

85 P. Mathias, *Retailing Revolution*, 1967, p. 73 et seq.

H. G. Ellis, *Broughs Limited*.

86 A. Watson, *My Life*, 1937.

4 The Problems of Social Adjustment to Industrialization

Housing and public health

The great series of sanitary investigations and reports accumulated in the years around 1850 demonstrated that the North East, in common with many other parts of the country, faced serious problems in such areas as housing and public health. They showed also that, while most of the worst conditions existed in the growing urban areas, those black spots represented concentrations of problems which existed also in various other communities within the region—country towns, rural villages and even fishing hamlets. Hexham was not a town at the centre of significant industrialization, but the inspecting engineer, Robert Rawlinson, had this to say of the state of Hexham in 1852[1]:

> I enquired for the return of the mortality, and found that, for the last 7 years, it was actually some 27½ in the thousand, but with 'cooked' returns it was 24 in the thousand. . . . I then traced disease to crowded room tenements, undrained streets, lanes, courts, and crowded yards, foul middens, privies and cesspools. The water I found was deficient in quantity and most objectionable in quality, dead dogs being lifted out of the reservoir. . . . I am staying at the best hotel in town, but there is no water closet, only a filthy privy at some distance.

It may well be that many of these conditions were of long standing, brought now for the first time under effective scrutiny and publicity.

Already, however, it was plain that the worst concentrations of social problems were to be found in those centres which had already seen substantial growth in economic activity and population. Rawlinson had this to say of parts of Gateshead in 1850[2]:

> Neither plan nor written description can adequately convey to the mind the true state and condition of the room-tenements and of the inhabitants occupying them. The subsoil on the sloping side of the hill is damp and most foul, the brickwork of the buildings is ruinous, the timber rotten; and an

appearance of general decay pervades the whole district. The buildings fronting to Hillgate have originally been erected as residences of a superior character, the stairs have had carved balusters; the rooms have been fitted up with various forms of decoration, which only serve at present to heighten the grim misery which pervades them. Single rooms are let off as tenements which are crowded with men, women and children; the walls are discoloured with age, damp and rot; the windows are broken, old rags, straw and boards occupying the place of glass, so that means of light and ventilation are alike absent.

To the problems which already existed at mid-century were now to be added the consequences of still more rapid economic growth and increase in population. In the second half of the nineteenth century the population of Northumberland almost doubled, rising from 304,000 in 1851 to 603,000 in 1901; the growth of population in County Durham was even more startling, from 391,000 to 1,187,000. Growth rates such as these would have imposed serious strain in any context; in a little-governed society which already possessed an accumulation of social problems the strains were especially acute.

Even in places where some kind of original planning accompanied early economic development, the unexpected pace of expansion could have adverse effects. The proprietors of the original Middlesbrough site had formulated a 'garden city' plan for the infant town envisaged in the first period of growth connected with the building of the early railways. A regular grid layout had been planned, with housing plots allotted the considerable area of 60 feet by 200 feet. These ambitious calculations were overthrown by the unforeseen boom in the iron and steel industry in the years after 1850[3]: 'It was soon found necessary to subdivide the 200-foot plots, and back-to-back houses were often built in the courts, within the reduced plots or in alleys which led on to the main streets.' The wife of one of the leading Teesside iron-masters vividly described the atmosphere in which the original 'garden city' concept was overtaken[4]:

There springs, and too rapidly, into existence a community . . . the members of which must live near their work. They must therefore have houses built as quickly as possible; the houses must be cheap, must be as big as the workman wants, and no bigger; and as they are built, there arise, hastily erected, instantly occupied, the rows and rows of little brown streets, of the aspect that in some place or another is familiar to all of us. A town arising in this way cannot wait to consider anything else than time and space: and none of either must be wasted on what is merely agreeable to the eye, or even on what is merely sanitary. . . . It is, unhappily, for the most part a side issue for the workman whether he and his family are going to live under healthy conditions. The main object of his life is to be at work; that is the one absolute necessity.

In some of the rapidly developing centres the pressures of population growth on an already inadequate housing stock were exacerbated by limitations on the supply of land available for new building. At Newcastle the extensive and inalienable Town Moor to the north of the town limited the possibilities of expansion away from the river in that direction. Gateshead was for many years ringed by landed estates, and it was only in the years after 1860 that substantial areas of land were released for house building. At South Shields the principal landowner was the Dean and Chapter of Durham, whose capacity to sell or lease was severely restricted by legal limitations. Even where such handicaps did not exist, urban land was normally expensive, often too expensive for the erection of workers' houses to be economically feasible.

Much of Newcastle's early industrial growth took place in or near the town centre. With such large works as those of Hawthorn and Stephenson in this district, and the absence of any effective system of local transport, there was serious pressure on the available housing stock, leading to some of the worst conditions to be found anywhere in Britain[5]. In 1865 the town's population had increased by about half in 20 years and amounted to some 122,000. A council report listed 9,639 families living in single-room homes, 6,191 families in two-room homes. Of these nearly 14,000 people were without 'water closet or privy accommodation of any sort'. Newcastle's death rate was then 36.7 per 1,000 annually; Liverpool, at 33.1 per 1,000 was the only other British city with a rate above 30 per 1,000. By 1901 Newcastle's population was to rise to more than 215,000.

The Public Health Act of 1848 had set a yardstick of a death rate of 23 per 1,000 as representing a situation so bad that the central government could insist on the creation of a Local Board of Health to take steps to improve matters. Newcastle had a crude death rate of 24.8 per 1,000 on average for the years 1874-9, Middlesbrough a rate of 23.96 per 1,000 in 1871-3 and Gateshead a rate of 22.9 per 1,000 in 1881-3. It was not until after 1901 that Newcastle's rate fell permanently below 20 per 1,000. The towns in the North East occupied regularly places near the top of the list in all contemporary assessments of such social problems as death rates, infant mortality and overcrowding. For example, in a table of urban areas, arranged to show the density of overcrowding in 1907, the top five towns in Britain were Gateshead, South Shields, Tynemouth (essentially North Shields), Newcastle and Sunderland, while West Hartlepool, Middlesbrough and Stockton, though not quite so bad, were still high in the comparative table[6]. In 1891, 34% of the population of County Durham was living at a density of more than two per room, while in Northumberland the situation was even worse, at over 38%. The figures for some individual towns were Gateshead 40.8%, Newcastle 32.9% and Sunderland 32.9%. In comparison London, at just under 20%, provided the worst situation outside the North East.

However, the same census material shows that the bad conditions were by no means limited to the towns, for the mining communities of Ashington in

Northumberland at 32.2%, and Houghton-le-Spring in Durham at 27.0%, were also notable black spots. In addition to overcrowding many mining communities showed the other evils which overcrowding and poor sanitation normally brought[7]. There was a striking difference, for example, in the pattern of deaths between mining and farming communities within the region. In the agricultural communities, roughly half the deaths occurred within the age group 0 to 60 years, and the other half at older ages. In mining communities, half of the total deaths occurred within the age range 0 to 5 years, a high proportion in the age group 5 to 15 years, with the remainder spread unevenly over the older age groups.

All this seems to present terrifying testimony to the adverse social effects of rapid industrialization. It is not, however, as simple as that. The overall county figures for overcrowding in 1891 are themselves very high, with the more rural county of Northumberland significantly worse than the more industrialized Durham. As late as 1911 Norham and Islandshire, an overwhelmingly rural area of North Northumberland, returned a figure of 34.1% living at a density of at least two per room. It seems then that we should be careful to avoid too easy an assumption that such social problems as overcrowding can simply be seen as an adjunct to industrial and urban growth. As in earlier periods, it may well be that these social problems should be regarded as regional features rather than as just urban and industrial. Other regions in Britain saw during these years comparable economic development and population growth without, for instance, comparable statistics of overcrowding; rural areas of Northumberland could produce very bad overcrowding figures without marked economic development or population growth. The evidence seems to suggest the existence within the region of a low level of housing expectation and provision when compared with other regions, and this too may represent a situation with roots deep in the past.

Yet if the towns and the other communities which were the focus of rapid industrial growth were not unique in their tribulations, the concentrations of the problems in urban areas made them more serious and more obvious. Before the end of the nineteenth century there were, however, already some signs of improvement. In the 1890s, for instance, although the population was still rising the density of overcrowded housing fell, though slowly; between 1891 and 1901 the proportion of the population living at a density of more than two per room declined from 34% to 28% in County Durham, and from 38% to 32% in Northumberland. The provision of additional housing was not a smooth or continuous progress, but a fluctuating trend. Gateshead, for example, saw two main bursts of housing activity in the later nineteenth century, both connected with the availability of land for building purposes. In the 1860s and 1870s land was released from the Park estate on the east and the Shipcote estate on the west side of the town. During these decades the construction of many terraces of small houses for workers took place, and the provision of houses grew more rapidly than population, so that despite an increase in population from 33,589 in 1861 to 65,845 in 1881 the numbers of persons per house dropped from 7.69 to 7.24. By 1881, however, the supply of available land had dried up again, and the trend was reversed during most of the 1880s, with population growth outstripping house-building. From the late 1880s further supplies of land came on to the market, and a second local building boom followed, with a significant improvement in the size of houses built in comparison with those of c. 1865–75. Even so, the renewed building did no more than keep pace with the increase in population continuing into the early twentieth century.

Similar fluctuations in the provision of new housing occurred in other towns, with a good deal of local variation despite the relationship which existed between housing activity and the prosperity of the communities involved. At Middlesbrough local government records show that, while 347 new houses were planned on average during the years 1865–70, the number rose to 1,027 between 1871 and 1876 and then fell from a peak of 1,416 in 1875 to only 31 in 1880. House-building in Middlesbrough remained generally at a low level in the 1880s at a time when it was showing higher figures on Tyneside—and even at West Hartlepool, only a few miles away. Within the region as a whole, however, there was a marked increase in house-building during the years on either side of 1900.

The slow progress towards higher standards of housing was to be seen too in the mining communities in the later nineteenth century[8]. The late 1860s and early 1870s were very good years for many collieries, and increased profits were often reflected in some degree of improved housing provision. Some of the new mining villages erected in these years, Cambois in Northumberland and Esh Winning in Durham, for example, were markedly better in housing and sanitation than many older ones. Much of the worst conditions within mining communities occurred in places like Bedlington, Spennymoor, Houghton-le-Spring, where the core of old villages became tenemented with the poorer strata of mining society, often including many Irish families. The 1872 Public Health Act was an important factor in clearing up the worst conditions in mining communities and in facilitating the provision of decent drainage and similar improvements.

Improvement in housing and sanitation brought with it improvements in health. While epidemics continued to strike in various forms, some of the worst varieties were in decline. Newcastle had suffered 412 deaths in the 1849 cholera epidemic; the rural town of Alnwick suffered 140 deaths in a month—12 times the town's usual death rate—so that again it was not just the industrial areas which suffered. Newcastle paid the price for neglect during the cholera epidemic of 1853, when a catastrophic 1,533 died. At the same time, however, the way forwards was pointed by the nearby town of North Shields, where only 12 died in 1853, largely because of the strenuous exertions of a reforming doctor, Greenhow. Smallpox continued to be a source of recurring epidemics. At Middlesbrough an outbreak of 1897–8 involved 1,411 cases and 198 deaths. Newcastle's smallpox outbreak of 1903–5 however was the last serious visitation of the kind, and this decline was typical of many of the great killer diseases of the past. Typhus saw a marked fall in the number of cases from the 1870s, and the combination of improvements in medicine, public health and housing conditions meant that local death rates, though still distinctly high by national standards, had shrunk considerably by the early years of the twentieth century.

A further significant factor of the same kind was an improvement in the water supply of many places, though again the timing of this improvement varied very considerably from place to place. At North Shields, for example, a report of 1851 had this to say about the water supply[9]:

> Nothing is more certain than that among the inhabitants of North Shields there is a great deficiency of water. In all parts of the town there is want of it and some of the most needy localities are entirely deprived of any regular supply. One of the worst of these is the township of Shields, where there is more filth of habitations and uncleanliness of person and much more disease and mortality than in any other part of the locality.

It was not until after an Act of 1897 that North Shields came to possess a decent supply of water, when Tynemouth borough council took powers to supersede the very unsatisfactory company which had prevailed earlier; as recently as 1892 the company had been forced by court injunction to abandon an especially polluted source. On the other hand, large areas of East Durham were better provided at a much earlier date, owing to the extensive work of the Sunderland and South Shields Water Company, founded in 1852. That company's chain of steam-powered water pumping stations—Fulwell 1852, Cleadon 1863, Ryhope 1869, Dalton 1877 and Seaton 1896—provided access to reliable water supplies to the towns of Sunderland and South Shields and to smaller communities in the area. Hartlepool received its water company in 1846, and the economic developments of the area necessitated the application of expanded facilities; in 1866, for example, the company's directors decided that[10] 'the workmen at the New Engine and Engine House have a Barrel of Ale and Bread and Cheese provided when the Engine commences to Pump Water'.

As late as the same year part of East Newcastle received water which had previously passed through a cemetery and had absorbed the graveyard drainage. Between 1870 and 1890, however, there was a major programme of new works; the Newcastle water company built a series of new reservoirs in rural catchment areas and continued to add new resources in the early twentieth century. By 1914 this company, which could not supply $1\frac{1}{2}$ million gallons of safe water in the early 1850s, could readily meet a daily demand of more than 20 million gallons. The improvement in water supply within the region in the later nineteenth century owed much to technical developments, and to the emergence of competent specialists in the field, such as the engineer, Thomas Hawksley, who was responsible for the design of more than 150 waterworks installations, including examples within this region at Darlington, Durham, Middlesbrough, Newcastle, Stockton, Sunderland and Weardale.

The problems of water supply also affected much smaller communities, such as mining villages, but here again substantial progress had been made by the end of the nineteenth century[11]. Especially in Northumberland, many smaller communities continued to depend on wells until far into the twentieth century, and the work of water companies was essentially confined to the more heavily populated areas in the south of the county. Some of the local sanitary authorities created after the Public Health Act of 1872 were soon active in this field, but many were not. The Bedlingtonshire authority had by 1876 brought a decent water supply to its whole area at a cost to the local ratepayers of some £13,000, and the nearby Cowpen authority spent £11,200 on similar work during the 1870s. In County Durham the situation was rather different, for in the more southerly county the work of water companies was more widespread. A number of mining communities received a supply from the Weardale and Shildon Water Company, for instance, a supply drawn from moorland sources and described by an unkind critic as being 'the colour of India Pale Ale, and a slight taste of pond'. It is probable that by 1880 just under half of County Durham's colliery villages had been brought into the network of supply by water companies, and those so supplied included many of the larger mining communities. In general, by 1914 polluted water supplies, for so long a killer, were rarely a problem within the region.

The share of official responsibility for the various improvements in social conditions which marked this period as a whole was for many years quite small, for the machinery of central and local government did not rapidly overcome the weaknesses which existed early in the nineteenth century. The attitude of many taxpayers and ratepayers towards increased public expenditure was not to be transformed overnight. The report of the commissioners appointed to enquire into the cholera outbreak of 1853, in describing how far the powers made available by the 1848 Public Health Act had been applied in Gateshead noted that[12]:

> . . . in the actual exercise of those powers, the Local Board does not appear ever to have lagged behind, but on the contrary to have been generally in advance of public opinion in the borough, and of the views and wishes of the ratepayers at large . . . the main obstruction thereto appears to have consisted in the impatience of sanitary rates on the part of the ratepayers at large, who have hitherto been more alive to the direct pressure of those rates than to the indirect effect of unremedied sanitary evils upon life and death, and ultimately upon the poor rates.

Time and again sanitary reformers resorted to prodigies of arithmetic to try to persuade ratepayers that a relatively small expenditure in prevention might save much larger sums in future costs incurred by the continuance of bad sanitary conditions. Proposals for new sewage works were often accompanied by inflated estimates of the likely profits to be obtained by entry into the manure trade, or by the growing of crops on land associated with sewage works. In 1892, for example, ratepayers at Alnwick, which was badly in need of improved sanitary provision, were told that[13] 'no profit is normally found to arise from Sewage Works, it being considered satisfactory if working expenses and labour, seeds and plants, be about repaid by sale of Crops—the object being to carry on the Works efficiently at the least cost practicable'. Many of these calculations appeared distinctly unconvincing, but there may have been some basis for them; one victim of a typhoid epidemic at Houghton-le-Spring in 1898 was said to have contracted the disease while visiting a local sewage works to examine an unusually large cabbage[14].

Local newspapers noted that the Tynemouth borough elections were unusually hotly contested in 1877; the heat had been imported by the council's decision to raise the salary of the Borough Surveyor, and councillors facing re-election who had voted for this were defeated[15]. After a considerable struggle local reformers as Wallsend were successful in bringing about the creation of an administrative Local Board, in 1866[16]. For many years this proved only a Pyrrhic victory, however, for at the ensuing elections for the new authority 'economists' swept the board. The board's expenditure for 1867–8 was as follows —scavenging, £2 14s. 0d.; rent of board room and cleaning, £6 9s. 4d.; sundries, 13s. 7d.; in addition a very small loan was raised to lay a short length of sewer, and that was all. Later in 1868 the growing area of Carrville managed to persuade the board to provide nine street lamps at an annual cost of £24; in Wallsend local politics of the day this was a substantial victory for progress. In September of the same year the board voted by six to two against a proposal to flag and drain one of the main streets; in December they turned down a proposal to light the short but important stretch of street connecting the railway station to the high street—the board's chairman remarked 'that such as were compelled to be in the place after dark might provide themselves, as their fathers had to do, with lanterns'. The population of Wallsend was nearly 10,500 in 1871.

Nor was it the case that all ratepayers were rich by any means. One important brake on the expansion of local government expenditure was that the level of rates could be a major item in the finances of the poorer ratepayers, especially in times of depression when demands for increased expenditure were likely to rise. During a major strike on Tyneside in 1886 the Newcastle Board of Guardians was reluctant to accept pleas for large increases in poor law outdoor relief, explaining that[17] 'a considerable proportion of the rates are drawn from a class very little removed from pauperism, who had a hard struggle to pay the demands made upon them by the Overseers, and that any considerable increase to their burdens would have the effect of causing them to become paupers'.

Where a very high proportion of local government expenditure had to be drawn from local rates, and ratepayers included many people—small shopkeepers, for example—who were by no means rich, local authorities elected by a ratepaying electorate were under continuous pressure for economical administration.

There is equally little sign of any great popular enthusiasm for increased intervention and increased expenditure by agencies of central government. In 1876, for instance, the members of the Crook co-operative society, mostly miners, met to celebrate the opening of a new shop. They warmly applauded the views expressed by a visiting radical from Newcastle[8]:

> When, in a country like this, they raise for the government yearly the sum of £70,000,000, and they had the confounded impudence to tell them it is not enough, was it not time the people stood upon their independence, and told the government that, if they could not conduct the business of the nation in a better manner than to be compelled to spend £75,000,000 a year, it was time they went away, and that somebody else took their places?

This kind of economical pronouncement was not simply the result of a selfish reluctance to part with money, for there was still a good deal of evidence about to suggest that official agencies were not necessarily paragons of efficiency or integrity. The records of the Hexham Rural Sanitary Authority provide eloquent evidence on this point[19]. In 1876 the Local Government Board, after repeated failures to elicit from the Rural Sanitary Authority any reply to a number of important queries, threatened to procure the dissolution of the local authority. Some years later the chairman of the Rural Sanitary Authority was complaining bitterly to the Local Government Board about ineptitude at the centre; the main grievance was the Local Government Board's protracted failure to confirm the Rural Sanitary Authority by-laws, and it subsequently transpired that the by-laws had been lost in the Local Government Board's Whitehall office. A County Durham incident of 1879 was of a similar import[20]. Plans for an extension to the workhouse hospital and for new building at the Wesleyan school at Houghton-le-Spring were sent by their respective sponsors to different sections of the Local Government Board. Both were confirmed, with the result that the workhouse's new wards for infectious diseases were sited next to the school extension, a conjunction which reflected no credit on the agents of either central or local authority. It is easy to assume that because an official agency takes up a certain task it can be accepted that the task will be carried out with reasonable skill. This may have been very often the case, but it was not always so.

Local government

Local authorities still found it difficult in the later nineteenth century to recruit and retain suitable staff, and ratepayers still objected to the paying of adequate salaries to public officials—salaries which would, of course, in some cases be higher than the incomes of many ratepayers. Although the general level showed improvement, there were still enough cases of officials of poor quality to substantiate popular doubts as to the efficacy of government agencies. In August 1851 John Scott, who combined the functions of paid assistant poor law overseer for a central Newcastle parish and local tax-collector, left Newcastle ostensibly on a visit to the Great Exhibition; it subsequently transpired that he had fled abroad after embezzling some £3,000 of public money[21]. Within the Houghton-le-Spring Poor Law Union, one of the union's original relieving officers survived 13 years of repeated complaints that he neglected his duties, until in 1864 he was forced to resign. In 1872 Joseph Elliott was appointed in place of his father, who had served as another of this union's relieving officers for many years in a competent fashion[22]. The son proved less satisfactory, and the mid-1880s saw repeated complaints against him for neglect of duty; in August 1885 he was suspended and then resigned after he had failed to pay the approved weekly allowances to 19 paupers in his district. During a severe trade depression in 1885–6 ratepayers in the South Shields Poor Law Union mounted an aggressive campaign for spending cuts, making reductions in official salaries a main target. The Board of Guardians bowed to the storm, and among other cuts reduced the stipend of their part-time clerk, G. W. Mitchell, from £220 to £125; when Mitchell retired a few years later, an audit showed that he had in the meantime evened things up by dipping his hand frequently into union funds[23]. In 1880 the Inspector of Nuisances employed by the Brandon Urban Sanitary Authority in County Durham fled to the U.S.A. with that authority's petty cash[24]. He seems to be the only example in the region of dishonesty among that category of official, but his colleagues in similar posts varied from the very good and effective to some who were barely literate. In 1899 Alan Cameron, collector of the water rate for Newbottle and Penshaw, was sentenced to 12 months imprisonment for embezzling public funds[25]. Throughout the period there was a constant trickle of cases, often well-publicized cases, in which public officials were shown as either incompetent or dishonest. Even if the general level of service was much better, these cases had a marked effect on a public opinion predisposed to view official activities with suspicion.

Central government agencies tried to persuade elected local authorities to pay decent salaries to their officials, but they met with little response. The Hartlepool Poor Law Union was frequently held up as a model to others because of the notable economy with which it conducted its affairs. The Poor Law Board in London, and its successor, the Local Government Board, were, however, unhappy about the cheese-paring attitude towards official salaries which was a part of this economical policy. During the 1860s, like some other poor law unions, the Hartlepool Board of Guardians adopted a practice of insisting that any application for a salary increase must be accompanied by a letter of resignation, so that the guardians could replace the official concerned if they could find someone to perform the duties more cheaply[26]. Even when legal authority existed for pensions to be awarded to retiring officials, some poor law unions sought to wriggle out of the commitment. For example, before pensions were made compulsory it sometimes happened that guardians would appoint a son as a replacement, on condition that he provided a home for the father, and the family waived a pension claim. It seems clear that in adopting practices such as these local authorities were reflecting the views of the ratepaying electorate.

Local police forces were another area of official activity which continued to face problems of recruitment, pay and conditions. During the third quarter of the nineteenth century police expenditure was often a major element in the total of local public spending, and therefore an obvious target for those seeking cheap government. Police were not well paid, and in addition they were subjected to strict discipline. During the prolonged engineering strike of 1871 on Tyneside, which involved a good deal of minor disorder, the Newcastle police force was in a turmoil, with mass resignations provoked by poor pay and cheese-paring administration, as well as the harshness of an overbearing chief constable[27]. As in earlier years the history of the local police forces in the later nineteenth century was punctuated by incidents which demonstrated the continuing difficulty in recruiting and retaining men of adequate calibre. Some of these incidents were not perhaps very serious; in 1887, for example, P.C. Landills of the Northumberland county force[28] 'while conveying two prisoners to Morpeth Gaol took them into a public house at Morpeth from which he delivered them over to gaol drunk, he himself being under the influence of drink'. In 1889, however, a much more serious scandal broke over the same force[29]. There had been in 1879 an ugly burglary at a country rectory, with shots fired by the burglars when they were disturbed. Soon afterwards two men, Brannagan and Murphy, both notorious poachers in the area, were arrested and charged with the crime; at the subsequent trial police evidence was responsible for giving them long terms of penal servitude. In 1889, however, the actual culprits confessed, and it became clear that the police evidence of 1879 had been fabricated. Brannagan and Murphy received a free pardon and £100 each in compensation for every year they had spent behind bars. One incident of this kind could have a much more significant effect on public opinion than a very much greater amount of unobtrusive good service.

In the case of the poor law, which remained a major area of public spending by local authorities, there was another factor which operated to limit public enthusiasm for extended official activity. It still remained the case in this period that the sums spent on relief payments were raised directly from the local community in the form of rates and were spent on local people. In a society which was much more locally orientated than that of later periods, local knowledge of recipients was not always conducive to greater generosity. It was much more likely that instances of fraudulent claims would be locally known, and ratepayers of the late nineteenth century were often well aware from their own knowledge of specific cases that the aged did not always grow old gracefully and that the sick and the weak were not always pleasantly pathetic.

Throughout the history of the old poor law, the new poor law after 1834, and subsequently, the history of the administration of welfare payments was punctuated by cases in which the system was exploited by unscrupulous applicants to obtain benefits to which they were not entitled. For example, during 1886 considerable pressure was put upon the Newcastle board of poor law guardians to persuade them to increase expenditure in doles to those rendered unemployed by a major strike. The guardians refused, partly because of the impact which rate increases would have on poorer ratepayers at a difficult time, but they also explained[30], 'Out-door relief has for many years been, for good reasons, kept down to the lowest point. Relieving officers have found imposture so rife among the applicants that they have wisely done all in their power to put and end to a system so fruitful of evil.' One kind of malpractice which frequently occurred is illustrated by a Durham case of 1910. The Houghton-le-Spring Poor Law Guardians discovered that Robert Richardson, who had been receiving relief for some time, had concealed the fact that he possessed £249 in the Post Office Savings Bank; he was ordered to repay the £65 9s. 6d. of ratepayers' money he had received through this deception. The same board of guardians had been so outraged by another kind of case in 1895 that they had deliberately arranged for full publicity to be given to it in local newspapers. Ann Clark of Dubmire village was recently widowed; on her husband's death she had received a £10 benefit from a friendly society, and had spent £10 14s. 0d. on the funeral, including a £2 10s. 0d. coffin, £1 on cab expenses and £5 on funeral clothing. She had then been destitute and had applied for poor relief for herself and her family; no doubt many ratepayers shared the guardians' view of this improvidence[31].

In addition to those who battened upon relief paid for by local rates when they were, or seemed to be, ineligible, there was another category of case which also tended to alienate the ratepayers whose money was spent on them. Again the Houghton-le-Spring Poor Law Union provides convenient illustration, in a series of cases affecting the workhouse there in the years around 1900[32]. In 1890 Elizabeth Bell, a workhouse inmate, received 14 days' imprisonment for disorderly conduct, and later in the same year two other women from the workhouse were before local magistrates, 'the one for tearing and destroying the bed-clothes, and the other for disorderly and refractory conduct in the workhouse'. In the following year another inmate, Sarah Graham, was before the magistrates for 'very cruel treatment' of an infant. In 1893 John Hall was in trouble for returning to the workhouse drunk, while on one Saturday night in 1894 Joseph Tweedy and John Newton returned to the workhouse drunk and in possession of a bottle of laudanum. In 1902 William Gribbin was given 7 days in gaol for drunkenness; after this escapade he 'on presenting himself for admission to the workhouse in a drunken condition, had owing to his violent conduct, been taken before a Justice and committed to prison for a further period of 14 days'. In 1905 the door of the relieving officer's office was kicked in by a tramp annoyed at being refused a ticket of admission to the workhouse's casual ward for a second night. Incidents of this kind could readily be paralleled, and, while they may have in a few kindled more active sympathies for the poor, it is highly unlikely to have been a general reaction among ratepayers who not only provided the money for relief expenditure but also exercised an effective control over the activities of the local authorities they elected.

It was probably true that both those who defrauded relief agencies and those in receipt of relief who behaved in ways likely to alienate influential opinion were a relatively small category, but their effect on public opinion could be very considerable. The concept of the undeserving poor died hard, if indeed it died, and it only required a small number of well-publicized cases of abuse to provide some kind of foundation for sentiments like those expressed by Alderman Richardson of Newcastle, in opposing a proposal for council-house-building in 1891[33]:

> There was a residuum of the population incapable of helping themselves. The residuum was the result, to a large extent, of hereditary causes, but mainly the result of a life of debauchery, sin and often crime. . . . If it was right and incumbent upon them to provide shelter for these people, it was equally incumbent upon them to provide food and raiment for them. Therefore the Corporation might begin and erect bakehouses and clothing establishments tomorrow. By that means, they would get themselves upon an inclined plane, which would land them in the vortex of pure municipal socialism.

Again this represented sentiments which would have been applauded by many ratepayers of the period, many of them by no means rich.

Yet despite this wide variety of adverse factors, the late nineteenth and early twentieth centuries saw very considerable increases in official government activity, by agencies of both central and local government. Parliament gradually elaborated a network of statutory provisions which brought an unprecedented level of central intervention in local affairs. Several local industries were among the first economic sectors to be subjected to effective systems of inspection and regulation. For example an Act of 1863 laid it down that 90% of the hydrochloric acid gas produced in alkali manufacture must be dissolved in the works rather than be emitted into the atmosphere. Coal-mining was increasingly subjected to an increasing body of regulations, and the Mines Acts of 1887 and 1911 were milestones in this process. Merchant shipping was another major local interest which was subject to an important series of Acts enforcing compulsory standards in such aspects as loading and other factors involving safety. Vested interests affected were often distinctly unenthusiastic about the introduction of controls; on the one hand the more enlightened firms in practice paved the way for national legislation and saw no reason for regulation by official sanctions, while recalcitrant enterprises did not like being forced to adhere to the standards already accepted by their more efficient or enlightened competitors.

Agencies of local government also saw very considerable expansion. In part this was caused by the implementation of national legislation. The Public

Health Act of 1848 and a variety of other piecemeal legislation brought extended functions to most municipalities within the area. The Public Health Act of 1872 completed the pattern of local sanitary authorities invested with powers in such matters as nuisance removal, drainage, water supply and overcrowding, with the new urban and rural sanitary authorities compelled to appoint medical officers of health whose regular reports provided increasingly complete awareness of social improvements which were needed. These officers presented regular monthly reports on the state of their districts to the elected local authorities, and annual reports to the central government. Inspecting officers of the Local Government Board were active in keeping the new sanitary authorities up to the mark. Before this, sanitary matters in most of the mining areas for example had been largely in the hands of parish vestries and overseers, and it was after the reform of 1872 that major improvements in the public health of mining communities were effected. Mining areas and rural areas were further affected by local government reforms of the early 1890s, which saw the creation of urban and rural district councils, a few years after the creation of elected county councils in 1888.

In addition to the creation of new local authorities, older agencies also saw considerable expansion. Once the Poor Law Amendment Act of 1834 had covered England and Wales with a network of poor law unions, it was soon found convenient to use them for a variety of other functions too. They provided the local machinery for the official registration of births, deaths and marriages, and they were often used as agents to gather information and statistics on a wide variety of matters when parliament or central government needed such services. They carried out major schemes of vaccination against smallpox, and in the 1870s and 1880s in particular they played an important role in public health improvement outside the corporate towns—the Rural Sanitary Authorities created under the 1872 Public Health Act were essentially the local poor law guardians wearing a different hat. The workhouses built by local poor law unions in the 1870s and 1880s were very different structures from those of 20 or 30 years earlier—larger, more complex, with much expanded hospital facilities; the present General Hospital at South Shields is a good example of the type, having been built as a union workhouse in the late 1870s. A lyrical 'review' of this new workhouse in the radical *Newcastle Daily Chronicle* on 28 January 1878 shows that contemporaries were themselves deeply impressed by the changes which had taken place.

The rapidly growing towns, however, were the centres of the most impressive growth in local government during the latter part of the nineteenth century, and of the increasing intervention of local authorities in tackling social problems. The regional centre of Newcastle provides good evidence of this but differed only in degree from other urban areas within the region. In 1873 Newcastle Borough Council attached only limited significance to its public health interests. The 'Sanitary Committee' was then in reality only a sub-committee of the Town Improvement and Streets Committee of the council; this situation however, changed during the remainder of the century. By the early twentieth century the Sanitary Committee was a main standing committee of the council. Its membership of 26 normally included some of the council's most influential members and itself had eight standing sub-committees to supervise different elements within its vastly expanded scope of activities. Even before this structural change developed, the council had begun to take a more effective role in such matters as housing controls. Under local Acts powers were taken to tighten the rules laid down to govern new houses, and under by-laws of 1865 and 1870 the council began to enforce such regulations as those governing minimum size of houses, minimum room dimensions, compulsory proportion of windows, and width of lanes and streets.

In 1882 Newcastle's Medical Officer of Health had a staff of a chief and four assistant inspectors of nuisances, a chief and assistant inspector of provisions, and two clerks. By 1907 this had grown to a chief inspector, assistant chief inspector and 19 assistant inspectors of nuisances, a chief inspector and two assistant inspectors of provisions, a superintendent of midwives, six health visitors and six clerks, not counting the substantial staffs employed in the city's own hospitals. By 1911 the city's cleansing department employed well over 500 men. For this function the city was divided into four districts, each controlled by an inspector; each district was divided into eight sub-districts with a foreman to each, and these were further sub-divided into smaller units of organization. After 5 years' service an employee was entitled to a week's holiday with pay, and even before this he could take off up to 8 days a year without pay; no one aged 25 years or over was paid less than £1.30 per week. The tiny band of scavengers of half a century before would have been astonished by the growth and complexity of such organizations; their councillor masters could scarcely have anticipated that in March 1907 the skilled professional who headed Newcastle's cleansing staff would be discussing his work with fellow experts at the quarterly meeting of cleansing superintendents of Great Britain and Ireland[34].

In 1880 the Newcastle Poor Law Union had an establishment of 57, which grew by five within the next few years; the duties assigned to these officials displayed a degree of specialization which would have astonished the handful of officials employed when the union came into existence in 1836[35]. At its creation in the mid-1830s the Newcastle police force numbered 85; by 1911 it had grown to 400[36]. Here too there was a marked increase in sophistication and professionalism as time wore on. For many years after their creation the county police forces of both Northumberland and Durham were headed by chief constables drawn from men who combined experience in the armed forces with an assured position in local society. In 1902, however, after Colonel Eden's retirement, the Durham county force was for the first time headed by a career policeman, who had previously headed smaller forces, first at Reigate and then at South Shields[37].

The multiplication of official positions and the gradual emergence of career structures and professional organizations brought to local government officials new levels of cohesion and influence. Professional administrators organized on both national and local levels. In the years before the First World War, for instance, the Newcastle Municipal Officers' Association published its own regular printed journal, and in its annual report for 1901 noted:

> Subjects of extreme importance to the members have been under consider-
> ation and action has been taken which it is hoped will be for the benefit of the
> members generally. . . . It is hoped that the small proportion of the staff still
> remaining outside the Association will see that it is in their own interests and
> also in the interests of their colleagues as a whole that they should join the
> Association without delay.

National publications such as *The Local Government Chronicle* also provided means for the exchange of information and opinions between local government officers and facilitated their emergence as a pressure group of considerable importance in any matters involving the work of local government.

Census figures give some indication of the considerable rise in the number of public officials during this period[38]. Outside the boroughs the number of those employed in government service rose from 500 in 1851 to 2,486 in 1911 in Northumberland, while the comparable figures for Durham were 385 and 2,587. Equivalent increases took place in the expanding urban areas—in Newcastle from 141 to 1,194, Gateshead from 34 to 291, South Shields from 12 to 225, and Tynemouth from 98 to 216.

One area of considerable growth in official activity was the provision of education. The period before 1870 had seen schooling mainly provided by voluntary unofficial organization, backed by increasing government grants and an expanding government system of inspection and regulation. The Element-ary Education Act of 1870 brought a leap forward in the extent of education directly provided by public sources, although the purpose of the Act was essentially to plug gaps not covered by the voluntary schools. The region's school boards, elected by a ratepaying electorate in the years after 1870, embarked upon a major programme of school-building in many areas. Even so, the achievements could vary considerably from area to area, depending to a considerable extent on local opinion and the capacity of the leading men on the new authorities[39]. At Tynemouth bickering between different local groups resulted in a local scandal at the 1871 school board elections, and the first prosecution for corrupt practices in such elections. Although the Tynemouth board went on to build important new schools for the borough, there was considerable local disquiet at the costs involved. The Western Board School at North Shields, opened in 1872, was designed to house 582 boys and girls in the main building, and 284 infants in another adjacent. The first estimated cost was £5,734, the final expenditure £7,500 with all fittings included; the discrepancy caused serious complaint from ratepayers, and one of the board members was at pains to explain that 'there is no ornamentation in the building . . . the cost about which so much has been said and written, is simply owing to the present high cost of building operations'.

Gateshead was a town which at first sight might appear an unlikely centre for particular success in the expansion of public education. Some of the town's leading employing enterprises faced serious difficulties in the late nineteenth and early twentieth century, including the closure of a number of important engineering works. A significant reduction in the rates to be drawn from such sources did not, however, prevent the Gateshead School Board from showing itself an unusually effective body. A main reason for this was the part played by Robert Spence Watson, a leading member for many years, and a very influential individual in a variety of ways, as well as someone very keen on the improvement of education. The Gateshead School Board was the fourth to be created and in the period 1871–1903 it built 21 schools; the 1902 Education Act abolished the separate education system in local government, but it was not until 1928 that Gateshead received another new school.

In general, however, the years after 1870 saw a rapid growth in the provision of elementary education and in the share contributed directly by public bodies. This growth is also represented in census figures, with a leap in the number of schoolteachers in the years after 1870. Northumberland county had 1,354 teachers in 1861 and 2,315 in 1881; comparable figures for County Durham were 2,086 and 4,349. The picture was the same in the towns; Newcastle's figure rose from 348 to 799, Gateshead's from 86 to 368 and Sunderland's from 245 to 559. Understandably this considerable growth rate was not continued, and in future years the increase in the number of teachers was more or less in step with the rate of population increase.

Overall then the later nineteenth and early twentieth centuries saw unprecedented increases in the scale of official activity by agencies of both central and local government. Although, as we have seen, there were factors such as some deficiencies in the quality of administrative staff, and ratepayers' distrust of increased spending, which acted as brakes on government growth, they were not strong enough to arrest the process. There were other factors at work which in practice outweighed such difficulties as these. In the first instance some of the problems facing the emergent industrial society existed in forms which unofficial activity could not hope to tackle effectively. Problems of housing and public health in places such as Newcastle, Sunderland or Middlesbrough required the intervention of overall municipal authorities armed with substantial legal powers. Despite the continuing trickle of examples of failure in official circles, the general trend was towards higher standards of honesty, efficiency and professional knowledge. There was, however, another factor of crucial importance to the process. The striking economic expansion which marked the second half of the nineteenth century played a part in making some of the social problems which already existed appreciably worse, but it also provided the increased wealth from which extended official institutions could be financed. In the mining area covered by the Houghton-le-Spring Poor Law Union, the population grew from 21,000 in 1836 to 34,000 in 1882, but the assessed rateable value of the property in the area grew from £46,000 to

£151,000[40]. Rateable value of property in Newcastle totalled £449,000 in 1870, but by 1907 had shot up to £1,641,000; comparable figures for Sunderland were £258,000 and £706,000, Gateshead £134,000 and £427,000, South Shields £125,000 and £421,000, West Hartlepool £67,000 and £262,000 and Tynemouth £112,000 and £243,000[41]. These impressive growths were in some slight degree due to improved methods of valuation, but much more to the effects of economic growth. In such circumstances it was possible for local authorities to equip themselves with extended resources without pushing up rate levels too high for ratepayers' distinctly limited tolerance. Even the most economical of local authorities could nerve itself to increased activities as potential rate income increased on such a scale. The Wallsend Local Board was still refusing to pave the High Street there in 1872 but appointed a medical officer of health in 1874 and raised his salary for this part-time appointment to £50 in 1877. In 1882 they added a surveyor at £52 and in 1883 an inspector of nuisances at £40. By 1891 the Wallsend Board was capable of agreeing to build a local hospital at a cost of £6,500. The rateable value had been under £30,000 when the Local Board came into existence; by 1891 it was very nearly £80,000 and was to grow to about £¼ million by the early 1920s with the continuing growth of shipbuilding and other enterprises. In these circumstances the Local Board and its successor, the Borough Council, could face substantial increases in local government expenditure with an equanimity which would have astonished their predecessors of the 1860s[42].

Charitable and other welfare organizations

Yet, if the official agencies of government came to play a much extended role in the region's affairs during this period, the role of unofficial agencies in ameliorating social evils and in pioneering new philanthropic activities continued to be important. Again this can be illustrated by instances of individual philanthropy, instances of the mobilization of charitable funds to meet temporary emergencies, and the work of long-term philanthropic foundations. At Jarrow and at Walker the first hospitals were built by leading local industrialists, Charles Mark Palmer at Jarrow and the shipbuilder, Charles Mitchell, at Walker. Successive building extensions at the Durham County Infirmary, which had been originally built in 1849–50, were made possible largely because of gifts of £10,000 in the 1860s by Dean Waddington of Durham and of £12,000 in the 1880s by John Eden of Beamish Park. At Newcastle the Diamond Jubilee of 1897 was commemorated by the rebuilding of the Infirmary; the contract for the new structure was fixed at £203,527. The Armstrong family and the local ship-owner, John Hall, each gave £100,000 towards the new Infirmary[43]. The first specialized hospital for the treatment of children within the region was opened in 1863 at Hanover Square, Newcastle; in 1888 John Fleming provided this institution with much improved facilities in a new building erected in memory of his wife, while in 1896 Lord Armstrong financed a further extension[44]. These are only a few examples of the many instances within the region of the continued provision of a wide variety of welfare facilities by private endowment. As we shall see the proliferation of such institutions—hospitals, asylums, clinics, convalescent homes, orphanages, sanatoria and many others —was to be a main ingredient in the process which led to the extended public welfare schemes of the later twentieth century.

The continued mobilization of charitable resources to meet pressing temporary needs was repeated time and again throughout the period, but perhaps one good example of this kind of event may suffice. The Hartley Colliery disaster of 1862, in which more than 200 men and boys died, was one of the region's worst colliery disasters. It was followed by a public subscription for the benefit of the dependents of those killed; most of the donations, though by no means all, came from within the region and the collection totalled £81,838. 19s. 5d. The committee set up to administer this fund made grants to meet immediate needs and then went on to work out a scheme of pensions and allowances. Widows were to receive pensions ranging from 10s. 6d. per week for a widow with one child to £1. 1s. 6d. to a widow with six children. These pensions were to cease on remarriage, but such an event would be sweetened by a grant of £20 from the fund. In this case donations received exceeded planned expenditure by about £20,000, and the surplus was invested to provide the nucleus of a fund to meet the need for provision for the surviving victims and dependents of future mining accidents. Similar funds had been established earlier to cope, for example, with the consequences of the cholera epidemic of 1853 and a great fire which devastated large parts of both Newcastle and Gateshead in 1854. The lists of the donors of considerable sums to these various local funds read like lists of the older and the newer dominant minorities within the region, with peers, bishops and landed gentry joined by banks, mines and factories.

Although the major charitable institutions founded in earlier years continued for the most part to carry out their work and to extend it further, there was also a continual creation of new institutions, as different needs became more readily recognized. The problems of getting to grips with the difficulties of the very poor were considerable. Most towns came to possess charitable funds for the supply of clothing and footwear to those who lacked them. In Newcastle, for instance, 2,676 pairs of boots were provided this way in 1909; police forces were in practice responsible for a good deal of philanthropic work among the very poor, and as in many places it was the local policemen who took on the work of distributing the footwear and trying to prevent the boots being subsequently sold[45]. At Sunderland the ship-owner, James Knott, began a similar scheme as a private undertaking, and this work was subsequently taken over in 1898 by the Poor Childrens' Holiday Association, with Knott providing an endowment fund for it.

The Poor Children's Holiday Association provides a good example of the ways in which charities continued to multiply and extend their work. The story of that organization began in June 1891, when the following passage occurred in a letter exchanged between two men involved in the charitable work of a Newcastle evangelical mission[46]:

> If there is anyone in your district convalescent or feeble to whom a *fortnight's stay at the seaside* would be of benefit, I shall be glad to pay for their lodgings, and, if necessary, for their board as well. Are there any street lads in your mission to whom a day at the seaside would be a treat? If so, we might organise a trip.

The first seaside trip organized for poor children took 120 boys and girls to Monkseaton for the day on 11 July of the same year. By 1912 the scheme catered for 12,000, and the Poor Childrens' Holiday Association founded on this basis went on to become the focus of a wide variety of welfare work within the region. It pioneered the provision of special institutions for the treatment of tuberculosis patients, long before there was any public provision of this kind within the area. Rescue work among waifs and strays and in the local courts was also undertaken, and the original holiday and convalescence basis became only part of a wide range of activities undertaken by this association.

An important change came over the administration of many important local charities during the second half of the nineteenth century. Previously the creation and running costs of such activities had been met very largely by donations from the richer groups in society, a situation reflected in the continuation of the patronage system for use of such facilities, described in an earlier chapter. From about 1870 an important change occurred. A significant element in the income of hospitals and similar voluntary institutions was increasingly derived from the multiplication of small regular subscriptions contributed collectively by workers in local factories, shipyards and kindred interests. The old patronage system, which reflected the dependence on substantial donations from relatively few people, ceased to be appropriate in a situation of many small subscriptions, and the constitutions of major local charities were altered to take account of the change. It was in 1861 that the Sunderland Infirmary first began arrangements for penny weekly subscriptions from workers in local firms; in the first year of the scheme's operation these subscriptions totalled £45, but this source of income rapidly grew, as groups of workers recognized the value of such arrangements which gave them ready access to the hospital's facilities. In 1877 the transition was recognized with the abandonment of the old patronage system altogether. At Newcastle Infirmary, a revision of the rules in 1887 abolished the patronage system there, and provided that nine of the governors elected to represent the regular subscribers should serve on the key house committee. Other charities came into line at various dates; it was not until 1899, for example, that the voluntary maternity hospital at Newcastle dropped the patronage system.

A rather similar development saw the arrival of some of the major local trade unions in philanthropic roles. From 1899 the Durham, and from 1900 the

Northumberland, coal-miners possessed subsidiary organizations financed by small regular subscriptions for the purpose of building aged miners' homes, and anyone travelling about the coalfield will see very many examples of the work of these bodies. The initiator of this development was a Durham miner, Joseph Hopper, born at Windy Nook in 1856, and he had a struggle to convince his fellow miners that they should dig into their pockets for this purpose. He received significant encouragement from the more enlightened coal-owners, however, and after 6 years' work the Durham Aged Mine-workers' Homes Association had built more than 200 cottages for aged couples, and a home for single men. By 1924 the figure had reached over 1,000[47]. The mixed pattern of charitable activity can be seen from the variety of origins which produced homes for retired miners—some were built by the miners themselves in increasing numbers, some continued the tradition of being built by the employers, some were built co-operatively in practice by both parties and some were built as war memorials.

There was also a continuing and expanding co-operation between welfare activities carried out by official and unofficial agencies. Society remained highly unequal in a wide variety of ways, and members of the dominant minorities were often found active in both local government and voluntary philanthropic activity. This applied to members of both the older landed aristocracy and the new industrialists. The conditions at Middlesbrough during the period of immense and unforeseen growth in the third quarter of the nineteenth century have been neatly caught in Lord Briggs' description of the town as 'the British Ballarat'[48]. Henry Bolckow played an important role in initiating this economic growth, but his part in the growth of the town was much more than this one contribution. He lived in Middlesbrough until 1856, and in these early years served as an improvement commissioner for both the town and the Tees port. He was the town's first mayor and first M.P., and one of its first magistrates. In addition he was governor of the voluntary infirmary founded there, and a generous benefactor to hospitals, schools, churches and recreational facilities. Bolckow was succeeded in both the mayoralty and the town's parliamentary representation by Isaac Wilson, manufacturer of both iron and pottery, and director of the Stockton and Darlington Railway. Wilson became chairman of the Tees port authority, principal agent of the Middlesbrough ground landlords, chairman of the school board from 1870 to 1888, a director of the local water company and first president of the Mechanics' Institute. With men like this active in public life, Middlesbrough received its first public park, a gift from Bolckow, in 1868, before Newcastle possessed such an amenity, while Middlesbrough attained corporate status as a borough in 1853—Darlington, a much older town, only possessed a local board of health with more limited powers until 1867.

We have already seen how official poor law authorities soon formed the habit of using the facilities of voluntary charities where special categories of poor people were concerned, such as the blind or the deaf and dumb. This process expanded with the multiplication of charitable institutions, and by the early twentieth century had reached impressive proportions, paving the way for the creation of a more extensive state welfare system. When official bodies placed their dependents in voluntary institutions, this entailed more than a trivial connection, for the spending of public money involved some form of public supervision, and it was normal practice for boards of poor law guardians to keep a close eye on the activities of institutions to which ratepayers' money was being paid for such purposes. Guardians were regularly commissioned to visit and inspect the services provided, and these duties were normally taken seriously; it was not uncommon for surprise visits to be arranged, and it was normal for visits to be thorough and followed up by the submission of full reports by the visitors. It is startling to realize just how far this system of co-operation had been taken by the early twentieth century. In 1913, deputations from the South Shields guardians visited the following institutions in which one or more of their board's charges were being maintained at public expense—Wigton Convent of Mercy, Carlisle; St Joseph's Home, Darlington; Lancaster Asylum; Border Counties Home, Carlisle; Carlisle Asylum; St Peter's Home, Gainford; St Mary's Home, Tudhoe; Hospital of St John, Scarton; Storthes Hall Asylum, Huddersfield; Edgeworth Children's Home, Bolton; Sunderland Boys Industrial School; Wellesley Training Ship; Green's Home for Boys; Shotley Bridge Training Home for Girls; Deaf and Dumb Institution, Newcastle; Blind Institution, Newcastle; York City Asylum; Beverley Asylum, Doncaster; Balby Home, Doncaster; Dr Barnardo's Home, Ilford; Field Heath House, Middlesex; Leatherhead School for the Blind; Stoke Park Colony, Bristol; Midland Counties Institution, Chesterfield; Middlesbrough Asylum; Sedgefield Asylum[49]. This one union was connected with a large number of specialized institutions, some of them by that time public in nature, but many of them still operating as unofficial voluntary activities. This kind of co-operation coupled with increasing inspection paved the way for the gradual takeover by official agencies of a varied range of social work first undertaken by unofficial agencies.

Co-operation between official and unofficial resources occurred in a wide variety of other ways too. Especially in the latter part of the nineteenth century it became common for charitable individuals or groups to provide amenities of various kinds for those living in poor law workhouses, for instance. Such donations might include gifts of books, pictures of musical instruments, or a barrel of beer at Christmas. Workhouse children were often taken to shows of various kinds, including pantomimes, or for a day either at the seaside or in the country. Let one example illustrate this increasingly common practice, which by the early twentieth century could be considered society's normal custom. The South Shields poor law guardians privately paid for the workhouse children there to visit the Newcastle Jubilee Exhibition of 1887, and after the trip was over the board of guardians received the following letter (original spelling):[50]

Dear Guardians,

We are glad to let you know that through your kindness we were taken to the Exhibition at Newcastle on Monday. The Guardians who met us at the Tyne Dock Station, wer Mr Thornton, Mr Proud and Mr Oldroyd. We spent such a jolly afternoon and saw lots of things. We always thought to go down a black hole, the pit we were in, we walked straight in We asked the gentleman if he wanted any putters he said he was full up. He took us through. By! what a black hole some of us got lost in the pit at last Mr Thornton and Mr Proud came to seek us to get some cocoa as it was so cold. By! what a canny man Mr Proud is. And by 5 o'clock we had such a good tea far more than we could eat we had to get paper bags to put some in. we went where we had a mind. The people at the Exhibition did not think we came from a workhouse they said we had such good clothes and looked so well, and we were so glad the master said that we had all behaved well. We do not know the Ladies and Gentlemen that gave the money for our Treat but you might tell the Newspaperman to thank them for us. A Gentleman some said his name was Mr Marshall and the Guardians that was with us bought two much big footballs and penholders one each and we spent an afternoon not soon to be forgotten we must not forget the kind officers who are over us.

We are your children

Christopher Thompson	Annie Spittlehouse
John Glancy	Margaret J. Gorman
John Findlay	Margaret Parkin
Thomas Peel	Minnie Hoey.

The improved activities of both official and unofficial welfare agencies, and their inter-action, did not solve the social problems of the area by any means, but they did much to mitigate them, and in general there was a substantial growth in welfare provision during this period. This expansion was not, however, the result of a universal interest in social problems and the welfare of the poor but rather the result of the work of smaller identifiable groups within the region who took an active part in pushing for the creation of better facilities and in the administration of both official and voluntary institutions to help those in need. In an unequal society the most effective contribution was normally made by those who possessed the means and the influence to ensure that note was taken of their views.

The influence of religion

At all social levels the region's society continued to present a marked lack of uniformity in interests, attitudes and aspirations. Instead there continued to be different, even clearly opposed, lifestyles to be found within those in similar economic situations and within even small local communities. One factor of continuing importance which made a significant contribution to the expansion of benevolent agencies was religion. While it remained true that wide reaches of society at varying social levels remained essentially unaffected by this influence, it does not require any very deep historical knowledge but merely modest powers of observation to appreciate that the building and serving of churches and chapels was one of the main communal activities of the later nineteenth and early twentieth centuries—all that is required is to keep eyes open when moving about the region, both in the towns and in smaller communities. Any survey of late Victorian communities will demonstrate the considerable re-sources devoted to church and chapel buildings, even if population growth frequently outstripped these efforts. During the second half of the nineteenth century Stockton received at least 17 new churches and chapels, Darlington at least 20, Sunderland at least 40, Jarrow at least 13 and South Shields at least 30. As the Newcastle suburb of Elswick grew with the expansion of Armstrong's works 15 churches and chapels were built there.

It is possible to suppose that this great investment was merely a pretence and that little genuine religious fervour lay behind this impressive accumulation of religious establishments. It is certainly easy to find examples of unconvincing or pretended zeal or markedly un-Christian behaviour by professed believers, but the evidence is plain for the existence in very many cases of sincere and genuine devotion, including the enthusiastic commitment of many men and women who at various social levels exercised considerable influence among their associates.

Henry Watts was a well-known Sunderland man; first a merchant seaman and then an expert diver, he saved at least 36 lives from drowning. His conversion was a dramatic experience. At the age of 31 years he was taken home dead drunk on New Year's Day 1857, in danger from alcoholic poisoning. On 2 January he became an active, professing and believing Christian, and so he remained for the rest of his long life[51]. The ship-owner and former seaman and captain, Walter Runciman, recalled a well-known local captain of the later nineteenth century, Archibald Wilkie[52]:

> He was a deeply religious man, who believed that the Sabbath should be kept as holy at sea as on shore, and if a gale obliged him to put his vessel under small canvas and it abated on a Saturday night, he would not make sail until midnight on Sunday. He was admired by everybody for his saintly mode of life, but his co-owners were averse to him carrying his belief to such eccentric lengths when on a passage.

It is not perhaps surprising to find that many mining communities were notable centres of religious zeal, in view of the uncertainty of life in both working and living conditions for many years. Although mining communities could also contain a considerable number of ungodly folk, a high proportion of the miners who exercised influence among their fellows—as, for example, office-holders in trade unions and co-operative societies—were to be found in the ranks of devoted adherents of churches or more commonly chapels. The consolations of religions were often exemplified in times of adversity. The doomed miners, trapped in the wrecked Hartley colliery in 1862, left behind notes which showed that they held repeated prayer meetings before the failing air supply finally triumphed over them. One of the survivors was Thomas Watson, who had been converted by Primitive Methodist missionaries only a few days earlier. He was left clinging to the shattered cage in the mine shaft after the accident occurred[53]:

> He had strong confidence in the Lord, and was favoured in a wonderful manner with the Divine presence and help. Leaving the broken cage, he slid down the signal rope to a place where two of his suffering companions were lying among the debris, with life fast ebbing away. One of these, George Sharp, was a member with the Primitives, and Watson and he conversed and prayed together. They also sung the first three verses of the hymn commencing "On Jordan's stormy bank I stand". . . . The other man possessed not religion; but oh, how earnestly did he enquire what he must do to be saved, and how fervently did he join with Watson and Sharp in the prayers they offered to the God of mercy! In these exercises Watson continued, until his two companions had yielded up their breath to Him who gave it. He then tried to re-ascend to the cage, but found it impracticable. He had, therefore, to remain alone with the dead until liberated many hours after. But, as he told the writer, his spirit quailed not—he was not alone, for God was with him. He spent his time in prayer, and in communion with Him who had graciously imparted to him, a few days previously, a sense of his forgiving love.

Throughout the later nineteenth and early twentieth centuries the major religious festivals, especially Good Friday, played a prominent part in the life of communities throughout the region.

Nor was it only among workers that deep faith was to be found. T. H. Bainbridge aimed at extending his Christian stewardship among the staff of his large department store[54]:

> We have a good many Christian salesmen in the house, and I should like some of them to take a personal interest in some one apprentice by gaining his confidence, becoming his friend and counsellor, and sometimes inviting him to tea on Sunday afternoon or supper on Sunday night, and having a talk with him after the Sunday evening service.

Bainbridge's faith was sincere; in 1912, facing a serious operation, he wrote:

> I am now face to face with the possibility of death. It is therefore a solemn moment. I have been a very unprofitable servant. I have no hope except in a penitent trust in Jesus Christ as my Saviour. The first verse of the hymn "Just as I am" represents, I trust, my attitude to Jesus Christ, on whose promise

"Him that cometh unto me I will in no wise cast out", I now rely for salvation.

Many similar examples could be cited to show that among the employing groups as well as the workers religion was a continuing influence. There were many links between the devout at different social levels. The inscribed stones on a Primitive Methodist chapel in the mining community at Bedlington Station in Northumberland illustrate this factor. The most impressive foundation stone was laid by a member of the prominent coal-owning family of Bates, but the walls also contain many inscribed bricks testifying to the contributions made by others associated with the building; they include the names of brick-makers who helped to provide materials, and the names of members of other working families in the area. Two bricks represent members of the Garrow family, for many years prominent in twentieth-century activities within the district, including trade unionism, local government, the Labour Party and the Methodist church. A few hundred yards away the Anglican church of St John also bears a foundation stone laid by a member of a coal-owning family, but the funds which built this early twentieth-century church included many small items, such as the making and selling of 'clippy mats' by womenfolk in working families. Religion in the late nineteenth and early twentieth centuries was a powerful force which cut across barriers of social status and wealth; there were variations of sect certainly, but these occurred in a context of shared faith and shared attitudes about matters which were felt deeply at many different social levels.

Crime and drunkenness

Yet if religion continued an important influence it was far from all embracing. While the outpouring of devout books, tracts and journals continued, it was not by any means the only kind of reading which reached a wide circulation. In the third quarter of the nineteenth century the *News of the World* and its principal rival, *Lloyd's Weekly News*, already enjoyed large and increasing circulations. The *Newcastle Daily Chronicle* of 17 July 1868 advertised the contents in the following number of *Lloyd's*[55]:

The Emperor Napoleon on Assassination.
Fearful stabbing case through jealousy.
Terrible scene at an execution.
Cannibalism at Liverpool.
The Great Seizure of Indecent Prints.
A man roasted to death.
A cruel husband and an adulterous wife.

Contemporary society continued to present much that was rough, vicious and criminal to fill the columns of such publications. If there was an overall increase in levels of civilization, it too was far from all embracing. Local newspapers continue to abound with descriptions of violent fights, some of them on a large scale. One incident of this kind was the battle which occurred in a very poor area of Newcastle on the evening of Sunday, 11 May 1851, commemorated in a local song 'The Horrid War i' Sangeyt'. The town's police came into collision with a large Irish crowd which refused to disperse and began to beat back the police. As the news spread in the neighbouring tenements, the equally rough native inhabitants sallied forth into the streets to aid the police against the Irish, and this unusual alliance drove the Irish from the scene of conflict. An interesting sidelight on this affair is the way in which the local song simply referred to the leaders of all three parties involved by their usual nick-names, confident that these would be readily understood in what was still very much a locally orientated community.

Policemen were not by any means always so lucky. At 3 a.m. one night in 1873 P.C. Gray of Eglingham surprised a poaching gang; he tried to arrest them but was shot and died the next day. In March 1875 Sergeant Hately tried to control a crowd of between 2,000 and 3,000 which had got out of hand during the Alnwick Hirings fair, only to be kicked and beaten to death; he was 38 years old, with eight children and had been in the Northumberland force for 17 years. In 1880 P.C. Scott was beaten to death by poachers near Paston; as late as July 1932 a constable was savagely injured, including the loss of an eye, in a poaching affray near Prudhoe on Tyne.

In 1878 the Tynemouth police could still record the following figures of the town's less prepossessing activities—914 offences of drunkenness and disorderly behaviour, 158 known thieves, 157 vagrants, 301 prostitutes and 682 habitual drunkards[56]. Prostitution remained common, with continuing reference to the inclusion of many young girls. In 1854, for example, a young girl found on the streets was taken to the Newcastle Penitentiary. She was badly bruised from beatings by her drunken mother, who regularly sent her daughter out on the streets on Saturday nights with orders not to come home without at least 5s.[57]: 'She did not care how she got it; have it she must, either by theft or prostitution.' Local newspaper reports make it plain that a number of local public houses were regular centres of this business; a case of January 1877, for instance, makes it plain that George Henry's Plough Inn, Spicer Lane, Newcastle, then enjoyed such a reputation. When J. A. Dickman was convicted of murder in 1910, it transpired that in addition to a variety of other nefarious activities he received letters about betting and other matters under the name of F. Black at an accommodation address in Newcastle styled 'Miss Hymen'. The impossibility of stamping out prostitution, especially in the region's ports but not only there, was widely recognized by the well-informed, and local police forces often had orders enjoining discretion. For example, the Newcastle police orders of 1863 stipulated that[58]:

With common prostitutes, not riotous or behaving indecently or disorderly, the constable is not to hold any communication whatever, but he must not allow them to assemble in crowds on his beat, or interrupt persons passing in the public streets or thoroughfares

These orders were essentially unchanged in the early years of the next century.

Drink remained a serious social problem which caused trouble in many sectors of society. As early as 1854 a Newcastle suburb had one public house to every 22 families[59]. In the early 1890s Sunderland had nearly 500 public houses, and South Shields about 250. National statistics of convictions for drunkenness in 1911 saw Northumberland at the top of the county league with 127.31 per 1,000 population. Newcastle had 97.91 and Middlesbrough 117.15. The major local fairs were often centres of drunken disorder, for example[60]: 'Sunderland Fair was held bi-annually, to which all the blackguards of the North of England came. The last fair was held in 1868 . . . great numbers of drunken men reeled about in the streets.' Contemporary accounts include many and varied examples of the family catastrophes caused by excessive drinking. The clergyman at Stannington village in the years up to 1870 was a drunkard, often found incapable in the fields, after being on the spree all night[61]. In the 1850s the schoolteacher at Tudhoe village either would give the children a holiday when he was incapable or would scrap lessons in favour of an informal dance[62]. A major contracting firm, McKay and Blackstock, held the construction contracts for Newcastle Central Station and the Berwick railway bridge; the senior partner, McKay, became a drunkard, and the firm was taken over by its creditors as a result of the confusion in its affairs from this cause[63]. A North Shields firm of solicitors, Fenwick and Crawford, suffered when two successive generations of Crawford partners took to excessive drinking[64]. Dismissals for drunkenness occurred on several occasions in most of the local police forces.

It was not surprising in this context that there were strong efforts to combat the drink problem. Some attempts were made to provide alternatives to the public house; various establishments set up to supply the worker with recreation accompanied by such innocuous beverages as cocoa proved disappointing projects and did not last long. There was some encouragement by influential sectors of society for the working men's clubs, though the great growth of that movement in the region was to come later. They appeared to present a more respectable and elevating place of recreation than many of the local public houses. The Durham club movement began to flourish in the early years of the twentieth century, with 58 clubs founded in the years 1898–1905. Northumberland was slower off the mark, with only 15 clubs in the national union of clubs by 1906.

However, the temperance movement was the more obvious alternative to the public house in the later nineteenth century. The North of England Temperance League was founded at Newcastle in 1858; by 1888 it possessed 105 affiliated societies, with active membership totalling 15,000; 5 years later the figures were 202 societies and 50,000 active members[65]. This was only one of a number of energetic temperance movements in the area. It is probable that in the years around 1900 the temperance movement aroused a much higher level of regular popular participation than any contemporary political movement, but of course it only obtained the support of a portion of society. Temperance societies such as Bands of Hope, Good Templars and Rechabites provided for many thousands of families, mainly but not exclusively among the workers, not only a safeguard against the heavy drinking which could and often did ravage a family, but also a wide and agreeable range of social activities. Moreover the temperance movement could always call upon considerable support from society's dominant minorities; the successive presidents of the North of England Temperance League were Sir Walter Trevelyan, Bt, Edward Backhouse, the Sunderland banker, Arthur Pease of the prominent Darlington banking family, T. W. Backhouse and the Countess of Carlisle. Many of these influential figures took their crusade against the ill effects of drink much further. The Trevelyan family of Wallington, the Middleton family of Belsay, the Atkinson family of Angerton and the Earl of Carlisle all turned their extensive estates 'dry' either by closing public houses or by transforming them into temperance establishments. This aristocratic example was imitated by some colliery companies, including those at Throckley and North Seaton. Evidence that the comfort and happiness of the communities concerned had been markedly increased by this paternalistic discipline existed in considerable quantity and was given wide publicity[66].

Campaigns against licences and for reductions in drinking hours were a common feature of local politics. On local boards of poor law guardians the question as to whether or not the inmates of the workhouse were to be allowed beer at Christmas often involved a degree of heated debate lacking in most other matters, and such issues often seriously divided guardians for year after year. Again the temperance question attracted support at many social levels but conspicuously failed to win universal acceptance at any level. In the 1892 general election at Newcastle the popular Tory candidate, Hamond, could still campaign effectively by appealing publicly for the support of 'all who loved a glass of beer'[67].

Sport and other recreational activities

Gambling was another common feature of Northern society. In 1853 a descriptive work on the mining districts remarked that 'the prominent vices of colliers are gambling and intemperance. The gambling consists in cock- and dog-fighting, bowling, card-playing and chuck-penny.' Large pitch-and-toss schools remained common features of mining areas until well into the twentieth century, and this too could lead to serious trouble for family life. Certainly mining communities evinced no uniformity of culture or interest; despite repeated condemnations from pulpit in church or chapel, denounced by 'respectable' mining society, gambling still remained a major feature of the lives of many miners. From the early years of the twentieth century increased interest in football was accompanied by the spread of football pools (which also provide illuminating evidence as to popular attitudes to the possession of substantial fortunes). The same paternalism which sought to enforce temperance also tried in some instances to combat gambling. The proprietors of the Throckley colliery, for example, not only enforced a ban on alcoholic drinks but also forbade the keeping of pigeons or dogs in their colliery houses, with the express aim of preventing the social ill effects of compulsive gambling[68].

Gambling was closely connected with the world of sport, and not only with the best side of sporting activities. An account of c. 1913 expressed grave doubts as to the likely effect of football pools upon the game[69]:

> This form of gambling is particularly obnoxious in that it is fraught with vital danger to one of the finest of our games, for it is to be feared that the methods which have led to the disrepute in which professional rowing and foot-racing on the flat are now held may utterly corrupt Association football also.

Despite such worries, there can be no serious doubt that the amount of popular interest and energy invested in sport and recreation of various kinds in the late nineteenth and early twentieth centuries made this aspect of society one of its most pervasive activities. Some sports maintained a wide interest throughout this period; others came and went. Boxing maintained a wide support, and even in the later nineteenth century sizeable local crowds would gather to watch open-air bouts—a crowd of more than 500, for instance, at one bout on Blyth Links in 1881[70]. A different setting can be seen in the next decade; the memoirs of Eugene Corri, a well-known referee of the 1890s, described the audience at a bout between Ben Taylor, 'the Woolwich Infant', and George Crisp, 'the Pitmen's Champion'[71]:

> Greater than the fight was the setting of it. The Standard Theatre, Gateshead was packed with pitmen (Shipcote Colliery was just across the road), who sat in their shirt sleeves, and I early observed that the majority of them had brought refreshments to contend with the great heat. Bottles were being handed about. Glasses were not necessary.

Fox-hunting was of course a traditional sport in the rural districts, but in the late nineteenth century it drew considerable support from workers in mining districts. At a meeting of the North Durham Hunt in 1873 there was 'a tremendous crowd of lookers on, many of whom were drunk'; about '60 or 70 yelling pitmen' encouraged the digging-out of a fox[72]. Hunting records of the period repeatedly mention that the field was followed by crowds of supporting pitmen. Horse-racing, and the gambling which accompanied it, were also matters of great interest to many at various levels of society. We have from the late 1880s a picture of two schoolboys playing truant to go to see Rothbury races and finding themselves in a railway carriage with a crowd of pitmen bound for the same destination[73]:

Evidently they had never been so far away from home before. They danced about the old-fashioned railway carriage simply boiling over with joy. The carriage seats had backs only half-height, making it possible to shout or climb over from end to end of the same coach.

The Newcastle race course, moved from the Town Moor—where it was replaced by a temperance festival which developed into a major fair—to Gosforth Park in 1881, drew very large gatherings of people from many social levels. Before the days of the trams many workers walked what we would consider very long distances to attend such events.

A sport which preceded Association football as the focus of an immense amount of popular enthusiasm was competitive rowing. Local newspapers in the 1840s already devoted considerable space to these events and testified to a wide popular following which was to continue to grow during the next few decades. From the 1850s a number of North East oarsmen were figures of national, indeed international, interest. At the great matches between the champions of the Tyne, the Thames and the Mersey, river banks were lined with huge crowds and very large sums of money changed hands in the accompanying gambling. Harry Clasper and his seven keelmen brothers were among the first North East oarsmen to achieve wide celebrity, as well as to pioneer improvements in the boats used for racing. In his heyday Harry Clasper claimed the title of champion sculler of the world. Perhaps even more famous was Robert Chambers, previously a puddler at a Walker iron works, who was taken under Harry Clasper's wing and surpassed his mentor in achievement before dying in 1868 at the early age of 37 years. When Clasper himself died at the Tunnel Inn, Ouseburn, Newcastle on 12 July 1870, aged 58 years, his funeral was one of the greatest scenes of popular mourning in the century. The *Newcastle Chronicle*, in general a reliable source, put the numbers attending the funeral at between 100,000 and 130,000. Clasper was buried in Whickham churchyard under a sumptuous monument 'reared to his memory, by the ardent affection of friends and admirers from every class, and from all parts of the kingdom'. Already, however, the sport was earning an unsavoury reputation for various kinds of malpractice. In the summer of 1871 the champion rowers of the Tyne headed by the reigning popular hero, Renforth, travelled to New York to face the top American oarsmen. Renforth had already learned to take stimulating drugs before matches; when his usual dose failed to bring the required effect, he took an overdose before a big race, with fatal results. The news of Renforth's death crowded all the other news from home and abroad from the headlines of the local newspapers. On 24 August the *Newcastle Chronicle*, the most popular newspaper in the region, devoted six and three-quarters columns to an account of Renforth's death, and it is an interesting point to note that this radical newspaper, very competent in matching public tastes, chose to give on that day only a quarter of column on the same page to the great strike which was then paralysing most of Tyneside's engineering works. The *Chronicle*, which had no hesitation in ascribing the tragedy to the effects of 'Yankee dope', continued throughout the remainder of August and the first half of September to give the Renforth story the highest priority, and it seems unlikely that in doing this it was running counter to the interests and preferences of the overwhelming bulk of its readers, largely drawn from the region's workers.

Rowing as the principal repository of popular sporting enthusiasms was to be eclipsed by the attractions of association football. An account of 1913 described how in mining communities and elsewhere within the region boys became infused with devotion to the game from childhood. Games were played in alleys, yards or any scrap of vacant ground. The ball might only be newspaper tied up with string, but it served its purpose. The dream of becoming a successful footballer of national acclaim was a day-dream shared by thousands of boys within the region. Games could be rough, and friendly societies commonly excluded football accidents or injuries from their coverage. The highest standards of sportsmanship were not always apparent, as may be gathered from this description of a local match of January 1885, reported in the *Northumbrian* magazine:

> On Saturday the West End and the Heaton Clubs met, and a very disagreeable game was the outcome. Darkness settling in seems to have had a great deal to do with it, but surely when umpires are on the field it ought to be possible to decide matters. But on Saturday neither side would give way, so that the game was abruptly brought to an end. The Heatonites claim having won by four goals to two, while the West Enders maintain that the score should be two goals each.

In 1889 an attendance of 10,000 was recorded at a local match at Sunderland, while 9 years later 20,000 turned out to watch Newcastle United's first game in the First Division. In the first decade of the twentieth century St James' Park received new facilities to increase capacity to 55,000. Football matches and other sporting events received a marked boost from the increasingly widespread Saturday half-holiday. Schools rapidly learned to field their own teams, and at Newcastle the local schools' own football league was organized in 1894. On Easter Tuesday 1895 a large crowd came to watch a match between Newcastle Boys and Sunderland Boys, and at least one of those playing had a distinguished career before him. Colin Veitch was to play for Newcastle United in five F.A. Cup Finals, to show an unusual versatility in playing position and tactical innovation and to be undoubtedly a leading local hero.[74] During the early years of the twentieth century Newcastle United and Sunderland consolidated positions among the country's leading teams in a sport which was increasingly the centre of wide popular interest. In addition to the big teams playing in national competitions, there were thousands of teams from a wide variety of local contexts—teams from villages, coal mines, factories, churches, schools, colleges and a variety of other origins. If the bulk of the participation and the audiences came from among the workers, football enthusiasm was by no means confined to them. John Fenwick, proprietor of one of Newcastle's biggest department stores, was a regular Newcastle United supporter, while in 1887 the officials of the Sunderland club included Thompson and Marr from among the leading Wearside shipbuilders and Tyzack from the ranks of local coal-owners.

There were many other kinds of recreational activities. The creation of local flower and vegetable shows grew increasingly common during the later nineteenth century; such foundations may not seem the stuff of which history is normally made, but they did in fact provide a focus of attention and enthusiasm for increasing numbers of people. On Saturday, 23 August 1879, for example, there were flower shows at Whitfield, Choppington, Shildon, Kenton, Gosforth, Shotley Bridge and Seghill; on the following Monday the Lumley and Harraton Agricultural Society staged its annual show, Ryton Flower Show was held and the Warkworth Horticultural Society opened its twentieth annual exhibition.

Further evidence of increased leisure, increased spending power and the ways chosen for their use comes from the development of the local music halls, from the primitive public house shows of the 1850s[75]. Thornton's Music Hall in Newcastle opened in 1885 with a seating capacity of 1,000; pit seats cost 6d., dress circle 1s. and boxes 2s. In February 1899, with greatly enlarged premises, this enterprise reopened as the Empire Palace of Varieties. Richard Thornton also opened the Alhambra at West Hartlepool in 1890, replacing it soon afterwards by a larger Empire; he also provided Empires at Sunderland in 1907 and Gateshead in 1915. This was only one of a number of similar chains established in these years. More highly cultural theatrical enterprises also flourished, while, on Tyneside and in some other places, still more edifying entertainment was provided. The Tyneside Sunday Lecture Society was active from 1884 onwards and provided such stars as Prince Kropotkin, Dr Nansen, Charles Bradlaugh and Oscar Wilde. At the turn of the century the first moving pictures appeared on the scene; in 1899 Newcastle could see a 'Bio-Tableaux' of the F.A. Cup Final between Derby County and Sheffield United, while it is not without interest in social history to note that among other very early examples of cinema shows presented in the North East by impresarios well acquainted with popular taste were 'The Grenadier Guards at Drill' and 'The Queen's Ships at Sea.'

These are only some of the immense range of sporting and recreational activities which absorbed so much of the popular energy and enthusiasm during this period. In general there was a considerable diminution of the more unsavoury aspects of popular entertainment which had marked earlier periods. In part this was the the work of enlightenment among the ruling minorities; a good example of this was the abolition of public executions. This was certainly not a response to the popular will, as was clearly demonstrated by one of the last of these events at Newcastle, in March 1863. Although earlier partial reforms had greatly reduced the degree of public spectacle involved, popular enthusiasm was scarcely abated[76]:

The whole length of the street from the Arcade steps to Carliol Street was barricaded strongly at very short intervals, forming pens to avoid accidents through the enormous crowd anticipated, and well it was so, for every available space was filled. The writer viewed the situation from the roof of a house immediately opposite the scaffold, which was erected on the top of the gaol corner opposite the railway bank that leads to Pilgrim Street; and looking down as far as the eye could carry, the whole thoroughfare had the appearance of a street paved with human heads. These people had assembled as early as 5.30 a.m. By 8 o'clock the crowd was so dense that dozens of people had fainted; and these were passed over the heads of the multitude to the outside. The story of the execution is soon told; the condemned man was under a minute in view before he disappeared from the gaze of the bloodthirsty crowd.

Blood sports such as cock-fighting were in plain decline during this period, again largely because of the war waged against them by established authority. The spread of religion also helped to curtail the followings of the rougher sports. Association football was a more innocuous pastime than bare-fist boxing, and flower shows markedly less vicious than bull-baiting.

It may seem frivolous in a book of this kind to devote so much space to a consideration of sport and recreation, and it would be so if for the many thousands who engaged in such activities they represented merely a trivial accompaniment to a life in which the highest priorities were directed to the problems of society as a whole. It was not so, however, for it is plain that sport and recreation occupied a central place in the preoccupations of very many people within the region. If for some the main ambition and dominating passion in life was to rise in the world of business and industry to become rich and powerful and if for others the affairs of church or chapel could predominate, for very many others the fortunes of a football club or a masonic lodge, or the annual administration of a prestigious local flower show, could be a matter equally absorbing, and this is an aspect of modern social history which has been far too neglected, mainly because of the exaggerated significance attributed to political matters in a society which was very far from besotted with ideological considerations.

Those groups, and they certainly existed too, which did take a profound and enthusiastic interest in political agitation often found the actual behaviour of contemporaries difficult to understand. During the Northumberland Miners' Picnic in 1910 one militant speaker, himself a miner, included the following passage in his speech[77]:

In last March or April, he remembered seeing a great crowd in Newcastle. The Lord Mayor was out, and bands were playing amid general excitement. He was told that Newcastle United had beaten Barnsley, and had won the English Cup! Thousands of people were there talking about the football match, yet that very day a father of three children had gone out on to the moor and cut his throat because he had been out of work for 18 months, and could not obtain bread for his family! He could stand the thing no longer, and ended his life; yet the thousands were more interested in the football match than they were in one human soul who wanted their help and aid so much. In conclusion, he would urge them to keep their heads right, and remember that a crust of bread to a starving being was of more value than all the Cups and League in the country. Let them combine, and not depend upon the employer classes, but on themselves, and themselves alone.

On the whole the evidence suggests that of North East workers the thousands who cheered Newcastle United's victory were much more representative than the political militant who found it so very hard to understand. No doubt he would find it equally difficult to understand those who joined the successive forms of the armed forces' reserves, but they existed in large numbers too. Other parts of the very complex fabric of contemporary society might well have appalled him; he could scarcely have liked the Conservative Working Men's Clubs that existed in the railway and mining town of Shildon in County Durham, or the Newcastle engineering centre of Byker and Heaton. He might also have been disappointed that workers at Armstrong's Elswick works could be found lending an ear to imperialist and big navy arguments, though perhaps it was not so very surprising[78]. It is very easy amidst the enormous volume of political noise which was generated by politically active groups during this period and subsequently to exaggerate the extent to which North East workers in the late nineteenth and early twentieth centuries did involve themselves in political matters. There were certainly very many other interesting things for them to be concerned with, while the evidence scarcely suggests that most workers were in the habit of parting with their hard-earned wages for the support of political movements.

Perhaps the greatest instance of popular celebrations within this period came in 1897, when the Diamond Jubilee brought communal rejoicings and excitement everywhere within the region. The biggest junkettings took place in the region's main centres, but we may take a more homely example from rural Northumberland, vividly recalled by a participant many years later[79]:

The year 1897 saw the whole country rejoicing over Queen Victoria's Diamond Jubilee . . . for us, the Jubilee consisted in the local efforts. These took the form of sports, competitions, tea and dancing on Barrasford Green, about a mile from us. The proceedings began with a procession of the schoolchildren from three villages, all waving small Union Jacks and wearing Jubilee medals presented to each child by the Parish Council (I think). They marched behind the Gunnerton Brass Band. I was given a flag and marched proudly in the ranks. Arrived at the Green, the races and sports began. . . . Music throughout the afternoon was provided by the Gunnerton Brass Band mentioned before, whose members were drawn from all over the estate; our gamekeeper, coachman, and both gardeners, the Station-master, the blacksmith, a road mender, and a few farmers. As the evening came on there was dancing on the Green till 10 p.m. The band then played Auld Lang Syne and God Save the Queen, and the great day was over.

It was not an equal society, in many ways, but it was not a society deeply riven with conflict; most people seem to have felt that they had better things to do with their time and their resources than to concern themselves primarily with issues of politics or society in general. This is an important part of the background to the region's economic development, for such growth would have been much less likely in a society obsessed to any marked degree with revolutionary fervour or beset by a continual stream of political disturbances. The relative social tranquillity maintained during a period of unprecedented stresses and rapid change was not the least remarkable achievement of regions such as North East England during the late nineteenth and early twentieth centuries.

Political activists

There were, however, groups who did take a deep, sincere and energetic interest in militant political activities to a varying degree. When in 1884 Newcastle was preparing a programme of festivities in connection with a royal visit, protest meetings were held to oppose the spending of public money on such activities; speakers contrasted this 'feasting and revelry in high places' with the 'semi-starvation and want' which were said to prevail among Tyneside workers[80]. The first socialist candidate to fight a parliamentary election in Newcastle was Fred Hammill in 1895; he obtained 2,333 votes. Only five Labour councillors appeared on Newcastle City Council by 1914, although two more were returned at the November elections that year. Between 1905 and 1907 a small group of North East workers were involved in smuggling arms to insurgent groups in Russia. In 1907 Daniel Currie of Sunderland was fined £20 for possession of ten boxes of cartridges found at King St, Sunderland; Thomas Keast was fined £6 for possession of over 30,000 cartridges and 65 lb of explosives at 42 Leazes Park Road, Newcastle[81]. This does, however, seem a very unusual activity for North East workers, while the sentences were less than Draconian. A deep concern with the Russian Revolution of 1905 is unlikely to have been a long-term interest of most workers in the region. Such small extremist political groups were certainly not a new phenomenon though; 50 years before the local manufacturer and politician, Joseph Cowen, had been sending messages to Polish dissidents either in hollow bricks or by using invisible ink on apparently innocuous commercial documents[82].

Perhaps more interesting were the small socialist groups which did grow up in many parts of the North East during the late nineteenth and early twentieth centuries. (For a study of the early history of Labour in North East politics see reference 83.) Although the national Labour Party was not to become strong within the region until after the First World War, earlier groups of workers associated with the Independent Labour Party and similar movements preceded it, and some of their members played important parts in establishing the position of the later Labour Party. Some of these men were very impressive figures. Often largely self-educated, their capacity for reading, thinking and organizing was such as to have earned them positions of high distinction in a society with greater opportunities than they did in fact experience. Others were perhaps less impressive in their intellectual attainments but were immensely engaging people. Arthur Barton has given as a fine portrait of such a man, his Uncle Jim[84]. Uncle Jim was a shipyard craftsman on Tyneside, and a fervent radical in a variety of ways. His favourite reading included Chesterton, Bradlaugh, Belloc, Darwin, Dickens and Hume. He was interested in neither football nor horses. Professing to be a militant atheist, he repeatedly issued challenges to God to strike him dead; when, however, he took some children to see St Nicholas' Cathedral, Newcastle, 'no believer could have followed the verger more respectfully. He even removed his hat, though with the muttered remark, "By, it's hot the day", as if that were the only reason.' Books and music were among his principal loves. He thought '*Messiah* held all the world's glory and grief', and he had 'a kind of rage for learning. He educated himself from the junk shops in Western Road. He read poetry, science, religion, mathematics. . . . From these sources he got the intoxication others took from the bottle.' He had a deep and angry hatred for injustice and oppression, and he was devoted to the idea of a socialist regeneration of society:

> Uncle Jim was a militant Socialist. He supported unpopular causes like the Boers and Home Rule for Ireland, and kept his cap on when the National Anthem was played. He never went to church. The Sunday of his week was the day the *Clarion* came out, and Robert Blatchford was the Holy Ghost to him. That romantic ex-soldier Socialist became my hero too. I remember standing at the window with Uncle Jim when I was about eleven. We had just read a particularly uplifting article. In the street outside a couple of drunks shook hands in an eternal goodbye outside the Engineers' Arms. A street singer shambled along in the gutter catterwauling something just recognizable as "The Rosary". Women hurried from the corner shop in broken shoes and their men's caps, with jugs of milk and bundles of firewood. And at the pavement edge, sexless small children in filthy garments played contentedly with chipped cups and old spoons.
>
> "It won't always be like this, lad," exclaimed Jim enthusiastically. "Them bairns' bairns won't cry for bread like you and me did."
>
> This was an exaggeration. We weren't exactly well off in the post-war slump, but we weren't yet starving. In fact by local standards we still did rather well. Uncle Jim could shower meat and drink on visitors. . . .
>
> Uncle Jim had all the wilful blindness of idealists. He thought all work people were as simple and great hearted as he was. Show him that some were cruel and cunning, shiftless and stupid, and he would reluctantly agree, but

he was sure education and a just wage would cure all that. All their faults were laid at the door of a wickedly imposed environment which he and Blatchford and Lansbury would sweep away.

Men like this were noble, but there were not a great many of them. Nor were they among the most influential workers in the period we are considering here. Indeed they must have put up with a great deal of leg-pulling, and sometimes worse, from their less intellectual fellows. Their interests to a considerable extent overlapped with another group, also deeply interested in learning in many cases but more concerned to work to improve the existing form of society rather than to seek to overthrow it root and branch and replace it with something quite different. This group included men like Thomas Burt, leader of the Northumberland miners, M.P., Privy Councillor, junior minister, honorary Doctor of Letters. Burt too was a much self-educated man, but his studies did not take him to socialism but to the radical wing of the Liberal party. Although a much older man, his career overlapped with that of Uncle Jim for many years. With powerful Liberal support from wealthier sectors of society, as well as his own union, his seat in parliament for Morpeth from 1874 was rarely challenged with any vigour. Throughout his life he worked for the cohesion of society as he saw it, and for its improvement. Burt was an outstanding example of a growing group of workers who in the later nineteenth century began to reach positions of influence in government. Many of them were involved mainly in local politics and administration. It was not until after the First World War that labour groups came to control any major local authorities, but long before then small numbers of respectable workers had begun to appear on town councils, boards of poor law guardians, urban district councils and the local magistracy. Joseph Hopper, founder of the Durham Aged Mine-workers' Homes Associations, was born at Windy Nook in 1856[85]. He was brought up as a Primitive Methodist, preached his first sermon at the age of 15 years and was on the list of regular local preachers at 18 years. He read avidly in such fields as political economy, history and biography; Macaulay and J. S. Mill were among his favourites. He became an elected member of Felling Local Board, Heworth School Board and the Gateshead Board of Guardians. Henry Kellett was born at Shincliffe in 1846, son of a miner; his parents planned a teaching career for him, but in the event this could not be afforded and so he entered the local pit. Injured in a serious accident he then entered the service of the local co-operative society, rising to become its manager at the age of 30 years. He was an active Wesleyan and served on Auckland Board of Guardians for 3 years. One of that same co-operative society's officials, Thomas Davis, was checkweighman at a local colliery and became one of the first working men to be elected to a local authority; he became a member of Barnard Castle Rural District Council and the Teesdale Board of Guardians, as well as a number of other minor elected bodies, before his election to Durham County Council in 1898.

Strong socialists such as Arthur Barton's Uncle Jim were rarely seen in elected public offices, though there were a few. It was the worker-politicians on the radical wing of Liberalism, the Lib–Labs, who made the first effective penetration into public office, and they still retained great influence in the major local trade unions. Their positions were not unchallenged by the champions of more militant causes, but in the later nineteenth and early twentieth centuries the Lib–Labs were the more influential section of the politically interested workers, and it was very largely on the basis of their work that the Labour Party was to develop in this region during the inter-war period.

Industrial relations

The picture in the history of industrial relations during this period is on the whole similar. Here too there were militant activist groups who believed that no common ground was to be found between workers and employers, but also strong influences directed towards more moderate causes. The second half of the nineteenth century saw considerable growth of trade unionism within the region, and the growth accelerated in the early twentieth century. Both Northumberland and Durham acquired stable mining unions, and in such trades as engineering and shipbuilding there were also marked advances[86a]. (The history of industrial relations in shipbuilding and engineering has been well analysed—see reference 86b.) Yet for many years unions such as the Amalgamated Society of Engineers only included a tiny proportion of those eligible to join—during the great engineering strikes of 1871 only about 10% of those involved were union members, though the active leaders were keen unionists. During the later nineteenth century there emerged an important group of trade union leaders who did much to establish the standing of unions within the region, not by the adoption of notably militant tactics but by espousing some of the attitudes which successful labour leaders had demonstrated in earlier years. Men such as Burt, William Crawford and John Wilson among the miners, John Burnett among the engineering workers, John Kane among the iron and steel workers, Robert Knight of the boiler-makers would have understood Henry Woodroffe of the seamen's union of the 1820s and 1830s. Like him they worked to give their organizations the respectability which would bring public acceptance and to elicit sympathy from uncommitted public opinion during disputes. They avoided any appearance of seeking conflict and stressed their adherence to law and order and to the established institutions of society.

They faced situations which were by no means easy. Society was in practice neither democratic nor egalitarian, and even among the ranks of the workers concerned there were difficulties, often serious difficulties, which inhibited co-operation. In shipbuilding, for instance, although the original changeover from wood to iron did not involve much internecine conflict between working groups, there was a sharp change in the pattern during the 1880s. The shipbuilding depression in the mid-1880s and the shock which it administered to men laid off brought the beginning of a long story of bitter inter-union conflicts arising out of demarcation disputes. During the years 1900-3, for example, major groups of shipyard workers were on strike in order to enforce claims to work as against other workers for a total of 35 weeks. The feelings which provoked these disputes were often very strong, stronger than any appeals to a sense of solidarity.

Another source of trouble was the strained relations which sometimes developed between skilled and unskilled workers. The skilled trades were the first to become effectively unionized, for the most part, and trade privileges were jealously guarded. Apprenticeships to the much more highly paid and regarded skilled trades were not freely available but were granted largely within a relatively closed circle of contacts; these contacts were often based on family links but could also arise, for example, from shared chapel membership or associations of that kind. A good example of the maintenance of this kind of privilege comes from the records of the Durham Colliery Enginemen's Association in January 1886 [87]:

> John Charlton, fireman, Stargate colliery, has applied through Blaydon branch to be taught the art of braking. This committee after carefully considering this case cannot see their way clear to depart from the resolution passed at a Delegates' Meeting held in 1875 which stresses that none but enginemen's sons be taught until the Executive deem it prudent to do so. There are a considerable number of our men out of employment at present, and your Executive have already refused to sanction many similar applications to learn to brake on this account.

In the shipyards of the later nineteenth century many labourers were not directly employed by the firm concerned but were paid by the skilled man whose work they assisted. For many years this was a source of friction, with frequent accusations from both parties to these arrangements. On occasion the friction brought about strikes by the unskilled men against the skilled, with the company concerned not a party to the dispute. In the early days of unionization among shipyard labourers, the skilled workers often showed themselves less than enthusiastic about such developments[88].

The rising union leaders of the later nineteenth century then faced serious problems. They were, however, operating in a situation in which their concern for moderation was matched by a similar concern among many important employers, though by no means all. Charles Mark Palmer, for example, while no great friend to trade unions, was careful to maintain good personal relations with his work force, a factor which ensured, for instance, that his enterprises remained at work during the strikes of 1871 which paralysed most other engineering works on Tyneside for many weeks. Some influential employers were anxious to reach amicable agreements with union leaders rather than to see production halted by repeated disputes. Both in the coal mines and in the iron and steel industry negotiated agreements prevented many disputes from escalating into major strikes during the later nineteenth century, though success was not always guaranteed. The work of David Dale in the iron and steel industry was a major example of the results which enlightened employers could obtain by patient negotiation rather than conflict[89]. After a series of serious strikes and disputes between 1860 and 1866, culminating in a lockout lasting several months in the latter year, the Board of Arbitration and Conciliation for the Manufactured Iron Trade of the North of England was created in 1869; on this board representatives of both employers and workers sat, and for many years it exercised an important restraining and pacifying influence in that major industry. Mining, shipbuilding and the North Eastern Railway were other major industries in which similar arrangements came into being.

There continued a strong tradition of settling industrial disputes by arbitration, as in earlier periods, and widely trusted individuals were repeatedly used in this capacity. Robert Spence Watson, a leading Tyneside Liberal, acted as arbitrator in more than 100 disputes, many of them complex and potentially the source of serious conflict, and in every case his award was accepted, though not always without grumbling, which might come from either side of industry. David Dale was also much called upon for the same purpose both within this region and elsewhere. The ranks of these conciliators received an interesting recruit before the end of the century in John Burnett, successively a largely self-educated worker, victorious strike leader, general secretary of the main engineering union and the central government's first senior civil servant concerned with industrial relations.

Although there were always groups which noisily derided any concept of common interests between employers and workers, this was scarcely the dominating spirit of industrial relations during this period. By 1914, while it would not be possible to maintain that the pattern of industrial relations had been invariably marked by conciliation and moderation, and the period had its share of prolonged and bitter disputes, in most of the region's major economic activities the trade unions were recognized as influential, responsible and respectable bodies to an extent which would have seemed incredible half a century earlier.

In a variety of ways the history of this period saw an advance in the position of the workers. Their trade organizations had as it were come of age, and there was the beginning of a penetration into positions of influence in regional and national administration. During this period of great economic development it had been easier for some workers to rise further and faster than in most other periods. Any list of leading North East citizens in the early twentieth century would include a number of plainly self-made men. In some cases this was marked by a rise to the ranks of major employers. Sir William Allan (1837–1903) began his working life in an engineering works, then went to sea as a merchant seaman and by hard work and good fortune ended his life as the owner of an important engineering company. James Craig (1834–1902) was the son of a Newcastle brush-maker, who made his way in the Tyneside business world by hard work and a notable absence of scruple, to become an important ship-owner and to serve as one of Newcastle's M.P.s from 1886 to 1892. George Luckley (1825–1911) began working life as an office boy and ended it as a partner in one of the world's greatest ship-repairing firms. Other workers could rise to positions of eminence without necessarily acquiring great wealth. Any of the many books listing important local dignitaries in the years around 1900 would include, together with county aristocracy and leading industrialists, men such as Thomas Burt and Charles Fenwick, miners' leaders and M.P.s When John Burnett, leader of the major engineering strikes of 1871, died in 1914 after many years as a senior civil servant, laudatory obituary notices were to be found in such places as *The Times* and the *Annual Register*. Society was still very far from equal, but at least the barriers were being lowered somewhat.

Concern for women and children

Some other groups in society which had not enjoyed much prominence earlier also began to receive more sympathetic treatment. Children and women can be included. In a number of ways more attention began to be paid to children as a group requiring special attention and special care. Children in the care of poor law authorities were during the later nineteenth century treated with more consideration; in the years around 1900 many poor law unions removed children from the workhouses altogether and placed them in separate groups of homes with a deliberate attempt to produce an atmosphere resembling that of a family home. The provisions of toys and treats of various kinds also became a normal practice. Poor law guardians were found not uncommonly congratulating themselves that the children in their care were much better treated than many poor children outside. This seems to have been in many cases all too true. An enquiry into the condition of poor children in South Shields in 1909 discovered that[90]:

> Many children were very poorly clad and their clothes showed no signs of being repaired and lacked any method of fastening except pins. It was even found at times that a child's underclothing was sewn on. . . . he often found that the main diet of a child was tea and bread which was not the proper food for the growing child especially when served as a mid-day meal by parents who were quite able to provide something of a more sustaining nature. It was also found a common practice for children to be sent to school without having a breakfast because the mother was unable to get up early enough in the morning to prepare any. In all the question of improper feeding was even more important than that of insufficient feeding as in many cases the only thing needed was a little more care on the mother's part.

Despite the distinctly patronizing note which colours this report, it was part of an increasing concern for the condition of children. As so very often happened, the intervention of Parliament in legislating for the protection of children was not so much an innovation as the setting of a legislative framework for an extended concern which had already made itself apparent within society. The idea that children were a special kind of creature needing special facilities tailored to their situation had long before been taken up by an enterprising local newspaper. From 1876 the *Newcastle Chronicle* published and publicized special features for children, beginning with specially written articles by 'Uncle Toby'. By 1886 this initiative had grown into a children's organization with about 100,000 registered members. The Dicky Bird Society, as this pioneer enterprise was called, numbered Ruskin and Tennyson among its honorary officers and emphasized in its proceedings the need for care and kindness towards animals, including both wild birds and household pets. While it remained true that many children within the region, and those not always among the poorest families, grew up in conditions of hardship or neglect, yet here too there were distinct signs of the development of a greater degree of sympathy and helpfulness.

Women too saw some improvement in their situation. There was of course a certain amount of suffragette agitation among those who possessed the leisure and the means to act in that way, and the region provided this movement with one of its most notable martyrs, Miss Emily Davidson, who sought to forward women's claim to the vote by throwing herself under the hooves of the King's horse during the 1913 Derby, with fatal consequences. There were, however, other signs of increasing freedom and opportunity for women, beginning for the most part in developments among the richer and more leisured sections of society. Legislation of the later nineteenth century opened some areas of local government to female voting and female membership, and a handful of women came to occupy seats on such elected authorities as school boards and boards of poor law guardians. In 1894 Miss Peel became the first woman guardian of the Houghton-le-Spring Poor Law Union; the Sunderland union had five women members by 1898, though their numbers dropped to only two a few years later. In 1913 the South Shields union had a woman as chairman of the board of guardians. Ladies such as these, however, were drawn from groups with the means and the leisure to forward their interests in social reform.

Employment for women

Employment prospects for women improved somewhat, though the North East remained a region of low female employment. The development of such professions as nursing and teaching provided openings for a few, though they tended to be ill paid. In 1932 *Blackwoods Magazine* published the recollections of a nurse at Sunderland Royal Infirmary in 1902; while the lady concerned appears to have withstood the conditions with admirable strength of mind, there is much of stern discipline, long hours, arduous work and very poor pay. Some progressive firms did take the plunge and recruited women workers; the shipbuilding firm of Wigham Richardson, for instance, employed a few women office workers from 1886, despite some doubts as to the wisdom of such a daring step[91], 'Afternoon tea was daily served to them, they were provided with wardrobes for their outer garments, and the drawer for their gloves was even scented with chips of cedar wood'. Not all firms displayed a like spirit of adventure. Near Wigham Richardson's Neptune Yard the Thermal Syndicate was in the early twentieth century technically a very progressive firm, but all its office work was carried out by a staff of 20 men and boys[92]. In 1905 J. J. Fenwick's secretary was the only woman member of the shorthand-speed class provided at Armstrong College[93]. Even in shops many of the jobs were occupied by men; in 1910 the staff of the Stanley branch of Brough's Stores consisted of 34 men and eight women; even after the First World War the figures were 42 men and 23 women[94]. Yet shop work did provide increased numbers of jobs for women and girls in the later nineteenth century, and a few even reached managerial positions which included some authority over men; in 1907 the Crook co-operative society, for instance, employed four women in important supervisory posts[95]. There were a few local industries which provided a substantial proportion of jobs for women; they included potteries and rope-making. Domestic service remained another major source.

Like many other social changes the tendency was for more enlightened concepts of women's role to filter down from the richer sectors of society. Even though in many working homes women might in practice exercise considerable influence, it was in many ways a patriarchal society. Here, for example, are two glimpses of the kind of relationships which were common in working homes in the earlier twentieth century[96]:

At half past five in the evening my father came back. He smelt of iron and oil and machinery, and he washed his hands with paraffin and dried them on cotton waste before sitting down to his tea. During the 3 or 4 hours left him before bed he did nothing—I mean nothing to help my mother. He might go out, or read *Titbits* or listen to Peter Dawson singing 'Boots' on the old gramophone, but everything he did was for himself. The eight and a half hours in the little cramped cabin of his crane high above the clash and roar of the shipyard were for us. What was left of the day belonged to him.

A year or two ago when I was once more in the north I went to see an old couple now in their eighties. There was no new-fangled equality here. The old man sat serenely reading his sporting paper. His wife, a shadow of the vigorous woman of my childhood, still crept around him in a sort of parody of her former bustling efficiency. Sixty years of bland unhelpfulness were eloquent in every puff of his glowing pipe.

The First World War was to do much to open the doors of employment wider for women, though not to bring about anything like a complete transformation to any concepts of equality. Much of the employment of women in novel spheres was essentially temporary; for example an emergency shell factory set up in the North Eastern Railway's Darlington workshops employed 150 men and 1,000 women, but did not of course outlast the war emergency[97]. However, in various jobs in offices, transport services and shops, there was some long-term increase in the number of jobs to which women could normally aspire, though this change was not on a sufficient scale to affect the region's generally low proportion of female employment in comparison with many other regions.

The impact of the First World War

The extended opportunities for women arising out of the First World War remains a well-known feature of the process by which the position of women was gradually improved, but there were other important effects of the First World War on the regions society which are perhaps less well appreciated nowadays. When war broke out in August 1914 recruiting at once began on a large scale. Official machinery for this purpose took some time to organize, and in the early months of the war much of the work of enlistment was done by voluntary agencies. By mid-November the Scottish community on Tyneside had provided a brigade of 4,000 men, and by the beginning of the next year the Tyneside Irish had provided 5,500 men for the army[98]. Local sporting programmes collapsed as the attention of both players and public went elsewhere[99]. Nearly 200,000 coal miners or about 19% of the national total of miners enlisted during the first 7 months of the war, and the Northumberland and Durham coalfield was at least as much engaged as other areas[100]. During the first 2 months of the war 10% of the staff of the North Eastern Railway volunteered, which meant some 5,000 recruits.

It is as well to place another range of figures alongside the recruitment figures[101]. Of the 1,543 men working for the Palmer company who joined the forces during the war 145 were killed. Of the 714 employees of the main Tyneside gas company who enlisted 90 were killed. Rutherford School at Newcastle had more than 830 old boys serving in the forces, of whom over 150 were killed. Dame Allan's School had 625 old boys serving, of whom 84 were killed. The Durham county police force contributed 420 recruits; 52 were killed and 98 wounded. Throughout the region the crop of war memorials, with their endless columns of names of the dead, testify to the enormous slaughter involved, while in a region such as this the toll of lost merchant seamen was another tragic list.

There were those in the region who were from the beginning strenuously opposed to the war and were willing to endure considerable personal discomforts for their opinions. The ranks of local socialist groups received a number of recruits from those who could not stomach the horrors of a world war. A few Independent Labour Party members in County Durham, for instance, formed a link in a chain of sympathizers seeking to conceal and protect conscientious objectors[102]. These were not, however, the prevailing opinions, and sympathy for conscientious objectors was not a prominent trait in a region in which so many families had one or more men serving at the front. It was not perhaps surprising, in view of the war's toll of death and injury, that anti-German feeling sometimes took a distinctly ugly turn. In Jarrow, for instance[103]:

The few Germans in our town were pork butchers, and they had a bad time. Their windows were constantly being broken, especially if a ship had gone down or an attack failed. Only the fighting men who sometimes came to tea . . . astonished us by speaking of the enemy in almost friendly terms.

In the Durham mining area around Crook, the news of the sinking of the *Lusitania* provoked a violent anti-German riot in which some 7,000 became involved. Two local butchers' shops with old German connections were destroyed, there were many arrests and some heavy fines[104].

For adherents of the various churches religious consolation could help to blunt the pain of bereavement. Here, for example, are extracts from letters sent to a Methodist padre from parents in County Durham[105]:

We were glad to receive your communication with reference to our son's faith and trust in God. It is a great consolation to know that there was no doubts and fears but a faith that would lay hold on the promises made to us; we know that if we are faithful we shall meet again in the better land. We thank you so much indeed for your kindness.

One is sometimes tempted to ask—has God forgotten to be gracious? Ours is a sad blow. Only a short while ago we lost our elder boy but not in this war. But we know the Lord giveth and the Lord hath taken away, and say, "Thy will be done."

For those who served in the war and lived, memories of shared experiences were to continue strong into the inter-war period. The numbers of ex-service and 'Comrades' clubs in the expanding inter-war working men's club movement was part of this. It is surprising how rarely it is remembered in our recent histories of inter-war Britain that organizations such as the British Legion involved very many more people at all levels of society, and exercised more effective influence, than many of the ephemeral political groups which seem nowadays to be singled out for exaggerated attention. It should be remembered that throughout the inter-war period 11 November was to mean much more to British society than 1 May. Not only for those who served, and their families, but also for those who came after as children in the inter-war North East the memories of the First World War largely endured[106]:

1914–18. To us these were the most significant figures of all time, and even today, half a century later, any one of those five fatal years rings out like the trumpets that soldiers of the Faithful Durhams sounded across our town every Armistice Day. The silence really was a silence then. The Armageddon of shipyard and steelworks was cut off at five to eleven like the gunfire on the Western Front that first November Monday. Horses were held; busses stopped; suburban trains sought the nearest station. You could hear the unfamiliar sound of sparrows chirping in the stubby plane trees across Ellison Street. We stood tense, not even breathing, behind our desks in school, while the red autumn sunlight slanted across from the playground where the Union Jack licked the misty morning air. Some of us raised secret adoring eyes to the engraving of John Travers Cornwell, the boy V.C., for ever at his post in the thunder and flame of Jutland. The weight and glory of death was heavy upon us. The heroes were all gone and we were young and guilty and alive. When I read Edmund Blunden's line, "Why slept not I in Flanders' clay with all the murdered men", that seemed to strike our note.

After the war

The end of the First World War closed what was in many ways a very significant period in the long history of human activity in North East England. The differences between Northumberland and Durham in 1850 and in 1920 were enormous. The population of the region had more than doubled, and its distribution had altered drastically, as had the ways in which the region's income was earned. The North East had acquired a relative importance on the national scale much greater than at earlier periods. While there still remained considerable areas of poverty, cruelty, vice and crime, there had been notable improvements in the standard of living of the great majority of the swollen population and a diminution in the rougher and barbaric elements inherited from earlier times. Other generalizations are much less easy to make, for the region's society continued to display a high degree of diversity and complexity. At all levels of society, instead of any gratifyingly simple uniformity of ideas, interests and aspirations, the evidence demonstrates variety and multiplicity of life styles and cultures. The more one attempts to impose upon the extensive evidence any kind of speciously simple pattern the less convincing does the result become. To say that the workers did this or that the employers did that, for example, represents not illumination but distortion, for neither workers nor employers acted in a monolithic way; they did not even act with sufficient general agreement to make such broad concepts viable as reasonable approximations. It is always tempting to search out a broad and general theory as a convenient umbrella under which to gather together a complex body of evidence. We do not yet possess a theory of society capable of reducing the complexity and diversity of society in the late nineteenth and early twentieth century into any form of convincing simplicity. Two examples may give some further indication of the difficulty of comprehending the variety of human behaviour within any such theoretical framework of uniformity and simplicity.

We have already noted that in 1871 the region's expanding engineering industry experienced one of its greatest and longest industrial disputes. Many engineering works on Tyneside were strike bound for many weeks. Some employers engaged in a strenuous resistance to the men's demands for a shorter working week, but two of the biggest engineering enterprises, Palmer's and Stephenson's, continued at work throughout because of the prestige which their heads enjoyed among their own workers. As the strike continued, public opinion rallied increasingly to the side of the strikers. They were supported by such unproletarian organs as *The Times, The Spectator* and *The Pall Mall Gazette*; before the strike ended, donations to strike funds were even coming from some engineering employers. During the strike the men's leaders constantly urged peaceable behaviour, but there was in fact a good deal of sporadic violence. In one case which came before a local magistrates' court, the evidence seemed clear enough that two local strikers had severely beaten an imported blackleg; the defendants were, however, acquitted, with the following words from the presiding magistrate[107]: 'The Bench are not satisfied that there is sufficient evidence to convict the defendants, and they are dismissed. And now, my men, take care and don't do it again.'

In view of the reputation which the poor law had acquired in many quarters by the early twentieth century it might be supposed that the institution of non-contributory old age pensions after 1908 would have been greeted with a united chorus of gratitude from the potential recipients, but even here it would be misleading to suppose general agreement, as the regional inspector of the Local Government Board, Elias, somewhat ruefully remarked in 1911[108]:

> Many even of the outdoor poor showed themselves reluctant to apply for the pension, some because the amount was less than they had been receiving from the guardians, two because "the guardians have always treated them well", thirteen "because they are as well off with their out-relief", three more "because they do not wish to be deprived of the visits of the medical and relieving officers" and so forth. . . . Of those who actually left the workhouses in this district not less than 27 (or approximately 8% of the whole) are reported to have returned during the first month of the year, many of them in a deplorable condition, bringing tales of cold treatment by friends and relatives or of futile adventures in the lodging houses and on the road. . . . The general attitude of the aged paupers on this question, although unconsciously complimentary, proved embarrassing to the various boards of guardians, whose financial advantage obviously lay in the wholesale transfer of cases to the pension lists, but whose efforts at "peaceful persuasion" were often times unavailing.

It would make things much easier for the historian if there had been a greater degree of uniformity and symmetry during this period of unprecedented changes, though a simpler story might be a good deal less interesting.

Shift in interdependence

There is, however, one further significant general change during this period, which, while not affecting everyone directly, did mark a profound transformation with very far-reaching consequences. This was a major shift in the nature of interdependence within society. In 1760 for most people life was still very much bounded by local horizons, and, where individuals depended on each other, they commonly depended on those among whom they lived and worked in locally coherent communities. Although there had been some shift away from this position by 1850, the pace of change in this respect markedly accelerated, so that by 1920 the extent of interdependence had been greatly extended. Alike in social, economic and political affairs the degree of localization had diminished, and interdependence no longer resided simply within the coherence of local communities. The point can be illustrated by a consideration of the growth of public utilities within the region. Even before 1850 a beginning had been made with the establishment of a number of companies formed to supply gas and water. By 1920, however, the network of supplies of water, gas and electricity was very much more widespread and pervasive. We have seen how the work of the Sunderland and South Shields Water Company in the later nineteenth century brought for the first time a reliable water supply to a wide area of East Durham. This was an undoubted benefit, but it also meant that the large population involved was brought into a new position of dependence on the continued operation of the pumping stations' steam engines by a few dozen specialized workers with whom in the nature of things most of those dependent on this supply could have not even the most remote acquaintance. Similarly the enginemen of the pumping stations were themselves increasingly dependent upon others whom they did not know for an increasing range of services and supplies. The coal-miners of the region could, and sometimes did, cut off by strike action the flow of the coal which was vital to both home and industry, but they too could not live of their own but depended for their food supply, for their children's education and for a widening range of other needs, on the continuance at work of a variety of specialized groups of other workers with whom they were unlikely to have any personal contact. In many ways the region's pattern of employment was interlocking, so that, for example, a slackening in demand for shipbuilding could have rapid repercussions on the jobs of many workers in iron and steel and in coal-mining. Whereas in earlier periods society was more effectively managed by unofficial patterns of influence and control existing within local communities, by 1920 the role of both central and local government had considerably expanded. The officers of local and central government depended on a wide range of services provided by many thousands of people whom they did not know, so too those thousands increasingly lived in a context in which the officials of government played a key role in managing the affairs of the society. This shift from a relatively intimate and local pattern of interdependence to a much more complex pattern of a more remote form of interdependence—which was none the less real—represented a major change, and one which had come about within only a few generations. The development was to continue and to become more pervasive in the years after 1920, but the process was by then well advanced. Nor was it confined only to developments within the region. A region which was heavily dependent on export markets depended to an unprecedented extent upon the continued demand from those markets, a factor which the region could scarcely control. By 1920 regional autonomy within the country had also diminished. We have seen how the region's banks were increasingly incorporated into larger concerns operating on a national basis. Employers' organizations and trade unions became during this period commonly organized upon a national rather than a regional basis, and the greater interlocking of the economy on a national basis was paralleled by an extension of the significance of national politics, and even for the increasing grouping of major elements of sport, recreation and entertainment on a national basis. This is not to say that regional organizations and regional characteristics had become defunct but rather to point a major shift in the relative significance of factors contained within the region and factors operating in much wider contexts. It was with this radically changed situation that the North East faced the problems which the succeeding period was to bring.

References

1 G. Cadman, *The Administration of the Poor Law Amendment Act, 1834, in the Hexham Poor Law Union*, M.Litt. Thesis, Newcastle University, 1976, p. 390.

2 R. Rawlinson, *Report to the General Board of Health . . , on a Preliminary Inquiry into . . . the Borough of Gateshead*, 1850, p. 27.

3 N. Moorsom, *The Birth and Growth of Modern Middlesbrough*, 1967, p. 8.

4 Lady Bell, *At the Works*, 1907, pp. 2–3.

5 J. Spence et al., *A Thousand Families in Newcastle upon Tyne*, 1954, p. 22.

6 E. R. Dewsnup, *The Housing Problem in England*, 1907, p. 49.

7 J. Y. E. Seeley, *Coal Mining Villages of Northumberland and Durham: A Study of Sanitary Conditions and Special Facilities, 1870–1880*, M.A. Thesis, Newcastle University, 1973.

8 ibid.

9 Anon., *County Borough of Tynemouth, 1849–1949*, 1949, p. 84.

10 Anon., *Hartlepool Gas and Water Company: 100 years of Progress, 1846–1946*, c. 1946, p. 9.

11 Seeley, op. cit., p. 309 et seq.

12 *Report of Commissioners Appointed to Inquire into the . . . Outbreak of Cholera in the Towns of Newcastle upon Tyne, Gateshead and Tynemouth*, 1854, p. xxxix.

13 D. Balfour, *Report on a Scheme of Sewage Disposal for the Town of Alnwick*, 1892, p. 7.

14 R. G. Barker, *The Houghton-le-Spring Poor Law Union*, M.Litt. Thesis, Newcastle University, 1974, p. 231.

15 *Newcastle Weekly Chronicle*, 5 November 1877.

16 W. Richardson, *History of the Parish of Wallsend*, 1923, p. 367 et seq.

17 Newcastle Central Library, volume of cuttings, *Newcastle Relief Fund, 1885-6*.

18 E. Lloyd, *History of the Crook . . . Co-operative . . . Society Ltd*, 1916, p. 141.

19 Cadman, op. cit., pp. 405, 70.

20 Barker, op. cit., p. 163.

21 Bank of England, Newcastle Branch, correspondence, 16 August 1851.

22 Barker, op. cit., pp. 91, 152.

23 P. Mawson, *The South Shields Poor Law Union*, M.A. Thesis, Newcastle University, 1971, p. 128.

24 Seeley, op. cit., p. 14.

25 Barker, op. cit., p. 206.

26 K. Gregson, his current work on the history of the Hartlepool Poor Law Union.

27 E. Allen et al., *The North-East Engineers' Strikes of 1871*, 1971, p. 137.

28 Anon., *Northumberland County Constabulary, 1857-1957*, pp. 16-17, 51, 57-9, 64-5.

29 J. J. M. Perry, *The Edlingham Burglary; or Circumstantial Evidence*, 1889. E. Grierson, *Confessions of a County Magistrate*, 1972, pp. 119-20.

30 Newcastle Central Library, op. cit.

31 Barker, op. cit., pp. 212-13.

32 ibid., pp. 170-1, 227.

33 Newcastle Council, proceedings.

34 J. Coote Hibbert and W. H. Wells, 'A Sketch of the Sanitary History of Newcastle upon Tyne', *Journal of the Royal Sanitary Institute*, vol. XXVIII, no. 4, 1907, pp. 161-75.
   Institute of Cleansing Superintendents, *Proceedings of 14th Annual Conference*, Newcastle, July 1911, p. 51 et seq.

35 Newcastle Poor Law Union, annual statements of receipts and expenditure, 1880 and 1889.

36 Institute of Cleansing Superintendents, op. cit., p. 89.

37 *Northumberland County Constabulary, 1857-1957*, pp. 16-17.
   Durham County Police, centenary booklet, 1940, pp. 21-3.

38 D. J. Rowe, 'Occupations in Northumberland and Durham, 1851-1911', *Northern History*, vol. VIII, 1973, p. 128.

39 M. Taylor, M.A. Thesis, Newcastle University, 1964.
   B. Everett, M.A. Thesis, Newcastle University, 1963.

40 Barker, op. cit., p. 150.

41 Coote Hibbert and Wells, op. cit., p. 170.
   Free Trade Union, *Free Trade and the Industries of Newcastle upon Tyne and District*, 1909, pp. 14-15.

42 Richardson, op. cit. pp. 413-15.

43 W. E. Hume, *The Infirmary, Newcastle upon Tyne, 1751-1951*, c. 1951, p. 52.

44 Anon., *The Newcastle Official Year Book*, 1930, p. 115.

45 Anon., *Newcastle upon Tyne Police-aided Association for the Clothing of Destitute Children*, 1908, p. 9.
46 Anon., *A Romance of Regeneration*, 1913.
47 J. Oxberry, *The Birth of a Movement*, 1924, pp. 10-12, 32.
48 *Victorian Cities*, 1968, p. 250.
49 Mawson, op. cit., pp. 96-7.
50 ibid., pp. 121-2.
51 A. Spencer, *Life of Harry Watts*, 1911, pp. 66-7.
52 *Collier Brigs and their Sailors*, 1926, pp. 282-3.
53 Anon., *Accident at New Hartley Colliery*, pp. 2, 3.
54 T. Darlington, *Memoir of Emerson Muschamp Bainbridge*, 1893, pp. 21-2, 39.
55 J. M. Milne, *Newspapers of Northumberland and Durham*, 1971, p. 30.
56 Anon., *A Brief History of the County Borough of Tynemouth Police*, c. 1969, p. 25.
57 J. Rewcastle, *Newcastle As It Is*, 1854, p. 14.
58 Newcastle Watch Committee, *The Borough Constable's Guide*, 1869, p. 21. *The Police and Fire Brigade Manual*, 1905, p. 244.
59 Rewcastle, op. cit., p. 25.
60 W. Robinson, *The Story of the Royal Infirmary, Sunderland*, 1934, p. 62.
61 U. Ridley, *Cecilia; The Life and Letters of Cecilia Ridley, 1819-45*, 1958, p. 192, no. 1.
62 J. J. Dodd, *The History of the Urban District of Spennymoor*, 1897, pp. 90-5.
63 Bank of England, op. cit., 8 April 1851.
64 ibid., 27 May 1859.
65 *The Northern Temperance Year Books*, 1894-7, p. 41.
66 ibid.
G. Hayler, *The Prohibition Movement*, 1897, p. 23 et seq.
67 E. I. Waitt, *John Morley, Joseph Cowen and Robert Spence Watson: Liberal Divisions in Newcastle Politics, 1873-1895, Ph.D. Thesis*, Manchester University, 1972, p. 352.
68 Hayler, op. cit., p. 25.
69 C. E. B. Russell, *Social Problems of the North*, c. 1913, p. 118.
70 *Northumberland County Constabulary, 1857-1957*, op. cit., p. 24.
71 Quoted by F. W. D. Manders, 'Theatres and Music Halls of Gateshead', *Gateshead Local History Society Bulletin*, vol. 1, no. 6, p. 92.
72 N. W. Apperley, *North Country Hunting Half a Century Ago*, 1924, pp. 31-2, 62, 142, 165, 176.
73 R. B. Charlton, *A Lifetime with Ponies*, c. 1941, p. 39.
74 W. Maw, *The Story of Rutherford Grammar School*, 1964, p. 155.
B. Dobbs, *Edwardians at Play: Sport, 1890-1914*, 1973, p. 71.
75 G. J. Mellor, *The Northern Music Hall*, 1970.
S. Middlebrook, *Newcastle upon Tyne, its Growth and Achievement*, 1950, new edition 1968, p. 305.

76 Newcastle Central Library, *Bruce Collection*, A Peep at Newcastle in the Fifties, vol. V, pp. 182–3.

77 *Northumberland Miners' Union Minutes*, 1910, pp. 33–4.

78 Waitt, op. cit., pp. 432, 442, 450–1.

79 Claudine Murray, manuscript on Victorian childhood.

80 Anon., *The Royal Visit to Newcastle upon Tyne*, 1884.

81 R. R. Challinor, *Gun-running from the North East Coast, 1905–7*, p. 15.

82 Newcastle Central Library, Cowen Papers, several examples.

83 A. W. Purdue, *Parliamentary Elections in North East England, 1900–1906: the Advent of Labour*, M.Litt. Thesis, Newcastle University, 1974.

84 *Two Lamps in Our Street*, 1967, chapter 10.

85 Oxberry, op. cit., pp. 10–13.

86a D. Dougan, *The History of North East Shipbuilding*, 1968, p. 124.

  b J. F. Clarke, *Labour Relations in Engineering and Shipbuilding on the North East Coast in the Second Half of the Nineteenth Century*, M.A. Thesis, Newcastle University, 1966.

87 C. Hiskey, 'Sources for Labour History in the Durham Record Office', *Bulletin of the North East Group for the Study of Labour History*, no. 8, 1974, pp. 20–1.

88 Clarke, op. cit., chapters 7, 8.

89 J. H. Porter, 'David Dale and Conciliation in the Northern Manufactured Iron Trade, 1869–1914', *Northern History*, vol. V, 1970, pp. 157–71.

90 Mawson, op. cit., pp. 122–3.

91 J. Wigham Richardson, *Memoirs*, 1911, pp. 283–4.

92 Anon., *The Story of the Thermal Syndicate*, c. 1956, p. 12.

93 R. Pound, *The Fenwick Story*, 1972, p. 61.

94 H. G. Ellis, *Broughs Limited*, c. 1952, p. 44.

95 Lloyd, op. cit., p. 208.

96 A. Barton, *The Penny World, A Boyhood Recalled*, 1969, pp. 168, 171.

97 R. Bell, *Twenty-five Years of the North Eastern Railway, 1898–1922*, c. 1951–2, p. 58.

98 Tyneside Scottish Brigade Committee, *First Report of the Honorary Secretaries*, 1915.

  F. Lavery, *Irish Heroes in the War*, 1917, p. 81 et seq.

99 C. Buchan, *A Lifetime in Football*, 1955, p. 52.

100 R. A. S. Redmayne, *Men, Mines and Memories*, 1942, p. 179.

101 S. F. Jackson, *A Short History of the Newcastle and Gateshead Gas Company*, 1947, p. 29.

  J. F. Davidson, *From Collier to Battleships: Palmers to Jarrow, 1852–1933*, 1946, p. 40.

  Anon., *Dame Allan's School, Newcastle upon Tyne, 1705–1929*.

  Durham County Police, op. cit., p. 25.

  Maw, op. cit., p. 113.

102   Private information from participants.
103   Barton, op. cit., p. 88.
104   Lloyd, op. cit., p. 59.
105   R. F. Wearmouth, *Pages from a Padre's Diary*, pp. 78, 130.
106   Barton, op. cit., p. 77.
107   Allen et al., op. cit., p. 140.
108   Mawson, op. cit., p. 134.

Part Three
1920–1960

5 Post War Economic Problems

Just as the unprecedented rate of economic growth which had characterized the period after 1850 was unforeseen, so the economic difficulties which afflicted the North East in the post-1918 period were unexpected as well as unwelcome. At the end of the First World War, there was a widespread anticipation of a return to pre-war patterns and practices. During the war years the main industries on which the region primarily depended, such as coal-mining, iron and steel, engineering, shipbuilding, had been busily employed, and there had been little to suggest that serious trouble lay ahead for them in the post-war years. Yet the inherent precariousness of the regional economy as it had expanded in the later nineteenth century remained, with a concentrated dependence on a few sectors of industry combined with a heavy reliance on export markets. These markets were vulnerable to the development of competing suppliers and were dependent upon the maintenance of a high volume of international trade, though the extent of these dangers was not very apparent in the first post-war years.

The coal trade
The coal trade had been at the heart of the region's industrial growth, and its early post-war history suggested on the whole that there was a good chance of its returning to pre-war patterns. In 1919, while Tyneside exports in other goods rose by 19% over the 1918 figures, the increase in exports of coal and coke was 25%. The next year saw a set-back, but one which could reasonably be attributed to merely temporary causes. The war-time coal controls continued, and in 1920 the national Coal Controller allocated to the North East ports an export quota of only 7 million tons, which was exhausted by the middle of the year. There was also some slackening in home demand, and the two factors combined resulted in a drop in coal consumption together with a marked underemployment of shipping and transit capacity[1]. Thereafter, however, the coal trade remained at a fairly high figure for the remainder of the decade except when interrupted by major strikes on the coalfield, as in 1921 and 1926.

During the French occupation of the Ruhr coalfield in 1923, there was a marked boom in the North East's coal exports; the river Tyne alone shipped $21\frac{1}{2}$ million tons, of which more than 18 million tons were exported. This record figure was, however, exceptional and could not be maintained when the temporary external circumstances which prompted it had been removed and the German mines resumed full production. The traditional pattern of destinations for the region's coal exports was essentially maintained, and in the 1923 boom Germany, France, Holland and Belgium took between them more than three-quarters of all foreign shipments. Within the coasting coal trade, London continued to be far and away the biggest market for North-East coal, with other British destinations taking only about 12% to 15% of coastal shipments[2].

The maintenance of a high level of coal shipments was reflected in the figures of employment on the coalfield during these years. In 1923 and 1924 the level of unemployment of North East miners stood at 2.6% and 3.9%, but in the aftermath of the prolonged stoppage in 1926 the figure jumped to 22.6% for 1927 and had only fallen back to 13.3% by 1929[3]. Although in 1929 the North East's mines produced 53.5 million tons of coal and employed a work force of 208,000, this already represented a drop in the number of miners employed since 1924. As economic depression deepened in subsequent years, the trend accelerated with falling demand. In the 10 years between 1924 and 1934 the coalfield lost almost 50,000 jobs, or about a fifth of the total employment afforded. For the most part this represented a serious reduction in the jobs available for adult men, though there was also a significant reduction in the number of openings for younger male workers.

The fall-off in demand which produced this rapid fall in employment had more than one root[4]. In 1929 about 17.8 million tons of coal mined within the region had been consumed by domestic or industrial consumers on or near the coalfield; this was much the same level as that of 1924 but was even then about 4 million tons lower than the 1913 figure. With many local industries hard hit by the depression, the figure for local consumption dropped to 12.3 million tons by 1933. There was a slight recovery in 1934, but this still left local consumption at about 5 million tons below the 1929 figure. The international economic depression and the severe shrinkages in international trade and exchange had severe effects on the export trade in coal which during the later nineteenth century had been such a major factor in the expansion of coal production within the region. In 1929 nearly 21 million tons of coal had been shipped from North East ports to foreign destinations, but by 1932 this figure had slumped to 12.6 million tons. There were slight improvements in 1933 and 1934, but this still left foreign shipments at about 7 million tons below the 1929 figure. The twin factors of economic depression and rival sources of coal production on the continent saw some of the North East's main overseas markets drop markedly, with shipments to Germany, France, Belgium and Italy all reduced by more than half. Coastal shipments held up much more strongly, with the 1929 figure of 11.3 million tons dropping only to an average of about 10.8 million tons for the years 1930–2. This relative stability in the coastal trade, however, could not compensate for the severe falls in coal exports and local consumption.

These blows fell heaviest on the older and less efficient collieries, and the loss of employment and income was most severe in areas where the cost of production had risen with the working-out of the most accessible and easily extracted seams of coal, as in many of the older Durham pits. A further contributory factor in reducing the level of employment was the increased mechanization of mining. As early as 1929, 55% of the coal produced was cut by machine in Northumberland, where many of the larger collieries were relatively new, and this figure had risen to 81% by 1933; for Durham the figures were 22% and 35%, reflecting a higher share of older and less competitive collieries in the southern county. Total figures of profitability for the two counties during the years 1929–35 show that overall the Durham mines were working at a loss in 1931–4, while the Northumberland mines were the same in 1932–4; these overall figures, of course, leave ample room for considerable diversity in the profitability of individual collieries in both counties. As late as 1937 the level of coal and coke exports from the Tyne was less than half the peak attained in 1923. The decline in both production and employment would have been even more spectacular had it not been for the effects of the important Coal Mines Act of 1930 which by enforcing arrangements for pooling income enabled the more competitive collieries of the region to subsidize the continued existence of some of the less profitable pits.

Even in these very adverse conditions some of the more modern and efficient colliery companies contrived to maintain programmes of expansion and improvement. In Northumberland, for instance, the Ashington Coal Company remodelled, and in some cases completely rebuilt, the surface installations of its five major collieries; although by 1931 there was only one colliery left in operation at Wallsend, this Rising Sun Colliery was taken over in 1934 by the Bedlington Coal Company, which sank new workings to the deeper Brockwell seam and erected expensive new surface installations for coal preparation. In County Durham, Horden Collieries Ltd was able to pay dividends of $7\frac{1}{2}$% in 1930 and 5% in 1935, though the figure sank to $2\frac{1}{2}$% in 1933[5]. All of these companies achieved significant improvements in productivity during the 1930s. In contrast many of the older pits in the Bishop Auckland area were amongst those hardest hit by adverse market conditions, and that district experienced very high rates of unemployment. In general the decline in the employment and income generated by the region's coal mines during these depression years was a major ingredient in the economic and social troubles experienced within the region during the inter-war period.

Part of the coalfield's difficulties stemmed from the troubles experienced by some of its main customers within the region. The iron and steel industry was a major consumer of coal as well as a major producer of materials for industries such as shipbuilding and engineering. By 1929 pig iron production within the region had reached 2.3 million tons and steel production 2.2 million tons. There then followed a catastrophic fall in demand from buyers both at home and abroad[6], which brought the 1932 production figures down to 880,000 tons for pig iron and 1 million tons for steel. A slow recovery then ensued, with pig iron production within the region rising to 1 million tons in 1933 and 1.7 million tons in 1934, with steel moving up to 1.3 million tons in 1933 and 1.8 million tons in 1934, both still significantly below the 1929 levels. Recovery continued in the following years, partly because of the impact on home demand of the adoption of rearmament programmes. In 1929, 14% of the insured workers in the industry within the region had been listed as unemployed, and in 1932 the figure touched 46% before declining again to 23% by the end of 1934.

As in coal-mining the overall experience of the iron and steel industry during the 10 years 1924-34 was a significant drop in the number of jobs provided, with a loss of 16,000 jobs in iron-ore-mining, blast furnaces and the rolling of steel. Again the process of technological improvement also contributed to a lower labour demand, even where productive capacity was significantly increased. In iron and steel, as in coal, the main root of the troubles during the depression years was a serious fall in demand from both home and export markets.

In coal-mining and in the iron and steel industry the North East region just about retained its previous share in national output, despite the severe overall falls in production. In engineering, however, the region was hit disproportionately hard during the worst depression years. Again a serious drop in demand both at home and abroad was experienced, followed by massive redundancies. Between 1929 and 1932 the numbers employed in the region's main engineering trades dropped from 56,491 to 33,171, a fall of 41.3% as against a national fall for the same period of only 23.9%, reflecting the regional dependence on various branches of heavy engineering which were hit hardest during these years. Marine engineering, for example, was hit by the slump in shipbuilding. Recovery in the North East engineering industry also lagged behind the national levels. In 1934 over the country as a whole engineering employed just under 10% fewer workers than in 1929, but the North East figure remained as high as 27.3%[7].

Shipbuilding and marine engineering

Even before the main international depression sharpened at the end of the 1920s, the North East shipbuilding industry had seen marked fluctuations in its fortunes, not unlike the experience of the immediate pre-war period[8]. There had been a prosperous situation just after the war, with the need to replace wartime ship losses, but this did not prove long lasting. In the autumn of 1923, for instance, 14,000 shipyard workers were unemployed at Sunderland and 6,000 at Jarrow. The early 1930s, however, brought a much more prolonged and serious slump. In 1929 the region launched 679,000 tons of new merchant ships, but by 1933 the figure had fallen to a catastrophic 37,000 tons and increased only to 67,000 tons in 1934. This was part of a national, indeed a world-wide, collapse in shipbuilding, reflecting the severe drop in international trade, but in shipbuilding, as in engineering, the North East did not even manage to retain its previous share of the greatly reduced British total of new tonnage. The 67,000 tons launched in 1934 represented a mere 14.5% of the national total, very different from the palmy days of the later nineteenth century. In March 1930, North East yards had in hand well over a third of the new ships under construction in British yards; in March 1934 the region's share of work in progress was down to as little as 10.4%. The rival yards on the Clyde contrived to do rather better and for the first time beat the Tyne in winning contracts for tanker-building, a field in which the North East had previously predominated for many years.

The collapse in shipbuilding orders from home and abroad was paralleled by a collapse in employment. Shipbuilding was an industry which had normally seen considerable fluctuations in employment on a short-term basis, and in 1929 the unemployment figure for trades engaged in shipbuilding and ship-repairing in the North East had stood at 26.6%, as against a national average of 22.5%. In 1931, with most building berths empty, 70.6% of the region's shipyard workers were out of work, and when things were at their worst in 1933 the figure touched very nearly 80%, as against national averages in these trades of 56.6% and 51.1%. As in engineering, recovery in the mid-1930s lagged behind national levels, though here again the rate of improvement speeded up markedly in the later 1930s.

The conditions prevailing in the earlier 1930s saw many companies in the industry facing a hard struggle for survival. At Sunderland, the Austin firm lost money in 1923-8 and then more in 1930-5, with recorded operating losses totalling £120,000. The much bigger Tyneside firm of Swan Hunter and Wigham Richardson saw profits drop from £150,000 in 1931 to £19,000 in 1933; the later recovery was marked by profits of £190,000 in 1935 and nearly £500,000 in 1939. Hawthorn Leslie returned losses in both 1932 and 1933 but again were making substantial profits by the later 1930s[9]. As they had done in earlier periods of slack trade, shipbuilders tried hard to find alternative occupations for their yards which would enable them to keep at least a nucleus of their work force busy. Some took up ship-breaking; others tried to keep going by building caravans, kitchen boilers and the like. However, no such palliatives could make a significant impact upon the problems facing an industry which possessed a great deal of expensive plant for which there was for a number of years no substantial business[10].

One possible way of adjusting the industry's resources to available demand was to reduce surplus capacity by the closure of less efficient units. This led in 1930 to the creation of the National Shipbuilders Security Ltd, an enterprise devised by the Clydeside shipbuilder, Sir James Lithgow, and backed by shipbuilding firms which between them built about 93% of British-built tonnage in 1930. Funds for its work were obtained partly by a levy of 1% on the value of new ships laid down in British yards, but the company also began with borrowing powers for up to £2.5 million. Its aim was to reduce capacity in the

British shipbuilding industry by buying up unprofitable yards and by sterilizing their sites as far as shipbuilding was concerned; initially this prohibition was to be for at least 40 years. A number of ailing North East yards were among early victims of this process, with Tyne, Wear and Tees all represented among closures of shipyards by these means. The most notorious instance of the company's work was the purchase and closure of the old Palmer shipbuilding enterprises at Jarrow. Jarrow was a town which had grown up with the development of the region's basic industries—coal, iron and steel, engineering and shipbuilding—upon which the town depended to a degree unusual even in the North East. During the years before 1934 there had been a number of blows to the town's economy with the closure of other major sources of income and employment, and this made the closure of the Palmer yards even more damaging. By the criteria adopted by the National Shipbuilders Security Ltd, these yards were obvious victims. The Palmer company was in serious financial trouble; the yards had no orders and no obvious chance of obtaining orders in present circumstances. The decision to buy out the company and to close its shipyards was taken on commercial grounds which seemed sound, but that decision could not remain merely a commercial one. The yards were the last major productive and employing enterprise which the borough possessed, and the social and political consequences of this decision were to be considerable, and notably long lived. The closure of the Palmer yards was to be a major ingredient in the story of 'the town that was murdered', to use Ellen Wilkinson's phrase. There was, however, more to come; early attempts to help the town by rebuilding iron and steel manufacture there were frustrated by opposition from other elements in that industry, which also faced surplus capacity and unemployment in other districts. However, even at Jarrow there were signs of recovery in the later 1930s. In 1936 Jarrow Metal Industries Ltd, with Palmer's old boiler shops converted into a steel foundry, began work, and by 1938 the Consett Iron Company had opened a rolling mill on another part of the old Palmer site. Palmer's old Hebburn shipyard was reorganized and modernized as a ship-repairing yard in time to carry out the conversion of the ill-fated *Jervis Bay* to her role as armed merchant cruiser. However, these developments, useful as they were, could not compensate for the loss to the town of the large-scale industrial enterprises which had supported Jarrow's early growth, and by 1939 Jarrow had certainly not recovered from the blows of the depression years.

The decline in these basic industries had far-reaching effects. For example, the marked drop in the region's trade brought unused capacity and widespread unemployment in shipping and a variety of port and waterfront activities. By 1933 unemployment in such sectors was running at about 50%. Although fluctuations and intermittent employment were common in such trades, this was far above normal experience.

Even before the cumulative blows inflicted by the major depression hit the region after 1929, some of the vulnerability to which the region's economy was exposed had been exemplified by the fate of the enterprise which had above all others symbolized the great growth period of the late nineteenth and early twentieth centuries—the Armstrong company. The great firm of Armstrong Whitworth, with its complex of shipbuilding, engineering and armaments activities, emerged from the First World War with considerable profits amassed but with very grave problems to be faced in a a world which presented less attractive opportunities for some of the firm's principal vocations. Shipbuilding as a whole was subject to fluctuating fortunes, but for Armstrong Whitworth the virtual cessation of the world appetite for warship-building was an especially severe blow. Warships were highly specialized costly vessels which had provided in the pre-war years of acute naval competition a very profitable line of business. Now naval construction, and indeed armaments manufacture in general, were at a very low ebb, which posed serious difficulties for this major company and endangered the livelihood of thousands of men at Elswick and the company's other plants. If the Armstrong company were to survive as a major firm, it was essential to find new forms of activity to replace the old military and naval stand-bys.

A number of possibilities were considered. Before the war the company had made some efforts to diversify into the manufacture of motor cars and aircraft, and some of the firm's war-time activity had forwarded these trends. During the war the firm had worked closely with the designer, John Siddeley, especially in aero-engine manufacture, and it seemed sensible to build on this link in post-war years[11]. In 1919 the Armstrong board of directors agreed to buy up Siddeley's own existing company; a new holding company, Armstrong Whitworth Development Company Ltd, was formed, with Armstrong Siddeley Motors Ltd as a subsidiary. This attempt to marry Armstrong's technical and manufacturing capacity to Siddeley's design skills began well but turned sour after a few years; by 1926 the main parent company was in serious trouble, as we shall see, while Siddeley had not found his new colleagues entirely congenial. In late 1926 the Armstrong Whitworth board of directors agreed to accept an offer of £1½ million from Siddeley and to hive off the joint enterprise, which thereafter continued its independent career in the motor car and aircraft industries.

The main trouble which beset Armstrong Whitworth in these years came from a completely different source. To meet the vacuum in orders for their equipment and workers in the post-war world, the directors decided to embark upon a bold new adventure, which it was hoped would provide suitable work for a variety of the great company's assets. This plan involved the exploitation of a large area of forest on the west coast of Newfoundland and included the creation of a new port, the erection of a hydro-electric power system and the building of complex paper mills of advanced design. The hope was that this gigantic project would provide work for the company in the building of the various kinds of machinery needed and the supply of the shipping needed to service the scheme. The war-time profits were not enough to cover the cost, and so the additional capital required was provided by a special issue of £3 million in debentures. This was a distinctly risky business, for this new issue raised annual interest charges on debentures to a total of $£\frac{1}{2}$ million at a time when post-war operating profits amounted to an annual figure of only about £650,000, with a very large share capital also to be considered. The adventure could only succeed if success could be made to come quickly and if profits from the grandiose new project began to flow quickly enough to offset any doubts about the company's financial stability. The reality proved very different. In such an unfamiliar field the company fumbled; the level of managerial expertise displayed was feeble, the planning defective, the cost control seriously imperfect and the expenditure spiralled upwards without adequate return. In 1924 the annual accounts of the firm disclosed a trading loss of £891,502, and by mid-1925 the giant company owed £2.6 million to the Bank of England and was only kept afloat by repeated injections of credit from the Bank. Share prices which had stood at £3 in 1914 plunged to a few shillings by late 1926. The Bank of England finally enforced drastic action; first of all a new top management was installed at the Bank's insistence, and then during 1927 arrangements were completed for a forced merger between the Tyneside-based company and its old rival, Vickers. A new company, Vickers Armstrong Ltd, now emerged, which took over the old armaments and shipbuilding interests of both firms, with the Vickers element in the new structure very much in the ascendant. Each party to the merger retained some commercially separate activities, but the bulk of their interests were now amalgamated[12].

The boldness of the ill-fated Newfoundland venture appears startling, but it had not been entirely unjustified, for the germ of the scheme was later to prosper in other hands, but the defective financing and execution of the project had fatally weakened the company and led to the loss of its independence. It was not the only element in the old Armstrong empire to face tribulations during the post-war years. The acquisition of additional naval shipbuilding capacity with the new Walker Naval Yard just before the First World War had then been very good timing, but the yard's prospects were not so rosy in the post-war years. The yard had to be closed because of a total lack of orders in April 1928. A gleam of light appeared 2 years later, when Vickers Armstrong obtained a contract to build the Furness Withy liner, *Monarch of Bermuda*, but no follow-up orders of any kind were to be found when that vessel sailed away late in 1931, so the yard closed again and the men were paid off. This time the closure was for 5 years, until the growing stream of British rearmament orders provided the yard with new life from May 1936; the cruiser, *Newcastle*, was followed by the *Sheffield*, the aircraft carrier, *Victorious*, the battleship, *King George V*, and a variety of other ships familiar in the naval history of the Second World War.

We may see then how the premier company of the region was battered by the economic difficulties which afflicted the region during the inter-war years. The impact of declining income and declining employment was not of course confined to productive industry but had repercussions throughout the regional economy, infecting a wide range of services which had developed apace in the more prosperous past before the First World War. Unemployment in the distributive trades within the region, which had stood at 6.8% in 1923, rose through 9.1% in 1929 to 15.6% in 1931 and continued to rise during the remaining years of the depression as many customers found their ability to purchase goods diminished[13]. Local building societies found the market for their mortgages markedly shrinking[14]. The retail companies which had shown such marked growth in the previous period found sales and profits sharply reduced. The shops which had belonged to the chain built by G. W. Duncan saw average branch weekly takings drop from £181 in 1930 to £129 in 1931; the profits of the shops which had been founded by the Brough family had been £55,000 in 1924 but were only £25,000 in 1932.

At the same time the extent of the depression ought not to be exaggerated. Throughout the region as a whole the majority of workers remained at work, and with the international depression bringing down many prices the 1930s were years of rising standards of living for many, even within this region. The problem was that the main impact of the depression fell upon a few major sectors of the region's economy with especial force, and it was the North East's ill fortune that those sectors were among those on which the region depended to an unusually large extent. Such elements as coal, iron and steel, shipbuilding and engineering were not only among the region's chief sources of wealth and work, but they had also for long been obviously the strength and pride of the region's expansion, so that the severe difficulties experienced there had psychological as well as economic impacts.

Chemical and other industries

There were of course some signs of continued success within a general pattern of trouble during these depression years. In the years after the creation of I.C.I. in 1926 the chemical industry on Teesside continued to show a strong capacity for growth. From the mid-1920s the I.C.I. base at Billingham replaced Middlesbrough as Teesside's boom town. This was one industry which escaped the major difficulties of the depression years, and employment in the region's chemical works rose from 6,500 in 1921 to 14,500 in 1931 and then continued to grow to reach 44,000 by the end of the Second World War[15]. Some other Teesside enterprises also missed the worst blasts of the depression; in constructional engineering, for example, a number of major bridge-building contracts for work both at home and abroad kept some major firms busy[16]. On Tyneside too the story was not wholly one of gloom and depression. The old soap-manufacturing firm of Thomas Hedley faced a severe financial crisis in the late 1920s but emerged from it in 1930, having become a part of the Cincinnati-based Procter and Gamble group. In the following years the rejuvenated firm found growing markets at home and abroad, with a series of new products launched and backed by skilful and expensive advertising campaigns—Oxydol in 1930, Sylvan Flakes in 1933 and Mirro in 1934, for examples[17].

If some established firms continued to show capacity for growth during the depression years, there was also a continued creation of new ventures. Some of the firms which succeeded in establishing themselves in these unpropitious years exhibited considerable ingenuity and managerial skills. One example of an enterprise which succeeded in establishing itself as a distinctly viable venture during the depression years was Victor Products Ltd, at Wallsend. The increased use of mechanical methods of coal-mining provided an opportunity for the establishment of new firms specializing in the design and production of mining equipment, and in 1929 two engineers, H. Crofton and R. W. Mann, decided to embark upon the manufacture of their own rotary drills for mining. Their original capital was very small and their original premises distinctly makeshift, but perseverance and skill paid off and Victor Products continued to grow during the early 1930s, with accelerated development taking place thereafter.

This successful initiative achieved in the worst years of the depression was certainly not unique, but the additional income and employment provided by companies which grew and flourished were not enough to offset those lost in the narrow range of major industries on which the region relied to a very considerable extent. In these circumstances the region increasingly looked for help in its difficulties to national agencies, especially the national government and legislature. During the previous period of massive economic growth there had been little disposition shown to invite any substantial government interference in the region's economic activity, but now times had very much changed. The experience of an unprecedented extension of government control of the economy which had taken place during the First World War had suggested that enhanced government intervention could be practicable and perhaps beneficial. In fact, the economic and social problems which beset the depressed regions during the inter-war period faced the national government with a kind of regional problem of a new and unforeseen kind. In so far as attention had been paid earlier to regional problems, they had mainly been seen as the question of predominantly rural areas facing difficulties from foreign food imports and declining populations. After the First World War, however, regional problems took on an abrupt change, with the areas concerned now to be found among those which had experienced massive industrial development in the recent past. Regions such as North East England, South Wales and Clydeside were dependent upon heavy industries which had been major growth sectors before the First World War, but they possessed a relatively small share the newer industries which were showing a much higher potential for growth in the post-war world. The problem was not so much a national predicament of industrial decline but the very great regional disparities in the distribution of older industries in relative decline and newer industries set upon a course of rapid expansion.

Government intervention
Government intervention in defence of the depressed regions during the inter-

war period was to become more extensive and more overt than in any earlier period but failed to make any very substantial inroads into the problems of the regions chiefly concerned. It is easy in looking back from a lengthy period of major increases in state intervention in the country's economic affairs to underestimate the difficulties involved in the early stages of this development. The deepening depression did not strike a community which had anticipated the trouble and carefully prepared contingency plans but came instead as something unexpected by the overwhelming majority. It was by no means clear what government could and should do in the early 1930s; the prevailing concepts of economics scarcely encouraged large-scale government irruptions into the management of the country's economy. Moreover both government and parliament were constrained by political circumstances, and it is very difficult to detect in the Britain of the 1930s any overall popular enthusiasm or support for a higher level of taxation to finance public involvement in economic activities on a large scale. Political parties which campaigned for much higher levels of government spending and government involvement did not fare particularly well in the electoral history of these years, despite the existence of a very wide electorate. The general elections of 1931 and 1935 clearly sustained in office the self-proclaimed national government, and even in a region such as North East England there was a substantial level of electoral support for the governments of the 1930s; in the general election of 1935, for example, 46.9% of those voting at Jarrow supported the Conservative candidate. There were certainly vociferous campaigns for a much higher level of state intervention and public spending, but it would be very difficult to establish that such campaigns succeeded in convincing the very wide national electorate who exercised voting power. Those who are contemptuous at the failure to solve regional problems during the 1930s must not be content with blaming governments but must blame also the mass electorate which installed and sustained those governments in office.

In these circumstances it is understandable that government intervention designed to help the economies of the depressed regions was not marked by a spirit of urgency or prodigality. The increase in unemployment on the coal-field, in the aftermath of the 1926 strike and the colliery closures which followed it, induced the Baldwin government to finance a scheme for the payment of small removal grants to encourage redundant miners to move to work in other regions. This scheme, inaugurated in 1928, was subsequently extended to certain other groups of workers facing a similar predicament and was then linked with a series of official centres established to provide retraining facilities. All this, however, while a new departure in government policy, was on a small scale in relation to the extent of the regional problems which were becoming increasingly apparent by the early 1930s. These modest exercises in inter-vention achieved an appropriately modest effect. The men who took advantage of the new facilities offered tended to be the younger and more venturesome workers, and the schemes did little or nothing for the very large number of older men among those whose jobs were lost during the depression years. It was also true that there was a high proportion of those living in the region who showed no inclination to go elsewhere or who soon returned after making the experiment. Moreover, during the worst depression years of the early 1930s even the country's more prosperous regions had little to offer in the way of additional employment.

As yet parliament and government had not gone beyond small-scale concepts of gingerly using public money to encourage some redistribution of labour between depressed regions and growth areas. The idea of using national tax revenue in direct subsidization of firms willing to offer employment in the depressed regions was a very much larger step, and one against which some very telling arguments could be levelled. How competent could government be in deciding which enterprises merited such government bounties? Why should taxes drawn from certain regions be used to subsidize economic competitors in others? Was not the principle of government subsidies an inherently inefficient economic policy?

Improvements in regional policy

It was not until 1934 that any further major innovation in regional policy was embarked upon. The Special Areas Act of that year followed upon a series of special investigations carried out in the depressed regions, and the wide publicity given to the resultant reports. The investigations had been instituted for two main reasons. In the first place the disastrous social effects of large-scale and long-term unemployment in the hard-hit areas were increasingly understood and were increasingly exploited by the political opposition. In the second place, however, the costs in public spending were a serious worry. Prolonged unemployment in staple industries within the depressed regions brought the need for high levels of spending in unemployment benefits and public assistance. While the central government had tried hard to maintain the principle of local autonomy and local responsibility, this veil was becoming very thin indeed by the early 1930s. Many local authorities simply did not possess the rate income to enable them to discharge their responsibilities in times of severe depression and large-scale unemployment. Time and again the central government had been forced to bail out local authorities in such regions as North East England by authorizing increases in borrowing by local authorities. It was sufficiently plain before 1934 that this kind of temporary palliative was wholly inadequate and that central government loans to local authorities were not likely to be repaid or serviced while existing conditions continued.

Wallace, the commissioner who reported upon the economic difficulties in Durham and on Tyneside, stressed in his report that the depression in the North East was due to causes which were beyond the control of the region itself[18]:

There is no likelihood that the same forces which have created the present situation will automatically readjust it, except after a lapse of time and at a cost of human suffering and economic waste which no modern Government would care to contemplate. Durham and Tyneside can only escape from the vicious circle, where depression has created unemployment, and unemployment intensified depression, by means of some positive external assistance.

Wallace pointed out that in June 1934 the national figure for unemployment was computed at 16.1%, while the figure for County Durham and Tyneside was 27.2%; in the Bishop Auckland district, hard hit by the closure of older coal mines, the figure was 50.4% and for Jarrow 56.8%. The report's figures, however, pointed not only to disparities between regions such as North East England and more prosperous areas but also to significant disparities within this region itself. Taking County Durham and Tyneside overall, nearly three-quarters of insured workers were actually employed in June 1934, while in some black spots the majority of insured workers were unemployed. The June 1934 figures listed a total of 165,000 unemployed in the area investigated by Wallace, and of these 63,000 had been totally unemployed for more than 2 years and 9,000 totally unemployed for more than 5 years. If anything, these figures are likely to be underestimates.

Despite these substantial figures, by the time these investigations were completed the depth of the depression had been passed. Any steps the government might take could scarcely be credited with weathering the basic crisis. In any event, the action that the government in fact undertook in the direction of job creation schemes was very tentative in relation to the scale of the problems still facing the depressed regions, and the results of the special areas legislation were trivial in comparison with the recovery effected by much wider factors which had nothing very much to do with official regional policy. Some revival in trade and demand, coupled with the growth of rearmament programmes after 1935, did more to improve the economy of North East England than anything designed by parliament or government specifically for that object. The regional legislation of the 1930s, however, has considerable interest for its recognition, on however tentative a basis, that the national government could and should intervene to curb unemployment by the direct use of national revenue to stimulate employing enterprises[19].

Under the Special Areas Act of 1934 two Commissioners were appointed— one for England and Wales and one for Scotland. The Treasury was to provide these officers with £2 million annually, which should be used to help the economies of those specified regions where the problems of depression were most pressing. In practice only a small amount of benefit resulted from this Act; there was an obvious disparity between the scale of the problems involved and the resources made available in this pioneering legislation, and the Commissioners were severely limited in their freedom to make grants by fears of unfair competition supported by public money. In the North East there was some significant help given, for example, to local building programmes for hospitals and housing, but little in direct stimulation of long-term employment prospects. The inadequacies of the 1934 legislation were speedily realized, and the remaining peace-time years saw further useful advances in regional policy. The use of public money to provide new employment by facilitating the development of trading estates was one early advance. In August 1935 the Commissioner for Special Areas in England and Wales reported to the central government that he had been converted to support the 'novel and unorthodox proposal of establishing trading estates financed out of exchequer Funds', and in the next year the government gave public approval to this conversion. The method of implementing this approach was to establish a non-profit making company in each of the 'special areas', or depressed regions, for the purpose of setting up estates. These companies were given powers to buy suitable sites and to prepare them for convenient industrial use; public money could be made available to buy the land, to drain the sites, to provide transport links, to provide gas, water and electricity installations and then to lease the prepared sites for industrial use. In the North East the main example of this kind of activity before 1939 was the Team Valley Trading Estate, near Gateshead. The original site area acquired there covered 700 acres, and by the outbreak of war in 1939 firms already planted there were providing 2,520 jobs. This was not a very large number, however, in comparison with the region's needs, and few of these new jobs provided catered for the employment of skilled adult men where the principal regional need existed.

A further significant enlargement of government intervention came in 1937, when the Special Areas (Amendment) Act loosened the official purse strings considerably. The Treasury was now authorized to make loans to companies willing to move into the depressed regions, and the statutory commissioners under the 1934 legislation were given a markedly enlarged discretion; they could now use their annual allocation of money to attract industry in much more direct ways, including the payment of part or the whole of a firm's liabilities in rents, rates or income tax incurred by a move into one of the special areas. It remained true, however, that such factors as the upswing of the trade cycle and the extended rearmament orders did more to reanimate the economy of North East England than any specifically regional policy on the government's part. There is a certain irony in contemplation of the extension of official regional policy in the later 1930s. The adoption of a more adventurous and far-reaching policy of direct official intervention to combat the effects of the depression owed something to the experience gained in the more tentative early ventures but much also to the increasingly buoyant national revenue which represented economic improvement and a diminution in the problems which the policy was designed to combat. If by 1939 the government was willing to spend more freely on regional policies, this was largely due to the circumstance that economic recovery had significantly expanded the resources at its disposal.

Economic recovery starts

A variety of indicators suggested that even by the mid-1930s North East England was beginning to rise out of the trough of the depression, even if the recovery was far from general. A perceptive retail shop-manager observed in 1935 that[20] 'the time is coming, when people are tired of going to cheap shops to which they were driven in the years of depression, and these people are now coming back to the better shops. The days of price only and nothing but price have gone, and trade can now be helped by keeping displays attractive and fresh.' In 1935 the Newcastle postal area handled 11.8 million more letters than in 1934, and 2½ million more telephone calls; wireless licences were also up by 10 500[21]. If the shops which J. W. Brough had built up before 1914 had seen their profits drop to only £25,000 in 1932, they were up to £52,000 in 1937 and a record £82,000 in 1939[22]. When the Housing and Building Exhibition was held at Newcastle in 1936 its catalogue could state thankfully that 'it is under much happier and prosperous industrial conditions on Tyneside that the second annual Building Exhibition makes its appearance'.

In 1932 the national level of unemployment was computed to be about 22%, while within the depressed regions figures like Middlesbrough's 40% and the Hartlepools' 48% could easily be found. By 1937 the national figure was 11%, the Hartlepools 23% and Middlesbrough 15%—a few miles away Darlington was down to 9%, appreciably below the national average[23]. Economic recovery within the North East region was real enough but over the region as a whole lagged behind the national level of improvement. Moreover by 1939 the amount of diversification introduced into the regional patterns of industry and employment was relatively slight in North East England. Compared with more prosperous regions, when war broke out in 1939 Northumberland and Durham still depended to an unusually large extent on the older basic industries and held a relatively low proportion of the newer industries which had during the inter-war period exhibited greater potential for successful expansion.

The rearmament programmes of the later 1930s and then the demands for war production after 1939 temporarily solved the region's unemployment problem, which had virtually disappeared by 1940, but did little or nothing to alter the basic situation which underlay the difficulties of the depression years. The embryonic regional policy, evolving in the last peace-time years to encourage diversification in the regional economy, was understandably engulfed in the more urgent needs of total war, and instead the demands of rearmament and war-time production served if anything to reinforce the regional dependence on the older heavy industries. Munitions of war required enhanced production of coal, iron and steel, shipbuilding and engineering; in 1938 these sectors had provided 35% of all jobs in the region, and the figure actually rose to 40% by 1943, though by 1946 at about 34% it was virtually back at the pre-war figure[24].

Moreover, as in the First World War, increased production for war purposes was obtained primarily by more intensive use of existing plant rather than by a high level of investment in replacement and modernization. There was some significant re-equipment in shipyards and steel works, but much more commonly the extension of shift working and expanded labour forces, and the diversion of civilian plant to warlike purposes, were the main sources of increased armaments production. At Wallsend, for instance, the growing firm of Victor Products Ltd had contrived to erect their first purpose-built factory for manufacturing mining machinery in 1937. Now this new plant was in great measure diverted to munitions production, and at the peak of this diversion 60% of the company's capacity was being used in such activities as the making of shell parts, equipment for the army's 3.7-inch guns and petrol pumps for Sunderland flying boats[25]. From 1943, however, as victory appeared increasingly assured, the pressure relaxed and the Wallsend factory could gradually return to its primary designed functions; as one of the firm's publications has it, 'considerable experience was gained in the art of changing swords to ploughshares'. This company was fortunate in that the kinds of machinery it employed were flexible enough to be applied to a variety of products for peace or war, and the growth engendered for warlike purposes could be transferred with relative ease to civilian uses. Many other firms within the region were during the war making do by more intensive use of plant which was already elderly when war began and was to be plainly obsolescent by post-war standards. There was, however, also a boost to the creation of new small factories on trading estates during the war; these sites were normally situated close to convenient supplies of labour, and by 1945 trading estates were providing a total of 12,000 jobs within the region[26].

However, the bulk of extended war-time production came from the older staple industries, and the achievement here was impressive, especially in the years before 1944. In shipbuilding the region's yards produced a rapid flow of new merchant ships, 240 from the Wear, 125 from the Teesside area and 74 from the Tyne during the war. The relatively low Tyneside total was due to the fact that the bulk of the region's share of warship work came to that river; for example, in a 21-month period in 1943-4 Smith's Docks at North Shields carried out by dint of intensive shift working an emergency programme which converted ten tankers into makeshift aircraft carriers for the anti-submarine war[27]. From the beginning of the war new service orders poured into the old Armstrong base at Elswick; as early as 1940 the company held naval contracts worth £12 million, and defence contracts totalling £20 million in all. During the war the work allotted to Elswick was governed only by the plant's capacity. From 1943 production of the Centurion tank was a main preoccupation there, and indeed that tank design was to provide work for Elswick for a total of about 16 years[28].

In another sphere the war years marked an economic turning point of another kind, as far as the coal trade was concerned[29]. War conditions inevitably shattered the export trade in coal, with the principal overseas markets under enemy control. Concentration on the vital East Coast route was of crucial importance, and even that was not easy; submarines, mines and aircraft were all used in German attacks on this vulnerable but essential link, and the crews of the collier fleet suffered severely. By the later years of the war coal shipments were running at a level well under half that of the pre-war years. From 1942 onwards, for instance, the Tyne was shipping well under 1 million tons of coal overseas, and in general the years of the Second World War marked the end of coal exports as a substantial asset to the region's economy.

The region's agriculture had suffered with other sectors during the depression years, including a serious collapse in beef prices in 1933. The later 1930s saw a recovery in demand with the result, for example, that by 1939 virtually the whole of Northumberland's Castle Ward—a large belt of agricultural territory around Newcastle—was dominated by pasture[30]. This development was abruptly reversed by war-time needs, for the need to increase home production brought about a crash programme to extend the area under arable farming[31]. The effect was especially marked in Northumberland. In that county the acreage under wheat expanded from 9,750 in 1939 to 71,728 in 1943, barley from 9,929 to 35,802 and oats from 27,720 to 56,358. The acreage devoted to potatoes went up from 4,728 to 13,793 during the same period. In contrast, the acreage of hay cultivation dropped from 102,277 to 53,604 and permanent grazing from 404,105 to 249,696. This enormous transformation within a very few years was a remarkable achievement, one of the most striking illustrations within the region of rapid and successful adjustment to the demands made by the war. Government initiative and government grants played a part in facilitating the shift, but much of the credit lay with the emergency war agricultural executive machinery which was rapidly and effectively improvized and which depended heavily on co-operation from the region's agricultural interest.

Agriculture was one sector which like many others saw a marked expansion in the employment of women under the pressure of war-time demands. The more complete mobilization of resources during the Second World War saw women take over a wider variety of jobs than had been the case in 1914–18. It was not surprising on the railways to find women appearing again as guards, porters and ticket-collectors, but substitution went much further than that, with women carrying and laying sleepers and repairing multi-core signal and telephone cables[32]. Shipbuilding too saw the enlistment of substantial numbers of women to carry out jobs hitherto regarded as impregnable male preserves; for example, at Hebburn Palmer's old yard employed during the war a growing work force which included 350 women working on ship conversion and repairs[33].

Some economic problems re-emerge

The end of the war saw the re-emergence of some of the problems which had afflicted the regional economy during the inter-war period. Indeed in some areas the post-war situation saw further losses in previous sources of income. The story of the coal trade, for so long the backbone of the region's strength, emphasized the need to find alternative sources of wealth and employment[34]. In

1947 shipments of coal from the Tyne to foreign buyers totalled a mere 216,000 tons—the lowest figure recorded since 1832. During the next 10 years coal exports comprised little more than a quarter of coal shipments. During the 1950s coal exports were running at not much more than half the normal figure of the 1920s, and even that low level was not to be maintained. Coastal shipments bore up much better, with London remaining far and away the most important destination; in 1952, a good year, London took 6.5 million tons of coal from the Tyne, or 87% of the total coastal shipments. Coal exports never came anywhere near their older significance, though within the drastically shrunken totals the old predominance of northern Europe remained. There were no significant shipments of coal to destinations outside Europe after 1954, while 10 years later—probably for the first peace-time years for centuries— no coal at all left the Tyne for either France or Germany.

This situation led to a marked shrinkage of employment in areas either directly or indirectly dependent on the winning and selling of coal. For instance, the number of coal-shipping berths on the Tyne fell from 34 in 1946 to 16 by the early 1960s, and this decline continued thereafter[35]. The decline of employment in coal-mining was the biggest single element in the serious fall in the number of jobs provided by the small group of staple industries which had underpinned the region's rise in the later nineteenth century.

The experiences of this and kindred regions during the depression years of the 1930s, together with the greatly expanded level of government intervention in the country's economic affairs during the 1939–45 war, provided an opportunity for the evolution of a much more thorough and sophisticated regional policy[36]. Before and during the war a series of important enquiries and reports had provided further foundations for such planning. In 1937, for example, the government had appointed a Royal Commission on the Distribution of the Industrial Population—the Barlow Commission as it has become known. Its terms of reference were:

> To inquire into the causes which have influenced the present geographical distribution of the industrial population of Great Britain and the probable direction of any change in that distribution in the future; to consider what social, economic or strategical disadvantages arise from the concentration of industries or of the industrial population in large towns or in particular areas of the country; and to report what remedial measures if any should be taken in the national interest.

This commission reported in 1940, and, while its main objective had not been the study of the structural weaknesses of the economies of the depressed regions of the 1930s, the report provided a reasonably thorough assessment of the problems involved. Not surprisingly, however, the commissioners found it less easy to agree on the best means to remedy these weaknesses. Although nothing much could be done to implement such enquiries during the war, a White Paper on Employment Policy in 1944 specifically accepted the need for a planned national policy for employment, together with a special need to tackle the employment difficulties of the regions which had been hardest hit by the inter-war depression.

Extension in government regional policy

In the post-war years a serious attempt was made to carry out the intentions of these reports and declarations. Official regional policy was to depend upon two main ingredients; on the one hand certain war-time powers were to be retained and applied to regional objectives, while on the other a new statutory frame-work was to be erected to replace the old legislation of the 1930s. In 1945 the Distribution of Industry Act repealed the old special areas legislation of 1934 and 1937 and replaced the inter-war 'special areas' with 'development areas' covering much the same districts. The Board of Trade was given powers to use public money to facilitate the movement of new industry into the development areas, though in fact these powers were in some respects less extensive than those made available to the old special areas commissioners under the 1937 legislation. During the war the government had introduced a system of building licences as a kind of rationing system for scarce building materials, and these powers were retained into the post-war period. During the immediately post-war years the Ministry of Works used these powers extensively to restrict new industrial building in the Midlands and the South and to facilitate industrial expansion and diversification with the development areas. This system of control was buttressed after 1947 and was eventually replaced by the statutory stipulation that before any new factory or extension over 5,000 square feet could be erected the industrialist concerned must obtain an Industrial Development Certificate from the Board of Trade. The combination of stick and carrot—inducements offered to build within the development areas together with a discouragement of developments elsewhere—made regional policy within the immediate post-war years more effective than it had ever been before. During the years 1945–7 the development areas, which contained about one-sixth of the manufacturing workers in Great Britain, received around 50% of the new industrial developments approved.

Within this general pattern North East England did well out of the various extensions of government regional policy. This region contained about 27% of the insured workers living in the development areas, but during the 10 years after 1945 the North East received 30% of the new factory projects backed by government help in the development areas, and these projects contained 32% of the total factory area involved in these schemes. The North East also obtained a large share in the advance factories set up by official initiative to provide ready-made accommodation for new industries in search of working accommodation. All this was useful, but, if the North East had been left to rely on these government initiatives alone, the region would have been in a sorry plight, for about two-thirds of the post-war industrial building within the region was financed by private capital, with the iron and steel industry and the chemical industry prominent among sectors in which substantial new capital was made available for development from unofficial sources.

One specific area of development in which government inducements were important was the continued growth of trading estates. By the later 1950s trading estates within the region contained 310 firms—an increase of about 200 since 1945—with a total employment provision of some 50,000. A quarter of these jobs was concentrated on the expanded Team Valley Trading Estate, near Gateshead, inaugurated in the mid-1930s. On these trading estates the bulk of the jobs provided came from clothing, chemicals, electrical goods and various forms of engineering. There was a notably high proportion of jobs for women on the estates—about half—and this helped to boost a significant change in the region's employment pattern in post-war years; previously North East England had been very low in the proportion of women employed, but the figure had now grown from 17% in 1938 to well over 30% by 1960.

Of course the North East region was in post-war years affected by government policies in many ways other than those specifically associated with official attitudes towards regional problems. The Labour Party's programme of nationalization saw such sectors as coal, railways, electricity and gas brought under public ownership, although for very many years the nationalized industries must depend heavily upon the continued service of those trained and perhaps to some degree moulded by pre-nationalization patterns. The iron and steel industry suffered the political uncertainty of nationalization, denationalization and renationalization. In addition to the direct effects of nationalization, in a wide variety of other ways the role of the state became more pervasive in the post-war years with, for example, the provision of a much wider range of official welfare services and the continuance of relatively high levels of taxation on both individuals and corporations.

The serious concentration of the post-war government on regional policy was severely curtailed after the balance of payments crisis of 1947 brought demands for economy. In the early 1950s a change of political control worked to the same end, with the Conservatives for some years much less willing to impede economic growth in other areas in order to bolster up the development areas. The partial withdrawal of government energies was made much easier by the trend in unemployment during these years. There seemed to be clear evidence that the steps already taken were working and that the adverse position of the development areas was declining, as the figures of unemployment for regions such as North East England seemed to be approaching parity with national levels. In these circumstances it was easier to argue that there was now little need to pursue extraordinary measures for the benefit of the development areas. In 1946 when the average unemployment for Great Britain was 2.4%, the figure for North East England was 7.7%; in 1952 the respective figures were 2.0% and 4.2%, in 1956 1.2% and 2.0% and in 1958 the difference was very small, 2.1% and 2.3%[37].

Any spirit of complacency engendered by these developments was, however, rudely shaken by a tendency for the figures to drift apart again in subsequent years; in 1960 the national figure was 1.7% and that for the North East 2.9%. The attempts of regional policy since 1945 to remedy the structural weaknesses in the region's economy had in fact enjoyed only limited success, and even in the early 1960s the unusual degree of dependence on a few industries remained. Nearly one-third of all male jobs in North East England still remained in coal-mining, shipbuilding, chemicals and metal manufacture, as against a national average in these sectors of 12%; in addition 11% of all male jobs in North East England still remained in engineering. The region still had seven out of every 100 workmen employed in shipbuilding, ship-repairing and marine engineering, amounting to 20% of the national total of those employed in this sector, increasingly vulnerable to very serious international competition. In 1962 10% of North East England's workers in these trades were unemployed. On the other hand the chemical industry, still a significant growth point, employed only $5\frac{1}{2}\%$ of the region's workers.

In these circumstances there was a renewed flurry of government interest in regional policies from about 1958. A new Distribution of Industry (Industrial Finance) Act was put on the statute book in 1958 to supplement earlier legislation but in practice marked no very significant improvement in effectiveness over earlier enactments. In 1960 a more determined attempt was made to tidy up the situation, when much of the existing regional legislation was repealed and replaced by the Local Employment Act. This new system has come in for a good deal of criticism; intended as a well-meant measure of rationalization and improvement the new scheme soon revealed some serious weaknesses. The existence of substantial disparities in need within the development areas had been accepted, and under the 1960 legislation the Board of Trade was now to maintain a list of smaller 'development districts', with the intention of channelling available help more directly to the actual spots where it was most needed. This could appear as a more skilful administrative device, but in practice the listing and unlisting of districts as local unemployment fluctuated could lead to some peculiar results in economic terms. For example, in October 1960 Haswell in County Durham was added to the list of development districts, while in the following year its neighbour, Houghton-le-Spring, was removed. This kind of shifting and piece-meal manipulation had serious defects, and later regional policy was to move back to a more sophisticated concept of concentrating help on larger areas with a coherent economic pattern.

In general, however, while the post-war years saw a whole range of devices elaborated and enacted to tackle regional economic and employment problems, the results were by 1960 far from perfect. It was not always easy to obtain substantial continuity of attention and policy in an area of government activity markedly subject to political pressures of various kinds, and in a period in which governments were beset by a variety of claims in competition for distinctly limited resources. There remained a sizeable differential between the growth of employment and income in the northern region and that in the country at large. Between 1952 and 1961 the numbers employed in Great Britain increased by 8.6%, while the region based on Northumberland and Durham found only 5.6% new jobs—the Midlands recorded 10%, Wales 4.6% and Scotland only 2.1%[38].

A further complication was the relationship between increased production and increased employment in some of the region's developing industries. The booming Teesside chemical industry was a very clear example. At Billingham, I.C.I. doubled the value of its products between 1946 and 1959, but the work force there actually showed a small decline, from 19,500 to 19,000. In general, technological progress in the chemical industry was not matched by the creation of new work opportunities. The point must not be pushed too far, however, for the growth was in fact important from both points of view. By 1960 the I.C.I. sites at Billingham and Wilton were Teesside's biggest employers, providing between them more than 30,000 jobs. The story of iron and steel on Teesside was a similar one, with increased productive capacity outstripping increased employment. By 1954 Teesside produced 25% of the national output of steel plates, 50% of rails, 33% of heavy sections, as well as other products, to a total annual output of some 2 million tons of finished steel, about half of which was destined for export markets. In occasional peak years, such as 1956–7 and 1960–1, with capacity fully employed, the annual total of crude steel produced exceeded 4.5 million tons. There was a considerable extent of capital investment and modernization of plant after 1945. In 1954 iron and steel provided 34,000 jobs on Teesside, or about 20% of all jobs in the district; in subsequent years productive capacity continued to grow, but the proportion of local employment offered by the industry dropped to 18.4% by 1961.

In shipbuilding the North East did well in the early post-war years. Of the 1,875,000 tons of shipping under construction in British yards in September 1946, 700,000 tons were in the North East, including 358,000 on the Tyne[39]. In the early 1950s a substantial boost in tanker-building, if not very good news for coal-mining, brought major building contracts to North East yards. In 1951 Shell had 14 tankers on order within the region, while in the same year an order worth £7 million for eight vessels for the British Tanker Company was also obtained. During the post-war period the North East's share in British shipbuilding did not change markedly, fluctuating about the 41% to 55% range. This was not the whole story, however, for the British share of world shipbuilding declined very substantially, with serious implications for a region such as North East England in which shipbuilding was so important. In 1901 British yards had launched 55% of the world's new tonnage, by 1929 the figure was only 39%, and in 1960, with the accelerated growth of foreign competition, the British share was down to 15%. This situation was to lead to drastic changes in the organization of the British shipbuilding industry in subsequent years. Already by 1960, however, the employing potential of this great North East industry was not holding up, and here too improved technology was not paralleled by maintained provision of work opportunities.

There were of course areas of employment outside productive industry in which there was significant growth in these years, but here too the region often lagged behind national trends. In the 20 years after 1951 the standard census occupation group 24—professional and scientific services—saw the numbers employed rise by 15% in North East England, but the overall national figure was 26%. Much the same was true of employment in general in the distributive and administrative services. There was then a continuing differential between the regions such as North East England—the 'depressed areas' of the inter-war period—and the more rapidly developing regions of the Midlands and South. It was not of course the case that the North East and kindred regions were becoming poorer but rather that growth and improvement came more slowly than in some other regions, whereas in the late nineteenth and early twentieth centuries growth had been relatively more rapid in regions such as this. The impact of government regional policies did mitigate these differentials somewhat but did not eradicate them. The nationalization of the coal industry made possible programmes of substantial investment and modernization in many collieries but could not arrest the inexorable decline of the coalfield as a source of employment, and 22,000 miners left the industry in the region during the 1950s[40]. There was some diminution of the old dependence on a narrow range of industries, and some successful fostering of new industries within the region, but the fact that in 1961 the region still had 15.8% of its total employment provided by coal, shipbuilding and marine engineering, as against a national average of only 4.4%, shows the intractability of the basic problems involved. What certainly has been amply demonstrated by the experience of regional policies in the inter-war and post-war periods is that major alterations in the economic structure of a region such as this are not a simple or an easy task.

Changes in population
Economic developments within the region were reflected also in the population figures. Even during the great growth period of the later nineteenth century there had been substantial outward migration from the region, amounting, for instance, to 19,000 during the 1880s. This had, however, been much more than compensated for by immigration into the region and a high birth rate. The twentieth century saw a very marked slowing-down in the growth of the population of Northumberland and Durham. In the first three decades of the century population growth for Northumberland moved from 15.5% through 7.1% to only 1.4%; the equivalent figures for Durham were 15.4%, 8% and 0.5%. There was no census in 1941; during the 20-year period 1931–51 Northumberland's population grew by 5.5%, but Durham actually recorded a small loss, −1.5%. In the years after the Second World War migration from the region kept the rate of population growth low, effectively cancelling out about half of the natural increase from births. As in earlier periods the outward migration

was only part of a much more complex pattern of movements in and out, but now the balance had tilted, and the overall effect of the movements was a net loss to the region. These net losses fluctuated with the economic health of the region; in 1951–2, for instance, the figure was 15,100, falling to only 2,100 in 1955–6 and rising again to 16,700 in 1960–1. The scale of these losses was not numerically very high, but, since a high proportion of those lost to the region were active younger people, the trend was not welcome[41].

Income and employment

The concentration on questions of employment and the role of the state in economic activity within the regions during the post-1920 period reflects the preoccupations of much of the source material dealing with these years. We are dealing with a society in which problems of unemployment and problems of regional disparities occurred on a large scale and aroused a great deal of contemporary concern. More sophisticated techniques of analysis in economic and social affairs also played a part in focusing attention upon the social impact of economic growth or decline. The enhanced national attention devoted to the problems of regions such as North East England also reflected a continuing decline in the separateness of the region's interests, and a continuing increase in the interdependence within British society. It was no longer possible to maintain that social problems could be seen as problems with which local resources or inexorable market forces could be expected to cope unaided. However halting and unadventurous the intervention of the national government in regional problems of the post-1920 period may appear from the standpoint of the later 1970s, even in the inter-war years it had progressed further than in earlier periods. By 1939 it was no longer pretended that economic and social problems in a region such as North East England were problems which a national government could ignore; instead it was accepted that government authority and national revenue could and should be applied to try to find solutions. Such increasing concern in regional matters was closely paralleled in the provision of much more extensive official welfare services during the same period. If the lessons administered to British society during the depression years of the 1930s were painful, yet at least to some extent the lessons were learned. The spectacle of rising unemployment now arouses a much wider degree of concentration and concern than was the case in earlier periods, even if it has also been learned that solutions to such problems are not always easy to come by.

A great deal of the extant source material on the modern economic history of North East England concentrates heavily on the problems experienced by the regional economy in the period since 1920, and it is necessary, too, to remember that in 1960 the regional economy supported a population living at a very much higher standard of living than had ever been the case at earlier periods. It would be wildly unrealistic to miss the point that the region has shared to a very great extent in the improved conditions which British society has experienced since the end of the Second World War. It is, however, true that there were in 1960 substantial differentials remaining between regions such as North East England and some of the country's more prosperous regions. Unemployment remained persistently higher than the national average, though nowhere near the appalling totals of the early 1930s. The region also continued to possess a relatively small proportion of the major growth industries of modern Britain. The push towards diversification of income and employment administered by government regional policies helped to mitigate these adverse factors, but it was plain by 1960 that the task of finding viable productive units capable of bringing to the region substantial new resources of income and employment was by no means easy. There was a continuing danger, for instance, that enterprises attracted to the region by direct or indirect subsidy might prove frail ventures in an adverse economic climate. Experiences under governments of various complexions have suggested that political theories are not in practice a satisfactory alternative to the skilful and efficient production and sale of goods and services for which real markets exist, though of course even in North East England this lesson has not been universally appreciated. As long as regions such as this remain below national averages for income and employment, there is bound to be a below-average consumer demand for a wide variety of goods and services stretching far beyond the immediate bounds of productive industry. The only viable long-term solution is an increase in the productivity and the competitive ability of enterprises within the region, and this is a solution over which official government action can have only a limited control.

In the period since 1920 North East England did not occupy the proud position of primacy in growth which it held in the period after 1850. However, the matter must be kept in perspective, for, if other regions have in the last half-century grown faster, the North East has not stood still. It will be obvious to anyone who has lived in this region between 1920 and 1960 that those 40 years could not be simply written off as a period of decline and depression. The years of severe social and economic problems of the inter-war period burned deep into the memories of very many people within the region, though as we shall see the history of the inter-war North East was much more complex than that, and the years of depression are far from the whole story. Moreover, those who remember the income levels, the levels of employment and productivity, the working conditions and the industrial relations in the North East of the inter-war period will not often be found sighing for mythical 'good old days' when they contemplate the economy of the region in the second half of the twentieth century.

References

1 H. Shaw, *Newcastle and Gateshead Trade and Commerce*, 1920, p. 53.
2 N. R. Elliott, 'A Geographical Analysis of the Tyne Coal Trade', *Tijdschrift voor Econ. en Soc. Geografie*, March–April 1968, p. 85 et seq.
3 Board of Trade, *An Industrial Survey of the North East Coast Area*, 1932, p. 98.
4 Staff of Economics Department, Armstrong College, Newcastle, *The Industrial Position of the North-East Coast of England*, 1935, p. 21 et seq.
5 Ashington Coal Company, sales brochure, March 1935, p. 4.
    Horden Collieries Ltd, *75,000,000 Tons of Coal*, 1946, p. 26.
6 Staff of Economics Department, Armstrong College, op. cit., pp. 25–7.
7 ibid., p. 27 et seq.
    J. Hodgson, *Changes in the Structure of Employment in the Northern Region of England, 1921–1971*, M.A. Thesis, Newcastle University, 1975, p. 181 et seq.
8 D. Dougan, *The History of North East Shipbuilding*, 1968, p. 140.
9 ibid., pp. 180–1.
10 J. W. Smith and T. S. Holden, *Where Ships are Born, Sunderland, 1346–1946*, 1947, p. 65.
11 O. Tapper, *Armstrong Whitworth Aircraft since 1913*, 1973, p. 14 et seq.
12 J. D. Scott, *Vickers: A History*, 1962, p. 153 et seq.
13 Board of Trade, op. cit., p. 417.
14 Anon., *Newcastle upon Tyne Permanent Building Society, 1861–1961*, p. 4.
15 J. W. House, *The North East*, 1969, pp. 135–6.
16 Anon., *The Cleveland Bridge and Engineering Company Ltd*, c. 1935, p. 5.
17 L. Hale, *Hedley of Newcastle*, pp. 5, 15.
18 Captain D. Euan Wallace, Durham and Tyneside report, *Reports of Investigations into the Industrial Conditions in Certain Depressed Areas*, 1934, p. 106, cmd. 4728.
19 A. J. Odber, *Area Redevelopment Policies in Britain and the Countries of the Common Market*, part 6, U.S. Department of Commerce, 1965.
20 P. Mathias, *Retailing Revolution*, 1967, pp. 89–92.
21 Tyneside Industrial Development Board, *Tyneside: the Natural Centre of Industry*, 1935, p. 3.
22 Mathias, op. cit., p. 89.
23 J. W. House and B. Fullerton, *Teesside at Mid-Century: An Industrial and Economic Survey*, 1960, p. 71.
24 House, op. cit., p. 68.
25 Firm's brochures, made available by Doris Snowdon.
26 House, op. cit., p. 68.

27 Dougan, op. cit., p. 192.
    J. Lamb, *Backward Thinking*, 1953, p. 174.
28 Scott, op. cit., p. 354.
29 Elliott, op. cit., p. 92.
30 H. C. Pawson, *A Survey of the Agriculture of Northumberland*, 1961, p. 72.
31 ibid., p. 9.
32 N. Crump, *By Rail to Victory*, 1947, p. 107.
33 Palmers Hebburn Co. Ltd, *Six Years Hard Labour*, 1946, p. 56.
34 Elliott, op. cit., p. 92.
35 ibid., p. 79.
36 Odber, op. cit.
37 House, op. cit., p. 77.
38 Odber, op. cit., p. 412.
39 Dougan, op. cit., p. 193.
40 House, op. cit., p. 106.
41 ibid., p. 55.

6 Improvement in Social Conditions

During the four decades after 1920, as in earlier periods, there were complex and varied trends to be seen in the experience of the region's population, but certain features stand out as especially prominent. One of the most obviously outstanding developments was a very marked improvement in the standard of living of the overwhelming majority of the people who lived in North East England during these years.

The variety of experience, and the overall improvement, existed even in the inter-war period, vividly remembered within the region as years of crisis and suffering. The crisis and the suffering were real, but it remains true that by 1939 there had been significant improvements in the quality of life within the region; in health, housing, diet, education, recreation and opportunity the situation in 1939 was appreciably better than it had been in 1920, despite the economic adversity which afflicted the region during this period. It is perhaps natural that the suffering is in practice remembered more vividly than the improvement, because the shock administered by the large-scale unemployment of the inter-war years came upon a region which had in the immediate past experienced a period of unprecedented growth and prosperity.

Shortage of revenue and relief policies
We have already seen some of the statistics of unemployment from these years. The social consequences of the economic troubles of the inter-war period were enhanced by the nature of many of the victims. The word 'deprived' is one which is frequently misused in our contemporary polemics, but it may properly be applied to many of the unemployed during these years. In the mines, the shipyards, the engineering works and similar enterprises, many of the men who found themselves unemployed and poor during the 1920s and 1930s were among those who in the immediately preceding period of massive economic growth had been among the more highly paid and highly regarded groups of British workers. Once the brief post-war boom had passed, unemployment and deprivation were a common experience among many members of the region's

premier working groups, culminating in the disastrous years of the early 1930s.

In the coal mines, for example, the lengthy strike of 1921 was sufficient to eat into any savings accumulated by mining families in previous years, and a few years of relative prosperity were followed by the more prolonged and bitter struggle of 1926, the effects of which persisted into the crisis years of the early 1930s caused by the serious fall in demand both at home and abroad. Comparable troubles affected workers in the region's other major industries.

In these circumstances workers who had been for many years relatively highly paid found themselves faced with major drops in income. In addition economic adversity imposed serious strains on the local resources available to relieve the difficulties experienced by many working families. We have already seen that a high proportion of the funds used for local public purposes were traditionally derived from local rates and were expended by local authorities elected essentially by a rate-paying electorate. There had already been times of stress in the nineteenth century in which economic depression reduced the resources available to many ratepayers, while the demands made on the available funds increased. The greater stresses of the inter-war period intensified these problems. Even if the development of such institutions as national insurance provided some relief to the burden placed on local authorities in difficult times, the greatly increased relief expenditure imposed by the inter-war depression involved costs which could not be sustained by the limited local resources.

The borough of Gateshead provided one good example of the difficulties involved in this situation. Before the First World War many of the employing and productive enterprises which had sustained the town's earlier period of rapid growth had closed down, so that the majority of workers who lived in Gateshead worked for employers whose firms were situated in other local government areas. Gateshead therefore possessed large areas of housing of low rateable value, without having access to rate income generated by the factories and other enterprises which employed the bulk of the town's workers. Social problems involving heavy expenditure fell upon the town's very limited revenue. In the early 1930s Gateshead's public assistance committee still carried a heavy burden of debt accumulated in coping with the General Strike of 1926 and its aftermath. In 1935 the town's rates amounted to 15s. 6d. in the £, of which more than 7s. went directly in public assistance to those in need. The situation was broadly similar within the administrative area of County Durham. Only about 3% of the county's houses possessed a rateable value of more than £20, while 76½% were rated at £10 or lower. In 1934, when the worst of the depression had already passed, 73 out of every 1,000 of the county's inhabitants were in some degree dependent on public relief, as against a national average of only 25.4. In that year public assistance payments required nearly £¼ million from rate income, even after special central grants in aid of distressed areas were taken into account. This involved a rate for this purpose alone of 8s. 6½d. in the £—more than that for all other local government purposes put together—at a time when the national average was 2s. 8½d.

Even in the later 1930s a penny rate in County Durham produced a sum of just over £14 per 1,000 inhabitants; the equivalent figure for Northumberland was over £20 and that for the county of Middlesex nearly £40[2]. At Jarrow a penny rate realized a total sum of about £400, while in Bedford at the same time a penny rate brought in £1,500 and in the London borough of Holborn £6,000. In addition to discrepancies between different regions, there were marked variations within the region itself. Some local authorities were heavily dependent on the small rates to be derived from the kinds of housing occupied by working families, while others possessed a very different pattern of property and rate income. Newcastle with its extensive commercial and industrial properties derived only 12.8% of its rate income from workers' housing, while in the neighbouring prosperous suburb of Gosforth the figure was as low as 7.7%; the equivalent figures for Felling, Hebburn and Jarrow were 58.3%, 53.9% and 48.5%. There was no correlation between population, the extent of social problems and the income enjoyed by local authorities. The situation can be illustrated by citing the varied figures for the population and the product of a penny rate of a group of Tyneside local authorities in 1939—Newcastle, population 290,000 (product of penny rate £10,216); Gateshead 118,000 (£2,125); South Shields, 111,000 (£2,083); Tynemouth, 67,000 (£1,499); Jarrow, 31,000 (£436); Whitley Bay, 27,000 (£1,091); Gosforth, 20,000 (£731); Newburn, 19,000 (£377)[3]. It was certainly not the case that the local authorities facing the most severe problems were those which possessed the largest resources; indeed the reverse was more commonly the case.

During the 1920s it became increasingly plain that some of the region's local authorities simply did not possess the necessary revenue to enable them to meet the demands made upon them for relief payments in times of economic adversity. Only subventions from national funds could meet the situation, and yet the tradition of local autonomy and local responsibility died hard. For a number of years the central government tried to limit the assistance which it felt obliged to provide to hard-hit local authorities to the form of repeated loans, in the belief that when good times returned it would be possible for local authorities to repay advances made to meet a temporary emergency. It was only when it became unmistakably clear that the emergency would not be short lived that different policies to help the region were embarked upon; during the 1920s many local authorities found themselves saddled with increasing loads of debt, without any real possibility of the loans being repaid.

Some of the problems experienced in earlier periods of the growth of local government continued during the inter-war years and complicated a situation already made difficult enough by the region's economic difficulties. It was not always possible to ensure that local authorities demonstrated a high level of fidelity to the standards and the rules which central government thought proper, and a few of the region's local authorities were at loggerheads with the central government during this period. Some of the ways in which local authorities could exasperate the central government were illustrated in the experience of the two bodies within the region which were superseded by the Ministry of Health for prolonged and deliberate refusal to accommodate their policies to the statutory duties laid upon them by national legislation. The two local authorities to which this extreme step was applied were the Chester-le-Street Poor Law Union and the Public Assistance Committee of Durham County Council.

By 1926 the Chester-le-Street Board of Poor Law Guardians had an over-whelming Labour majority, two-thirds of its members being miners[4]. The board already had a long record of conflict with the Ministry of Health for operating relief policies markedly more generous than the prevailing national regulations allowed, and the union was already heavily in debt. Matters grew much worse with the approach of the 1926 strike. On 6 May the Board decided to appoint an emergency executive committee consisting of five of the Labour guardians; this committee met the following day and co-opted all of the other Labour members of the board, thus effectively excluding the minority of non-Labour guardians from the conduct of the union's affairs during the crisis. The union's authorities continued to defy central regulations by, for example, channelling all orders for relief in kind to the local co-operative stores and by expressly forbidding relieving officers to inspect the pass books recording applicants' deposits in local co-operative societies when assessing the financial position of claimants. In the sub-district of Birtley administrative impropriety was taken much further, for there applicants for relief were invited to contribute to a fund collected for the benefit of the local poor law guardians. By July 1926 the union had 14,000 cases of outdoor relief on its books, and it was plain that very little effort was being taken to check the validity of such claims, especially claims emanating from mining families. This was perhaps an entirely intelligible standpoint on the part of those responsible during a prolonged coal strike, but it was scarcely likely to recommend itself either to central government, whose rules and specific instructions were being flouted, or to the ratepayers, whose money was being spent so freely. The central government reacted strongly; after repeated warnings and reprimands went unheeded, emergency powers were invoked, and the elected board of guardians was replaced by com-missioners appointed by the Ministry of Health. By the end of 1926, after a thorough check, the number of outdoor relief cases was down to only 3,000.

After 1930 the functions of the old poor law authorities were vested in the public assistance committees of the principal local authorities, and the new authority in County Durham was soon in serious conflict with the central government[5]. After 2 years of constant tug of war over the relief policies to be operated, the public assistance committee of Durham County Council was superseded by appointed commissioners at the end of 1932. The new com-missioners, headed by a Liberal ex-Home Secretary, Edward Short, found that their elected predecessors had been refusing only about 1% of applications for relief and had been paying out maximum levels of relief in the case of 92% of applicants, with only 7% at lower levels, which scarcely suggested any punctilious regard for the existing regulations. The new authority embarked upon a careful review, while claiming to be completely fair, as a result of which the proportion of cases allowed full benefit was reduced to 70%, reduced benefit was given in 23.5% of cases and 6.5% of applications were disallowed.

Moreover, even in these hard times, there remained cases of those who deliberately exploited the relief system to obtain benefits to which they had no legal claim. The lax administration by County Durham's public assistance committee had allowed relief payments to be made to some individuals who possessed considerable resources. For example the report of their appointed replacements showed that the elected authority had paid £1. 3s. 6d. per week to a family which enjoyed a weekly income of £5 from house property, while a number of regular payments had been made to few families with undisclosed resources running well into the four-figure category. We also have the frank recollections, published in 1938, of a very intelligent and likeable man of marked left-wing sympathies who during the early 1930s spent some time in a lodging house in County Durham catering for unemployed men[6]:

> The lodging was rough, the bedding sparse, and the food consisted mainly of thick slices of bread and margarine, with milkless tea, fried blackpudding and onions and a little cheese. The talk at mealtimes was mostly about football or sport and hardly ever about politics or women— the main subject of interest to all was 'fiddling', i.e. the various means by which they could supplement their relief without reporting to the authorities.

This is, no doubt, an entirely intelligible viewpoint, but not one calculated to endear those concerned to ratepayers in a district paying a rate of 8s. 6d. in the £ for relief purposes alone, as against a national average of 2s. 8½d. There were other complications in such matters. The strict family means test for relief of the early 1930s aroused bitter and lasting resentment; a father who had lost his job in a skilled and highly paid trade could find his meagre relief payments reduced because of the earnings of adolescent or adult children, and normal patterns of family relationships and mutual respect could be severely strained as a consequence.

As in earlier periods the numbers of those who took illicit advantage of welfare payments may well have been statistically very small, but their existence could have a disproportionate influence on public opinion, and especially the opinion of those who had to provide the money for relief payments. The task which faced the elected councillors and poor law guardians who had to administer relief arrangements during the inter-war years was rarely simple or easy. Time and again the records of local authorities reflect a pattern of intense and conflicting pressures. The unemployed and their champions naturally pushed for the adoption of policies of greater generosity, while ratepayers and their organizations pointed to the genuine difficulties brought about by sharply increasing rate demands, especially for poorer ratepayers and those among them who were themselves hard hit by the consequences of economic depression. Both sides had a case, and councillors and poor law guardians did not find it easy to manoeuvre among these conflicting pressures.

There were other sources of friction in the administration of public relief systems during these years. Many skilled workers, who had previously enjoyed positions of relatively high income and status among their fellows, now found that for the much smaller sums of money granted to them in relief payments they must attend upon the local official agencies and must justify their claims to junior officials. Many of these officials were both sympathetic and competent, but this was certainly not always the case. It is still common to find stories of official lack of sympathy and understanding within these years current among local people; some of these incidents may have become exaggerated during the intervening period, but there can be no doubt that they reflect a genuine foundation, which can be illustrated by a single example which is far from unique. An unemployed man of considerable intelligence and ability, trying to improve his education while out of work, had an opportunity to attend a course for adult education teachers at Reading, but he could only afford to go if his unemployment benefit continued while he was there[7]: 'I was met by a most astounding refusal. "Supposing work turns up here for you while you are away?", they said. And then added with unpardonable effrontery, "You can't go".'

John Mill, General Secretary of the Boiler-makers' Society, made the point in restrained terms in a speech of December 1934[8]: 'To entrust wide discretionary powers over craftsmen workers to young clerks without industrial experience seems likely to create a dangerous form of official despotism, and to be resented by the workers.' In some local government areas, as we have seen, domination of the local authorities by political groups representing local workers could produce a sympathetic administration at local level, but there was no guarantee that this situation would always prevail.

Mutual support and solidarity among the workers

The harsh experiences of the region during the inter-war years brought many instances of mutual support and helpfulness, but they also demonstrated that coherence and unity at various social levels was far from complete. The political history of elections within County Durham, where Labour was appreciably stronger and where many constituencies were dominated by the votes of workers and their families, does not suggest any very high degree of uniformity[9]. The Hartlepools sent Conservative M.P.s to Westminster in 1929, 1931 and 1935, while Darlington, Stockton and Sunderland all sent supporters of the self-proclaimed National Government to the parliaments of 1931 and 1935. In the general election of 1931, Labour fared badly in North East England as in the country as a whole, and the predominantly mining constituency of Seaham Harbour gave Ramsay Macdonald a comfortable win, although it did not compare with his huge majority there as Labour candidate in 1929. Even in the

1935 general election, after the experience of the worst years of the depression, the Labour party's recovery in the region was much less marked than its more sanguine supporters had hoped. Labour made significant gains in the Durham county divisions, and Seaham Harbour gave Macdonald a trouncing, but seats such as Houghton-le-Spring. Barnard Castle and even Jarrow were only won by distinctly narrow majorities.

The magnificent solidarity of the turn-out in support of the miners during the General Strike of 1926 might at first sight point to a different picture of solidarity and determination, but even here the evidence is mixed rather than simple. Whatever truth there may have been in the often-repeated claim that the workers were badly let down by their leaders, it remains true that many of the labour leaders who shared responsibility for the end of the General Strike remained in their elected positions within the labour movement for many years after 1926. The only action which could have saved the position of the miners after the failure of the General Strike was the imposition by other workers of an effective embargo on the introduction and movement of imported coal, and nothing substantial was done to that end.

The position is even clearer when we come to the 1930s. It is difficult to see how anyone in the Britain of the depression years could have remained ignorant of the continued presence in their midst of substantial areas of large-scale unemployment and deprivation. Apart from the worst depression years in the early 1930s this was a time when very many people in Britain at various social levels were enjoying improved standards of living and genuine falls in price levels. There were many schemes to try to help the victims of the economic troubles of the depressed areas, but this was very far from being a continuing and general preoccupation at any level of society. While the Durham coalfield was hit hard by falling demand in the early 1930s there were other coalfields which remained more prosperous, but there seems to have been little enthusiasm on the more fortunate coalfields for the reintroduction of national wage systems which would have involved readjustments in wage levels to the advantage of the more depressed coalfields. It is understandable perhaps that miners in Nottinghamshire, for instance, were less than keen on proposals which would have involved acceptance of some reductions in their own earnings. It went very much further than that, however. In the Britain of the 1930s there were very many people who were prepared to make loud noises of sympathy for the victims of the depression. Those at any social level who were prepared to make any very strenuous efforts to bring more concrete help to bear were a smaller number, while those at any social level who felt obliged to make any very significant personal sacrifices for this purpose were a smaller number still. While sympathy for the unemployed was widespread, it was not a uniform or continuous preoccupation, and even in North East England events such as the abdication crisis of 1936 and the coronation celebrations of 1937 were capable of weaning a great deal of public attention away from the social problems of the day.

At the same time there were many efforts to bring help to those sections of society which needed help so obviously during the depression years. If very many people at various levels of society did not in fact exert themselves energetically in such efforts, a wide variety of interests did.

Within the affected areas families, friends and neighbours did much to help the unemployed and their families. Many small neighbourhood shops were generous in the extension of credit to customers in difficulty; when more prosperous times came many, though by no means all, of these loans were punctiliously repaid. On the other hand, some substantial help came from sources far removed from the hard-hit communities in North East England. During relief efforts in the 1930s organizations in Surrey 'adopted' Jarrow as the focus of their endeavours, while Hertfordshire chose to 'adopt' a group of Durham mining villages[10]. Apart from government measures some of the biggest contributions to relief measures came from sectors of society far removed from those adversely affected by the depression. The Lord Mayor of London's Relief Fund for the depressed mining districts in the late 1920s was one example of this, as was the £2 million fund established by Lord Nuffield in 1936 to help the victims of depression.

Nevertheless if there were substantial attempts from a variety of sources to bring ameliorative resources to bear, they were not enough to do more than to mitigate the serious social consequences of economic depression. The groups who suffered most often felt that they were largely forgotten by the remainder of the national community, much as many miners felt after the failure of the General Strike in 1926 that they had been left to struggle on in isolated weakness[11].

Attacking the social problems

Yet there is another and a very important side to the experience of the region during the inter-war period, for these were not merely years of economic crisis and social problems. They were also years of substantial progress in some important respects. We have already seen in earlier chapters that in a number of ways this region had lagged behind national standards in such matters as housing and public health. The drastic drop in regional resources associated with the depression years did in some respects slow down the process of improvement, especially in the communities which saw the highest levels of economic troubles and unemployment. The region's figures in such matters as overcrowding, infant mortality, tuberculosis and similar indicators all continued to show the North East region in an unenviably high position in the tables. Here again, however, overall figures for the region concealed major variations within North East England as well as contrasts with other regions. The level of overcrowding provides a good example of these local disparities. The 1921 census computed the following figures for overcrowded housing occupied by the inhabitants of various Tyneside communities; at Newcastle a total of 88,000 people, or 33.6% of the population, were living in conditions of overcrowding, while figures for nearby communities were Hebburn 11,000 (46.9%), Jarrow 15,000 (42.5%), Gateshead 45,000 (37.0%), South Shields 42,000 (36.5%), Tynemouth 21,000 (43.4%), Gosforth 2,000 (13.8%), Whitley Bay 2,100 (10.4%). Some of the most striking disparities, however, existed between communities within this region and levels prevailing elsewhere. In 1935 the infant mortality rate per 1,000 live births was 42 in the Home Counties, 76 in County Durham, 92 in Sunderland and 114 in Jarrow. During 1931-5 the death rate from tuberculosis among young women in Gateshead and South Shields was more than twice the average for England and Wales.

Despite these fearsome statistics the inter-war period, with all its difficulties, was a period which saw an increasing attack on the region's social problems. Although there were local variations and temporary set-backs to the process, there had by 1939 been overall a significant improvement in the social environment of North East England. If in some respects parliaments and governments moved warily in accepting wider responsibilities for regional problems, there was an increase in the resources made available from national revenue for the tackling of some of the region's old problems. We have already seen how limited was the rate income of many local authorities, yet how serious were, for example, the housing problems existing in many of the region's communities. The availability of somewhat more generous subsidies from central funds was an indispensable prerequisite before local authorities could afford to tackle housing problems on any large scale. This applied both to the improvement of the existing housing stock and to the building of new houses. For example, in the mid-1920s local authorities could call upon central grants in aid for the replacement of old dry lavatories by water closets and modern drainage, and this enabled many local authorities to embark upon this kind of sanitary improvement. It was this aid from central funds which enabled Gateshead, a borough with little income to spare, to install nearly 19,000 water closets in houses previously without them in the years 1925-7. Gateshead also obtained a new central library in 1926; of the total cost of £27,000, the greater part came from external sources, with £16,500 provided by the Carnegie United Kingdom Trust. A new isolation hospital could be built for the town in 1936 because a grant of 75% of the cost could be obtained from central funds under the 1936 Special Areas Act. Without these kinds of external help the borough council would have been incapable of embarking on expensive improvements, at a time when the public assistance committee spent half of the town's rate income and when more than 800 in every 10,000 of the town's inhabitants were in some degree dependent on relief payments.

The availability of central subsidies made it possible for many local authorities to embark upon new housing schemes and to tackle the worst of the slums inherited from earlier periods. At Sunderland, for instance, 445 families were rehoused in 1934-6. In their new accommodation they occupied a total of 1,671 rooms, in contrast with the 881 rooms in their old homes. Each family now possessed such amenities as a bath, scullery, garden and water closet. The gain was not unmixed, however, for their new rents worked out on average at 3s. 8d. per week higher, and from this point of view it can have been little consolation that they now paid only 2s. 5d. per room compared with 2s. 10d. per room in their old slum dwellings[12].

In the county borough of Tynemouth, mainly in this respect the town of North Shields, about a quarter of all children born in 1920 were born in one-roomed homes. By the mid-1920s this situation had deteriorated to about one-third, but thereafter, despite the increasing depression, there was a clear change for the better. Tynemouth Council responded to the Housing Act of 1930 and its proffered subsidies by working out a 5-year programme of slum clearance and rehousing, including the erection of almost 2,000 new houses on the Ridges Estate and adjacent areas. In 1936 only 10% of new babies in the town were born in one-room homes, and by 1938 the figure was down to 5.7%, very much lower than had ever been the case before[13].

At Blyth the borough council built more than 1,200 houses between 1918 and 1935, and here again subsidies were vital in keeping the cost to ratepayers down to a tolerable figure[14]. Darlington eliminated much of its worst town centre slums before the outbreak of war in 1939, while by that time Middlesbrough had rehoused more than 4,000 families on its new council housing estates[15]. Gateshead had by 1935 built a total of about 2,300 council houses, and this enabled the borough to eliminate or diminish some of the older slums which had come to possess wide notoriety stretching back for many years[16]. Newcastle also saw substantial improvements in its housing stock during the inter-war period. A total of 5,549 new houses were built there in the 1920s, but under the impetus provided by central subsidies the figure jumped to 22,160 for the 1930s. If most of these were still built by other agencies, the council's share mounted considerably; in the 30 years between 1890 and 1920 Newcastle Council had built a total of 454 homes, but during the 1930s 8,130 council houses were built, and by 1939 the city's own housing provided homes for more than 22,000 people[17].

In many other ways too the 1920s and 1930s saw significant improvements in social conditions. The disappearance of the old poor law authorities in 1930 saw a rationalization in local government which in general, despite the pressures of the depression years, brought a continuing improvement in welfare provision. At Newcastle, for instance, the new authority markedly improved the level of medical facilities provided by the old workhouse hospital, now the Newcastle General Hospital. The number of patients admitted rose from 3,048 in 1930 to 6,695 in 1936, and during the same period the number of operations carried out rose from 596 to 2,722[18]. The new authorities worked under the Relief Regulation Order of 1930 and its successors, which explicitly abandoned any policies of deterrence towards the poor and aimed at rehabilitation and wherever possible re-employment[19]. The new authority for public assistance in Newcastle after 1930 immediately abandoned the traditional practice of using differential relief scales for summer and winter, and now the more generous winter scales prevailed throughout the year. When in 1931 the Ministry of Health, alarmed at the growing cost of relief in the depressed regions, asked local public assistance committees to make economies, the Newcastle authorities replied that they had given careful consideration to the Ministry's request but saw no possibility of reduced spending. In 1931-2 the annual expenditure of the city's public assistance committee amounted to nearly £340,000[20].

In a variety of ways, even if North East England continued to lag behind national averages, the inter-war years saw some narrowing of the gap between North East England and more prosperous areas. In 1923-5 Gateshead exhibited an annual infant mortality rate of 100 per 1,000, as against a national average of 73 (Newcastle, 96; South Shields, 104; Jarrow, 101; Gosforth, 70; Whitley Bay, 57). By 1935-7 the Gateshead figure was down to 86, an improvement but still well above the then national average of 58 (Newcastle, 89; South Shields, 82; Jarrow, 97; Whitley Bay, 67; Gosforth, 65). By 1939 Gateshead's infant mortality rate was down to 60 per 1,000, still uncomfortably above the national average, but representing a substantial improvement during the inter-war years[21].

These improvements in health and housing in years which were so unpropitious in economic conditions were not due to any very widespread popular pressures but much more to the continued exertions of identifiable minorities of keen social reformers. As had been the case in the nineteenth century doctors were prominent in this category, including a group of reformers among doctors holding public positions as medical officers of health. A good example of this type of social reformer was Dr McGonigle, medical officer of health at Stockton. Like other reforming doctors of the same stamp, he pulled no punches as far as his analysis of social conditions was concerned, and his annual reports contained carefully gathered statistics in support of the case for urgent reform. He measured and published figures showing marked disparities in the death rates between the households of employed and unemployed workers, and differentials in various measurements of health between richer and poorer groups in society. Some of his findings helped to demonstrate the fallacy of some of the more simplistic conceptions of social amelioration. He pointed out, for example that the removal of a poor family from a slum dwelling to a modern council house did not necessarily produce a great improvement in the family's standard of living; if the exaction of much higher rent levels impaired the family's ability to feed itself properly, there might even be a deterioration in condition rather than an improvement. Similarly at Newcastle Dr James Spence, a distinguished pioneer in the study of child health, carried out on behalf of the city council an extensive survey of the health of local children. He emerged from this unprecedentedly thorough investigation with such uncomfortable conclusions as a finding that while anaemia affected only about 16% of the children of professional groups, the figure could be as high as 81% for the children of the very poor. He also showed that among the children of the very poor there was eight times as much pneumonia and ten times as much bronchitis as among the children of the city's richer families[22].

The activities of social reformers such as these, whether or not they were in public office, were part of a continuation of the philanthropic activity which we have seen at work in earlier periods too. The continued creation of new charitable societies to meet social needs continued during the period after 1920. In the regional centre of Newcastle the Citizens' Service Society worked from 1920 onwards to carry out a number of charitable activities of its own and at the same time to act as a kind of co-ordinating agency for other welfare activities within the district[23]. It was supported mainly by contributions in cash and kind from the wealthier sections of local society, who also provided the bulk of the voluntary workers who staffed its services. At a time when there were a substantial number of educated women of means for whom a working career did not exist, such an organization could call upon substantial reservoirs of talent and interest. In its work there was a deliberate attempt to cope with the problems of individuals rather than broad classifications of those in need. In some cases the Citizens' Service Society passed on applications to more specialized charitable organizations which were better fitted to deal with the problems concerned. For other categories, however, the Citizens' Service Society devised and operated a variety of services. For those suffering from tuberculosis or other illnesses the society would provide money for extra food, spare beds or warm clothing. The provision of home helps for a family household while the mother was ill was part of the society's work long before any official agency was able to provide such a service. As new council estates developed in the 1930s the Citizens' Service Society helped to foster community associations on them. A good deal of work was carried out in the rehabilitation of discharged prisoners and Borstal boys. The society bought a number of large houses and converted them into flats to be let at moderate rents. The work of the Citizens's Service Society was only one part of the continued activity within the region of voluntary agencies trying to create new social services before such activities were provided by official resources.

In some ways the pattern of philanthropy reflected more general changes in British society. Although the work of specifically local organizations continued to be important, a much higher proportion of charitable work came to be carried out by local agencies of major philanthropic societies operating on a national basis, as for instance in the work against cruelty to children and animals. There was also, however, a continuance of trends which had been active in earlier periods. One of these was the continuing inter-action between official and unofficial agencies of relief. As in earlier periods local authorities continued to make grants from public funds towards the work of voluntary organizations which complemented their own activities. Semi-official bodies such as the National Council for Social Service received official grants in aid of their social work in the depressed areas. The process by which official agencies took over social services pioneered by voluntary societies also continued; in 1920, for instance, Newcastle City Council adopted nine 'mothers' and babies' welfare centres' which had been founded in previous years by voluntary efforts.

Many charitable organizations created in the nineteenth century continued to maintain and expand their activities. During the inter-war years, for instance, the Poor Childrens' Holiday Association extended its facilities for the treatment of tuberculosis, especially among children, and in 1930 the association opened a large new holiday home at Whitley Bay for mothers and children from poor homes. Unofficial philanthropic resources also made a contribution to the improvement of the area's housing. The Sutton Dwellings trust built sizeable estates in Newcastle in 1918, 1928 and 1935, and another in South Shields in 1929, which between them provided nearly 1,000 new homes. On a much smaller scale the bible class of a North Shields presbyterian church raised funds with which to build about 100 new houses[24]. The trustees of Sir James Knott's estate spent considerable sums in providing improved facilities in North Tyneside, including an expenditure of about £100,000 on a large modern youth centre for North Shields and the building of the Knott Flats at Tynemouth, a huge modern housing block overlooking the Tyne.

The old-established medical charities also continued to play a large part in providing medical services in a period in which the state's official provision remained limited. An appeal in 1927 raised £143,000 (including one donation of £75,000 from Lord Runciman) for major extensions to Newcastle's Royal Victoria Infirmary, the region's principal voluntary hospital[25]. It became increasingly common for the work of local hospitals to be supported by the work of organized groups of voluntary helpers, such as the Guild of Help at Sunderland Royal Infirmary, founded in 1931[26]. In 1936 Sir Angus Watson gave Newcastle a large house at Rothbury to serve as a convalescent home for sick children. Support for the expanding range of voluntary charitable activity came from a wide range of society. Much of the money and many of the voluntary workers came from the richer sectors of society which possessed the money and the spare time needed, but it was also a normal occurrence for such bodies as working men's clubs to make regular contributions to such institutions as hospitals and convalescent homes. ·

Another feature of the inter-war years was the improvement of the region's resources for recreation and entertainment. Sport, especially association football, continued to provide a deep and abiding interest for a very large proportion of the region's inhabitants, and it may well be that the levels of enthusiasm devoted to these activities remained greater than those expended in contemporary political organizations of any kind. The growth of the cinema during the inter-war period was marked, and the region developed an above average interest in this area of entertainment[27]. The inter-war years were also an important period in the expansion of working men's clubs in North East England. In 1925, for instance, the Prudhoe Working Men's Club spent £3,000 in buying the Palace Theatre, while the Westerhope Excelsior Social Club spent £5,000 on a new building in 1935. From 1921 the clubs' Federation brewery provided not only good quality beer but also a continuing source of financial strength to the clubs of the region. (Reference 28 gives much information on the histories of individual clubs and of the federation brewery.)

The experience of the region during the inter-war years was in reality more complex and varied than is normally remembered now. It was a period of shattering blows from prolonged and large-scale unemployment, and the means test of the early 1930s still occupies a powerful place in the region's memories. It was, however, also a period of improved housing, improved health and improved recreation. Substantial areas of poverty and very great inequalities of wealth, comfort and opportunity continued to exist, as they had done in all earlier periods. There were, however, other elements present, and they included a continuing expansion of efforts, by both official and unofficial agencies, to try to tackle the social problems which existed. By 1939 those problems had not disappeared, but many of them had been substantially reduced, notwithstanding the economic difficulties which beset the region during the inter-war years. It seems probable that when the Second World War broke out the majority of the region's inhabitants were enjoying a higher standard of living than they had possessed in 1920. By 1939 there had been for the first time a significant attack on the slum areas which had disfigured the region's towns for generations, even if much still remained to be done in post-war years. By 1939 the unemployed lists had shrunk markedly in most places within the region. The improvement which took place during the inter-war years was not equally shared and may have meant little to the long-term unemployed, but for the majority of the region's people it was real.

The impact of the Second World War

The coming of war in 1939 produced a variety of effects. By 1940 the demands of the war effort had effectively mopped up the remaining areas of unemployment. The overriding priorities of war interrupted the process of social improvement in some ways, such as the provision of new housing, but brought also a considerable expansion of public acceptance of responsibility for the food and the health of the country's population. Medical services, whether provided by local authorities or voluntary agencies, were increasingly absorbed in an emergency system of public medical services which foreshadowed the post-war national system. By 1939 the extended resources of central and local government possessed resources in trained professional staff on a scale much larger than in earlier periods, and it was relatively easy to bring into operation emergency administrative arrangements to meet the needs of war. At Darlington, for instance, the staff of the public assistance committee coped with the need to provide emergency centres capable at need of looking after 7,000 people and the task of finding homes for a total of some 10,000 war workers and evacuees, as well as the conversion of the old workhouse building into an emergency hospital. The tradition of co-operation between the resources of official and unofficial welfare agencies proved a very useful asset in the rapid improvization of new administrative and welfare facilities to meet the sudden needs of war.

As in the First World War there was large-scale recruiting for the armed forces, though now of course conscription was employed from the beginning, in itself an indication of the state's greater administrative resources. In some cases mobilization revealed the continued existence of an older pattern of society. When the Northumberland Hussars mustered for war service in 1939 its squadron commanders were Major Lord Ridley, Major Lord Ravensworth and Major T. Eustace Smith (of the Smith's Dock family), and the junior officers showed a considerable sprinkling of the county's gentry families[29]. This was, however, an exceptional case, for in general the army's regional regiments depended less on local links and local recruitment than had been the case in the previous war[30]. During the First World War casualties involved in individual actions by units with a high level of local recruitment could often come as catastrophes for local communities, but this was less the case in the later war. The overall casualty figures were also on a somewhat smaller scale, and war memorials will often provide eloquent indications of the differences involved; at Shildon, for instance, the village war memorial lists 271 deaths from the first war, 138 from the second. The casualties of 1939–45 were, however, serious enough. During 6 months in 1944, for example, the Fiftieth Division, including the Durham Light Infantry, saw 113 officers and 1,045 other ranks killed, 338 and 4,967 wounded[31]. A region such as North East England, with its important maritime traditions, suffered heavy naval casualties and a tragic loss among merchant seamen, a loss shared by deep sea seamen, coastal crews and fishermen. The region also provided its share of those serving in the greatly increased Royal Air Force and bore its share of casualties there too.

Unlike the First World War the threat of death and injury from enemy action was not confined to the fighting services and the merchant marine. The police records at Tynemouth showed 329 bombing incidents within the borough between June 1940 and March 1943. Both North and South Shields, like some other towns, suffered many civilian casualties from bombing, and both towns saw serious local tragedies caused by direct bomb hits on crowded air raid shelters. The ports of the region were among the principal targets. The railway stations at South Shields, Sunderland and Middlesbrough were hit, while the destruction of Newcastle's principal goods station in 1941, the biggest single instance of material damage within the region, provided a spectacular enemy success. In North Shields bombing destroyed 166 properties, severely damaged 1,307 and slightly damaged 9,928; at South Shields 482 properties were destroyed, 1,324 severely damaged and 9,706 slightly damaged. Despite the immediate danger to which the civilian population was exposed in this way, and the natural hostility to the enemy states, it is probable that the level of hatred and hostility towards the enemy was somewhat less frenetic and uncontrolled than had been the case in the First World War. Especially in the crisis years of 1940–3 there was a very marked spirit of national unity. There were strikes in various places during the war, some of them, as in coal-mining, of a serious nature, but they were insignificant in comparison with the determination to stick it out together until victory had been secured. There were a few people within the region, especially before the German attack on Russia, who saw the conflict as a capitalist war in which the people had no true interest, but this was certainly very far from a prevailing viewpoint.

Post-war problems and achievements

The coming of victory in 1945 ushered in a period in which, while the social problems were not equivalent to those faced in the inter-war years of depression, the region still had difficulties to face. As we have seen, the rebuilding and modernization of the regional economy was not an easy task. In a number of ways, however, war-time experiences and advances contributed to social improvement in the post-war years. The very high levels of taxation imposed to meet emergency war expenditure provided opportunities for maintaining at least higher levels of public spending for social purposes than earlier periods would have willingly accepted. There had been during the war many expressions of a determination, widely shared, to ensure that post-war society would provide a more just and wholesome environment. To this end a number of important enquiries and reports had been accumulated during the war years. In some more practical immediate ways war-time developments were to help to curb some of the older social evils. In particular medical discoveries brought into practical application during the war could be used after 1945 to mount sustained and successful campaigns against some of the killer diseases of earlier years. Improved techniques of preventive medicine as well as new drugs contributed to the virtual extinction in the post-war years of scourges such as diphtheria and scarlet fever, while the toll of others such as tuberculosis were reduced to relatively tiny proportions. In 1938 there had been 100 deaths of children under 15 years on Tyneside from tuberculosis; there were 85 in 1947, 18 in 1951, four in 1954[32]. The figure of 100 for 1938 in itself represented a major drop from earlier figures, but the scale of the post-war achievement was certainly a very striking one.

In housing too the coming of peace was followed by a resumption of the process of improvement which had already marked the inter-war period. Even a relatively small local authority such as Castle Ward in Northumberland built 1,000 houses in the decade after 1945, at a cost of £1½ million. Between 1945 and 1957 more than 40,000 new houses were added to housing stocks on Teesside[33]. In other directions parallel improvements were effected; in the early 1950s, for instance, 400 miles of main electricity cables were installed in Northumberland, bringing this service within reach of many homes which had not possessed it before[34]. These improvements were not immune from their own problems. The movement of large numbers of families from overcrowded and inadequate, but long-established and intimate, communities in slum areas did not always prove an entirely unmixed blessing. The creation of large peripheral housing estates in the region's towns often meant that main social, shopping and recreational facilities became more distant from the homes of large numbers of people, though this problem could be mitigated by the extension of both public and private transport and by the creation of suburban shopping and community centres. Large new housing estates understandably found it difficult to recreate the closeness of the old neighbourly communities of the older urban areas. Victorian Britain was not the classical period of urban sprawl into rural areas, and in the towns of North East England even in the early twentieth century open country was rarely more than a short distance away. The unprecedented urban expansion of the later twentieth century has made this much less the case. It is, however, easy to exaggerate the appetite of urban populations for the recreational possibilities of rural tranquillity.

Overall, however, the improvements in social conditions effected between 1945 and the early 1960s were very substantial. The prosaic figures of successive census reports testify to some of the more obvious material improvements. There was no census in 1941, but the evidence from the 1931, 1951 and 1961 returns is eloquent enough. In 1931 the proportion of households in County Durham living at a density of more than two persons per room was 13.1%, and this included more than one-fifth of the county's total population; by 1951 the figure was 3%, including one-twentieth of the population. The same 20 years saw an increase of 34% in the number of dwellings in Newcastle, 72% in Gosforth, 57% in Longbenton, 45% in Whitley Bay and 43% in the Castle Ward Rural District. In 1951 the proportion of households in County Durham living at a density of more than 1.5 persons per room was 11%; by 1961 the figure was reduced to 4.9%, while the equivalent figures for Northumberland were 10.7% in 1951 and 5.4% in 1961. By the time of the 1961 census 96.5% of Durham households had their own internal cold water supply, 78.5% had a hot water supply, 72.8% had their own fixed bath and 92% their own water closet; equivalent figures for Northumberland were 97.1%, 81.3%, 77.6% and 91.5%. This does not represent the attainment of perfection but a move to standards of domestic facilities which were much better than those of any previous period and which marked a very substantial improvement effected during the years since 1945.

Not everyone would agree that this improvement in material comforts was paralleled by the continuing spread of civilization, but, depite some conflicting currents, the evidence suggests that this was the case on the whole. There remained substantial areas of vice and crime within the region, but that was certainly not new. There was a marked decline in the support given to organized religion, which came to affect a much smaller proportion of the population than it had done in the late nineteenth and earlier twentieth centuries. The temperance organizations failed to hold the support of their older mass following, but for this there were a number of reasons. The region continued to consume considerable quantities of drink, though the intake of spirits remained markedly below the national average[35]. The widespread increase in purchasing power, however, meant that a moderate indulgence was less of a pressing danger to family life than it had been at a time when very many working families had very little money to spare for this. Brutish drunkenness could still be found within the region but was less common than it had been in the past. There were 477 convictions for drunkenness at Newcastle in 1947, a figure which would have astonished a late nineteenth-century chief constable by its moderation[36].

Other murkier aspects of life within the region continued. Prostitution was by no means dead, with the unsettled war years probably marking a peak. A report of 1944 noted that[37] 'the women who are promiscuous or who have become prostitutes appear to form the habit very early, even as young as 16 years'. In 1953 Newcastle clinics reported a total of 2,587 new patients suffering from venereal disease[38]. The continuance of this social problem, despite the clear availability of greatly improved medical techniques, has been attributed variously to an increase in promiscuity or to the survival of significant inhibitions affecting sexual matters; conceivably it reflected both.

Worries about vandalism in many forms became increasingly vocal. Some older people felt that their younger contemporaries displayed a growing reluctance to accommodate themselves to older concepts of social discipline. Certainly the earlier tendency, already referred to, to see in the young a separate category of people needing special facilities blossomed in an unprecedented range of separate tastes and interests for them. The massive popularity accorded to new recreational resources aimed specifically at younger age groups was a new phenomenon in its scale, and the North of England was often in the van here[39]. Some of these developments seemed strange and worrying to many older people. Here, for instance, is part of an official report of 1955 on a youth club in Newcastle[40]:

> Young people seem able, through the various social techniques and therapies at their disposal, to create for themselves a society which is colourful, healthy, satisfying and harmless but lacks much contact or concern with some of the traditional virtues and values, particularly those which are roughly called 'spiritual'.

Yet, if there were worries, and the population of North East England was certainly not converted into a heavenly host, on balance the improvements outweighed any disadvantages of the post-war changes. Educational provision within the region improved during the 1945–60 period, both for schools and for higher education, though the region remained low in the national tables for the proportion of children who received more than the statutory minimum of schooling. Facilities for recreation and entertainment continued to improve. The availability of radio and cinema was to be supplemented by the arrival in general use of the new medium of television. Perhaps no development exemplified higher standards of resources and recreational facilities better than the experience of the working men's clubs of the region. Many of these institutions blossomed in post-war years into amenities for workers which would have astonished any earlier period[41]. The Chirton Social Club at North Shields spent £22,000 on club extensions in 1955, and in the same year the Bedlington Station Working Men's Club spent £27,000 on a concert hall to seat 200 and two new lounges. The Hazlerigg and District Victory Social Club also spent £16,000 on a new concert room in 1955, and a further £2,000 to provide an Alpine Lounge in 1960; in 1967 a further £8,000 was to be spent on a Beachcomber Lounge. These were not unusual ventures in the club world of the post-war years and symbolize the higher standards of comfort and enjoyment available to many workers within the region during those years. The growth of holidays, and holidays abroad, were further indications of higher standards of recreation and opportunity. It would be a brave man who sought to equate all the material improvements of the post-1945 years with a considerable increase in happiness, a notoriously difficult commodity to measure, but there was certainly a considerable extension of the opportunities for happiness insofar as these opportunities were governed by such factors as health, income, comfort, leisure, recreation, tolerance and the availability of help and support from communal resources.

Not everyone was satisfied with the substantial improvements in material conditions achieved during the 15 years or so after the end of the Second World War. It is understandable that many of those political activists who had campaigned energetically and persistently for social improvements should feel that the changes had not gone as far or as fast as they should, but there was more to it than that. For many radical reformers the improvement of material conditions was not to be welcomed just for its own sake but as something which would provide the necessary setting for a very different society from that which had existed in the past, a society marked by cultural, intellectual and ideological changes of a fundamental kind. In an earlier chapter we saw Arthur Barton's perceptive and attractive portrayal of his radical Uncle Jim. By 1960 that old campaigner had indeed seen the substantial alleviation of the poverty and its consequences against which he had fought in the past. He was not satisfied with the wider implications of these changes, and his reactions were described in an account published in 1967[42]:

Well, he saw it come—most of it anyway, for he lived until the other day. He saw slums wiped out, churches diminished, council houses multiplied. He saw the bairns' bairns come down the street in pseudo-Edwardian finery where their ragged parents had played. And he puzzled over the emptiness of heart and mind that a security beyond his modest hopes has brought. I visited him a few years ago in the same house in the same street. It will be gone now and a block of flats or a bowling alley will have risen on the site. He looked incongruous in a gay pullover knitted by a grandchild, but the usual striped flannel shirt was underneath and he still fingered the black leather belt he wore at the forge for 40 years. He looked up from a famous review, pushing back a pair of steel-rimmed spectacles and delivered a sharp tirade against scientific humanism and angry young novelists.

We looked out of the window at the street. Forty years hadn't made all that difference to the houses. There were a few fancy front doors with glass panels and chromium knockers, a forest of television aerials and a car of sorts at every other house. Uncle Jim sighed. He looked like a defeated general. He turned sadly back to his pile of penny poets and his 1920 *Clarions*, an old fighter whose victory had turned sour, a rebel without a cause.

"What went wrong, hinney?" he asked.

The verdict was much too harsh, though it represents a kind of judgement which comes easily to those whose concepts of society are drawn more from ideological theory than from the consideration of the realities of human nature and human behaviour. It is possible that those who dream dreams and see visions deserve a major share of the credit for progress and improvement, but they must often suffer disappointment when the progress and improvement attained fail to make of their dreams reality. Some of those who struggled against adverse circumstances for many years in order to diminish poverty and suffering and to provide increased comfort, leisure and opportunity were buoyed up by the hope that the attainment of these objectives would naturally lead to the creation of an unselfish society in which individual gain would cease to be a widespread preoccupation. This was in many ways an attractive vision, but it was scarcely realistic.

It is possible to take a more favourable view of the state of society in North East England by the 1960s, especially if it is compared, not with a utopian dream but with the reality which had existed in any earlier period of the region's history. A more favourable account would have to take note of conflicting factors, for the continued existence of brutality, cruelty and vandalism could not be denied. Yet it is plain that the level of material prosperity experienced by the overwhelming majority of the region's inhabitants was higher than that of any previous period. This was important in itself, but the results went beyond the provision of material comforts on an unprecedented scale. A society which had on the whole grown markedly richer over the previous few generations had devoted part of this increased wealth to the provision of more sophisticated and complex resources for social improvement. The region was now firmly part of a national society which had evolved public institutions for which the term welfare state could reasonably be coined. These were certainly not perfect but marked a significant advance on the facilities available in any earlier period, and the acceptance of an unprecedented level of public responsibility for the provision of welfare services over a very wide range of social difficulties. In the space of a few generations the development of a more sophisticated and inter-locking economy, and the great expansion of the activities of central and local government, had produced a much more complicated and inter-dependent society than that of earlier periods.

A major source of historical distortion has been a widespread tendency to devote a disproportionate amount of attention to things in the past which have gone awry and to pay relatively little attention to those which have gone well. The history of modern Britain is an area which has suffered especially from this kind of lop-sided approach. There is no difficulty in finding within the modern history of a region such as North East England a sufficient range of conflicts, hatreds, inequalities, oppressions, tragedies to provide a high degree of gloomy satisfaction, but it is important to remember that this provides but one side of a complex story. The most diligent student of the region's past will find it extremely difficult to fix upon any period in earlier times in which the condition of the people can be seen as more attractive than the position reached by the early 1960s. Such a student may well conclude that the region's society in the third quarter of the twentieth century was very far from perfect and that the region still faced serious economic and social problems, but he will probably conclude that the overall tendency of the 200 years after 1760 was one of progress and achievement rather than of decline and deterioration.

References

1   D. Euan Wallace, Durham and Tyneside report, *Reports of Investigations into the Industrial Conditions in Certain Depressed Areas*, 1934, pp. 89–90, cmd. 4728.

2   D. M. Goodfellow, *Tyneside, The Social Facts*, 1940, pp. 36–7.

3   ibid., pp. 70–1.

4   M. Rose, *The English Poor Law*, 1971, p. 311 et seq.

5   *Report to the Minister of Labour by the Commissioners Appointed to Administer Transitional Payments in the County of Durham*, 1933, p. 10 et seq.

6   J. Common, *Seven Shifts*, 1938, pp. 125–6.

7   G. Hitchin, *Pit Yacker*, 1962, p. 145.

8   *Newcastle Journal*, 7 December 1934.

9   M. Calcott, *Parliamentary Elections in County Durham, 1929–35*, M.Litt. Thesis, Newcastle University, 1973.

10 N. Branson and M. Heinemann, *Britain in the Nineteen Thirties*, 1971, p. 61.

11 Hitchin, op. cit., p. 81.

12 N. Dennis, *People and Planning*, 1970, pp. 150–1.

13 Goodfellow, op. cit., p. 32.

14 J. D. Reynolds, *The Governance of Blyth*, 1935, p. 25.

15 J. W. House and B. Fullerton, *Teesside at Mid-century*, 1960, p. 65.
    R. Glass, *The Social Background of a Plan, A Study of Middlesbrough*, 1948, p. 49.

16 *Municipal Government Centenary, County Borough of Gateshead*, 1935, p. 21.

17 *The Newcastle Official Year Book 1930*, p. 45.
J. Spence, *A Thousand Families in Newcastle*, 1954, p. 23.

18 Newcastle General Hospital, *Nurses' League Journal*, 1937, p. 3.

19 Newcastle City Council, *First Report of the Public Assistance Committee*, 1930, p. 1.

20 Newcastle City Council, *Second Annual Report of Public Assistance Committee*, 1932, p. 13.

21 Goodfellow, op. cit., p. 28.

22 Branson and Heinemann, op. cit., pp. 206-7.

23 Newcastle Central Library, collection of published reports of Citizens' Service Society.

24 Anon., *County Borough of Tynemouth, 1849-1949*, 1949, pp. 162-5.

25 W. E. Hume, 'The Royal Infirmary, Newcastle upon Tyne', *The Medical Press and Circular*, 1 October, 8 October, 1941.

26 W. Robinson, *The Story of the Royal Infirmary, Sunderland*, 1934, p. 86.

27 D. Elliston Allen, *British Tastes*, 1968, p. 178.

28 T. Elkins, *They Brewed their own Beer*, 1970.

29 J. Bright, *History of the Northumberland Hussars Yeomanry*, 1949, p. 13.

30 S. G. P. Ward, *Faithful, The Story of the Durham Light Infantry*, 1963, p. 466.

31 E. W. Clay, *The Path of the 50th*, 1950, p. 313.

32 F. J. W. Miller, *Growing up in Newcastle upon Tyne*, 1960, p. 112.

33 House and Fullerton, op. cit., p. 418.

34 H. C. Pawson, *A Survey of the Agriculture of Northumberland*, 1961, p. 37.

35 Elliston Allen, op. cit., p. 173.

36 Spence, op. cit., p. 22.

37 Anon., *The Social Background of Venereal Disease*, 1944, p. 7.

38 Newcastle Hospital Management Committee, *Clinical Review for 1953*, p. 21.

39 Elliston Allen, op. cit., p. 42.

40 *Report by H.M. Inspectors on the Rye Hill Youth Club*, 1955, p. 8.

41 Elkins, op. cit., passim.

42 A. Barton, *Two Lamps in Our Street*, 1967, pp. 130-1.

Bibliographical Note

We are fortunate in the possession of a comprehensive and up to date bibliography of the economic and social history of the region for the greater part of the period covered by this book. *The Economy of the North-East in the Nineteenth Century: A Survey with a Bibliography*, by D. J. Rowe, first appeared as a paper in *Northern History*, vol. VI, 1971 (pp. 117–47). Subsequently this paper was republished separately by the North East Regional Open Air Museum, Beamish, County Durham. A much enlarged and more comprehensive second edition will be published by that museum in the latter part of 1978. In view of the existence of this valuable survey of the available source material it is unnecessary to embark here on what would be to a very considerable extent a work of duplication.

One or two specifically twentieth century sources should however be added. H. A. Mess, *Industrial Tyneside: A Social Survey* was very much a pioneering work when it appeared in 1928. In 1935 a short book on *The Industrial Position of the North-East Coast of England* was produced by the staff of the economics department of the then Armstrong College, Newcastle. D. M. Goodfellow's *Tyneside: the Social Facts*, published in 1940, brought together a useful body of evidence on the region's recent experience. Since the text of the present book was completed, Dr James Hadfield's 1977 Sheffield Ph.D. thesis on *Health in the Industrial North-East, 1919–39* has provided much additional evidence for the substantial social improvements experienced by the region in the inter-war years.

Index